McKay's Guide to

ALASKA

Also by *Robert G. Hart*

HOW TO SELL YOUR HANDICRAFTS

McKay's Guide to

ALASKA

by
ROBERT G. HART

DAVID McKAY COMPANY, INC.
NEW YORK

Library of Congress Catalogue Card Number: 59-12261

MANUFACTURED IN THE UNITED STATES OF AMERICA

VAN REES PRESS • NEW YORK

Second Printing, June 1960

Dedicated to my friends

CHARLOTTE ZENK

DON PARK and JOE BALOGH

for that first unforgettable year
in Alaska

ACKNOWLEDGMENTS

The author is indebted to the following agencies and organizations for their helpful information and use of material: Alaska Communication System, Alaska Department of Education, Alaska Department of Health, Alaska Employment Security Commission, Alaska Historical Library and Museum, Alaska International Corporation, Alaska Native Arts and Crafts Clearing House, Alaska Native Health Service, Alaska Resource Development Board, Alaska Rural Development Board, Alaska Rural Rehabilitation Corporation, Alaska Visitor's Association, American Baptist Home Mission Societies, American Friends Service Committee, Canada National Employment Service, Civil Aeronautics Administration; the Department of the Interior's Alaska Railroad, Bureau of Commercial Fisheries, Alaskan Geology Branch, Bureau of Indian Affairs, Bureau of Land Management, Bureau of Mines, Bureau of Public Roads, Fish and Wildlife Service, Indian Arts and Crafts Board, National Park Service; the Government of the Yukon Territory and Provinces of British Columbia and Alberta; Jesuit Missions, Lutheran American Missions, Methodist Board of Missions, Presbyterian Church USA, Royal Canadian Mounted Police, University of Alaska, Veterans Administration, Western Electric Company, Incorporated; and the many Chambers of Commerce and Postmasters in Alaska.

Special thanks to John Latham for his invaluable assistance in the editing and preparation of the manuscript, and to the following friends and acquaintances who assisted in making this book a comprehensive guide to Alaska: Lillian Berman, Barney Blumenstein, A. J. Breitenstein, Joyce Brunette, Dan M. Burlison, Don Burrus, Mrs. Archie M. Byers, J. Edward Davis, Frederick J. Dockstader, Norman Donohue, S.J., Margaret Draper, George Fedoroff, Joseph A. Gallagher, M.D., Pauline Galliano, Arvid A.

Hamberg, Mrs. Gail Hatcher, Frances Hediger, Nat Hiken, Bernard R. Hubbard, S.J., Celia M. Hunter, Clarence M. Irrigoo, Sr., Max Jacobson, M.D., Alice Jayson, Edward L. Keithahn, Carroll Kennedy, Kay J. Kennedy, Edward Leight, Frank Long, W. D. MacBride, Herman J. Mack, Alf Madsen, Jay B. Mallott, Angelo Mango, Charles R. Mountjoy, Park Munsey, Alfred Rice, Frank Ryan, Verna C. St. Louis, Ronald Senungetuck, Roy Smith, Geoffrey E. Stamm, Avis Ann Tobin, W. S. Upson, Gizella von Waltherr, Arthur Walker, Hal Waugh, H. D. Williams, and Robert L. Wing.

CONTENTS

LIST OF MAPS

McKay's Guide to
ALASKA

CHAPTER I. THE FORTY-NINTH STAR

On the morning of January 3, 1959, forty-two years after the first official request for Alaskan statehood was initiated in the city of Nome on the Bering Sea, the President of the United States signed the official proclamation.

The most significant paragraph of the proclamation reads:

> Now, therefor, I, Dwight D. Eisenhower, President of the United States of America, do hereby declare and proclaim that the procedural requirements imposed by the Congress on the State of Alaska to entitle that state to admission into the Union have been complied with in all respects and that admission of the State of Alaska into the Union on an equal footing with other states of the Union is now accomplished.

But after the forty-two years of debate, demands, struggle, defeat, and final victory, the "admission of the State of Alaska into the Union" was received in every outpost, village, and city across the rugged land without any of the fanfare or the great celebrations that usually greet a long-awaited and historic event. Alaskans everywhere reflected the same quiet and dignified acceptance as their governor, William A. Egan, who said, "We accept the proud challenge of statehood and will seek to enhance the radiance of America's forty-ninth star."

The 230,000 people of the 586,400 square miles of state had already celebrated the fact of their statehood. On July 7, 1958, Congress had taken the final vote to admit the vast frontier territory as a state, and on that night the demonstrations were compared to the "wild rejoicing that Alaskans got used to back in the gold-rush days."

With whistles, sirens, horns, and bells, with bonfires and fireworks, street dancing and parades, the "sourdoughs" and the "chechakhos," the old and the new Alaskans, cheered and toasted the victory together as they watched a river turn to gold at Fairbanks when the exultant residents strung thirty pouches of gold dye across the Chena River near the memorable site of one of the big gold strikes at the turn of the century, and, for a short time, the waters of the Chena were a spangled gold flowing to the sea.

At Skagway, the gateway of the Klondike strike in '98, housewives paraded in the streets wearing badges with the embroidered words, "Bigger than Texas, better than California. Alaska—God's country." At Anchorage the long twilight was ablaze with a bonfire built of fifty tons of timber, one ton for each state of the Union, and an extra one for Hawaii. In the capital city of Juneau a replica of the Liberty Bell was struck forty-nine times as the people danced in the streets. The Ketchikan Junior Chamber of Commerce issued certificates declaring that the bearers were in Alaska when the territory became the forty-ninth state.

In the Arctic city of Nome, and in the Eskimo villages along the icy coast of the Bering Sea, the bonfires were so big and bright that one observer said, "The illumination of the celebration will go across the water to Siberia, to another continent."

That other continent, only a few miles across the Bering Strait, had made its contribution to the great statehood celebration. Many, many years ago the contribution was made through one of the most renowned real-estate deals in history, arranged by the czar of Russia, the man who owned the monumental land and did not know how rich it was in all its forests of timber, its unmined veins of gold, copper, silver, and lead, its wilderness of fur-bearing animals and waters choked with fish.

The royal owner of the fabulous land knew that his days were numbered and that, so long as he lived, he and his country would be in need of money. He instructed his minister in Washington, Baron Edward de Stoeckl, to sell the land for $10,000,000. But William H. Seward, the United States Secretary of State who negotiated the deal, didn't know if his government would approve the sale and give him the money for it. Nevertheless, he offered $5,000,000 for it and, on a day in March, 1867, Seward of the

United States and De Stoeckl of Russia agreed on the sum of $7,200,000, less than two cents an acre.

Half a year after the agreement was signed for "Seward's Icebox," the double-eagle emblem of Imperial Russia was replaced by the American flag in the official ceremonies at Sitka, and the commissioner of the czar, Captain Alexei Pestchourov, saluted the new flag, saying, "By authority from His Majesty, Emperor of all the Russias, I transfer to the United States the territory of Alaska." And with that transfer Russia's great adventure in the remote territory was ended, an adventure of important discovery and exciting exploration that began in the year of 1741 when the Dane, Vitus Bering, was an officer in the Russian Navy.

Under orders from Czar Peter the Great, Bering sailed on an eighty-foot ship to explore the waters lying east of Siberia. He sighted the mainland at Mount St. Elias, less than ten miles from what is now the Alaskan-Canadian border, and his observations established the fact that Asia and America were two separate continents.

Approximately fifty years later the most important of many Russian expeditions was that of Gregor and Natalya Shelikov, the ambitious husband and wife adventurers who dropped anchor at Three Saints Bay on Kodiak Island and established the first Russian settlement in North America.

Shelikov, who dreamed of building a great Russian empire in the New World, led many of his countrymen in establishing trading posts along the shores of some of the main rivers and, under the new-formed Russian-American Company, the furs of the new country were profitably exploited for the Imperial government. The company, which was granted a royal charter, was the instrument of exploitation of the fur trade and the organization that brought the white man's governing power to the people of the new land.

Before Shelikov had time to expand his dream of empire, he died, and Alexander Baranof was named head of the company. He immediately strengthened its power by forcing a temporary peace with the natives and organizing one thousand of them in a hunting fleet that sailed into the Pacific and returned with a rich cargo of skins from sea otter and fur seal.

Meanwhile, British, French, Spanish, and American vessels were exploring far into the north country, and their interests, particularly those of the British and the Hudson's Bay Company, clashed with the interests of the Russians, who had finally stripped the country of valuable otter and seal so that, by 1867, only a few remained of the hundreds of thousands of fur-bearing animals. It was that depletion of Russia's most profitable resource that helped to influence the czar's decision to sell the "barren field of ice."

The sale of Alaska and the fabulous years of the gold rush have become legend, told and retold in chapters of history and in tales of adventure. But there was an important pledge written into the sale that is not often mentioned. It is the pledge, exacted by the Russians, which states that the inhabitants of Alaska "shall be admitted to all the rights, advantages and immunities of citizens of the United States, and shall be maintained and protected in the free enjoyment of their liberty, prosperity and religion."

The actual fulfillment of that pledge came ninety-one years after it was signed, when, finally, Congress voted the full rights of citizenship under statehood for Alaskans and, at long last, admitted them "to all the rights, advantages and immunities of the United States." And during that great celebration, a real-estate man in Fairbanks stood in the crowd watching the Chena River run gold. The man, happy as everyone else, turned to the crowd around him and said in a jubilant voice, "I wonder how many people in Texas knew what they were getting when they got us?"

The golden waters had almost disappeared into the Yukon on their way to the sea when the crowd's laughter died away. The celebration continued and the man's question was left unanswered. But it is a good question and well worth some good answers.

What did the Union get when it got the "last frontier"? And who are the people who fought so hard for "the rights and immunities of the United States"?

The Alaskan governor of World War II years, Ernest H. Gruening, gave one of the answers when he wrote of Alaska's people: "Theirs is a friendliness and a forthrightness which the frontier breeds. Frontiersmen have never been much interested in where you came from, in what you had been, in what wealth and position your family had. It is what you are. It is what you can do in these surroundings." Then Gruening concluded: "More or less everybody knows everyone else. It is a long way from Ketchikan to Kotzebue. But persons and performance throughout the Territory are common knowledge."

There are many different kinds of people, different races, tribes, and colors in the old and modern communities on the "long way from Ketchikan to Kotzebue." Identification of native Alaskans is simplified by some historians and census takers who have divided them into four groups living in four scenically different areas. The storm-swept islands of southwestern Alaska are inhabited by the Aleuts. The proud Tlingit Indians and tribes of the Tsimshian and Haida live in the majestic southeastern region, the Athapascan Indians inhabit the wonderlands of the southeast and interior, and in the vast north and northwest are the Eskimos, living along the coast of the Arctic Ocean and the Bering Sea. White residents, those who were the pioneers, explorers, gold miners, and those who are now the businessmen, the missionaries, teachers, homesteaders, the government workers, and the many others have settled in all regions, restricted only by their kinds of work and interests in the territory and the people.

Approximately half of Alaska's Indians are the Tlingits, pronounced *Klinket,* a vigorous, warlike people, proud, shrewd, and physically strong, who had to battle for their ancestral forests when the white man came because they have always depended on timber for their fishing boats and canoes, for beams and rafters that support their homes, for the boxes which have always protected the family treasures, and for the dancing masks, drums, shields and weapons, and totem poles.

The Tlingits and their branch tribes were skilled carvers of wood and stone; they worked copper, wove blankets from the hair of wild goats, and made beautiful baskets and elaborate ceremonial masks, but their livelihood came from the sea.

Although modern Tlingits have lost many of their former ways of life, they are still a fishing people. Many of them own and operate their own fishing boats; some work in southeastern canneries during the summer and, in fall and winter, supplement their incomes by trapping and hunting, while others carry on the traditions of carving, woodworking, and weaving.

In the past, Tlingit people did not remain rich for long. When one of them saved a number of blankets, which were used for money, he held a great feast, called a potlatch, where he gave everything away. The more he beggared himself, the more he was honored. It was a form of attaining social security, because those who had received the gifts from him were obligated to assist him in time of need. This custom is almost extinct today, but the Tlingits continue to be shrewd business people and occupy positions of importance in the economy and development of the state.

In the same area of Alaska, the Tsimshian Indians settled on Annette Island when they came from British Columbia in 1887, led by the missionary William Duncan. In their model village of Metlakatla they developed a successful type of co-operative living. Though individuals own their own fishing boats and operate the stores in the village, their salmon cannery, water system, community hall, electric plant, and sawmill are operated on a co-operative basis.

The Haidas came to southeastern Alaska from British Columbia several generations ago and settled the southern part of Prince of Wales Island. Though most of their income is from fishing, they are as noted today, as they were in their regal past, for their slate carvings and wood inlay of bone and shell.

The Athapascan Indians are a poor, quiet, and introverted group with a genius for making and decorating useful and ornamental objects. Far from the small Athapascan villages are the Aleutian Islands, the Pribilofs and Kodiak Island, homes of the stoic and happy Aleuts who are able seamen and fishermen with deep respect for their religion, their burial grounds, and their Russian Orthodox churches.

More than any of the other natives, the Eskimos have preserved their ancient customs and habits even though they have the ability to adapt themselves to the changing patterns of life in Alaska. They are a hardy, resourceful people with a strong sense of fun, and, unlike the Alaskan Indians, they do not stand in awe of the new methods and environment brought to the Arctic by military and construction men because they alone will always be masters of their environment.

But no one, Indian, Aleut, Eskimo, or white, will ever completely master the land. Alaska is, as the Aleut word of origin, *Alayeksha,* describes it, the "great land"—too great, too overwhelming and violent for any people to master.

It is a land one-fifth the size of the combined forty-eight states, a fantastic wonderland wrought by nature and all the natural elements. It is a land of glaciers formed by millions of tons of ice, of vast mountain ranges spotted with active volcanoes, of hot springs that well up out of the frozen Arctic soil and provide water for the people of communities like Nome and healthful mineral baths for those at the hot-spring resorts. It is a land of rivers and creeks that fill with spawning salmon so great in number that the hand can scoop them out of the shallow waters.

The "great land" occasionally rumbles with mild earthquakes and with springtime icequakes when the shore ice rises and settles before it cracks and breaks. It is the temporary or permanent homeland of such creatures as the Alaska fur seals that converge by the thousands on the Pribilof breeding grounds, of the walrus that blanket the rocks of Walrus Island in Bristol Bay, of moose and caribou that range the mountains and forests, of bear, wolves, wolverine, mountain goats, marten, mink, and abundant others. Millions of birds from all the lands to the south migrate to their Arctic nesting grounds.

Summer carpets of midget wildflowers cover the Arctic landscape, and a galaxy of poppies, purple iris, creeping dogwood, fireweed, Jacob's-ladder, wild roses, wild dandelions, chives, skunk cabbage, and acres of blueberries and low-bush cranberries grow in seasonal abundance over the state, fed by thousands of streams and rivers.

The Yukon is one of the great rivers of North America, rising in British Columbia and flowing through part of the Yukon Territory across the width of Alaska. Almost all of this noted river is navigable and, in summer, it is one of the important waterways for the interior. Second in size is the Kuskokwim, which rises on the western slope of the Alaska Range, winds through the southwestern regions, and empties, like the Yukon, into the Bering Sea.

Several of the large rivers, the Unuk, Stikine, Taku, and Alsek, the Copper, Matanuska, and Susitna, flow into the Pacific, and the Kobuk, Noatak, and Colville are principal streams that empty into Arctic waters.

Alaska is a land of long days and long nights, a startling element for newcomers traveling northward into the Fairbanks area and beyond to Point Barrow at the "top of the world" where there is an almost round-the-clock darkness in winter and twenty to twenty-four hours of summer daylight.

In the vicinity of Fairbanks the midsummer sun rarely sets until ten or eleven at night, and three hours later or less, after a brief twilight, the dawn breaks and a bright new day begins. On the longest day of the year in Fairbanks the sun rises at 12:57 A.M. and sets at 11:48 P.M.

At Point Barrow the sun does not go below the northern horizon from early May to August. It circles the sky and at noon in the south it is at its highest; it is at its lowest in the north horizon at midnight, adding another descriptive name to Alaska—"the land of the midnight sun."

But during the winter at Barrow, the sun stays below the rim of the horizon and is not seen from late November until late January. At Fairbanks on the shortest day of the year, the sun rises at 9:58 A.M. and sets at 1:40 P.M. But the long winter nights are bright with snow, with a crystal-clear, fog-free atmosphere, and the ever-present luminous light that comes from below the horizon and gives a mysterious and wondrous beauty to the great land. But the most radiant phenomenon of the winter sky is the aurora borealis.

Popularly known as the "northern lights," this eerie pageant of color is one of the most dramatic winter high lights in the world. It may be equaled by an unknown phenomenon in outer space, but it is still unequaled by anything seen on earth. High in the atmosphere the display of light looms bright and colorful from early August through early April, swinging in folds like silken draperies, undulating or drifting, then billowing lightly on a phantom breeze. Reaching from one horizon to another in a shining path from Alaska to Labrador, this iridescent spectacle often makes crackling and swishing sounds.

Scientific analysis has indicated that the lights are produced by electrical discharges in oxygen and nitrogen with the sun as the source of energy, but it is easier to believe that they glow from the luminous magic and myth of Aurora, goddess of dawn. But for all the existing phenomena of Alaska, there is one which exists mostly in the stories and speculations of many people. It is the climate.

As unpredictable as it is in most places, weather forms the basis of Alaska's favorite pastime—betting; local residents make up pools and hold contests to see who can guess "tomorrow's high or low" or "which day it will rain the hardest." There is rarely such a thing as a "sure bet" on the weather because it is varied, dramatic, and uncertain. Depending on the time of year and the susceptibility of the individual, Alaska's climate can be described as "deadly cold," "very cold," "fairly cold," "cold," "cool," "springlike," "fall-like," "almost warm," "warm," "quite warm," but it would never be described as "too hot" or "too dull." And because of the various descriptions and speculations, climate is a major consideration for most people who plan a visit to the state, and it is a vital consideration for those who plan to settle there.

Alaskans advise, jokingly, "If you don't like the climate in these parts, it's easy to find some you do like. It's a big country and there is plenty of weather for everyone."

But they have a real concern for the welfare of newcomers and they don't hesitate to describe the problems of climate, mainly that all forms of transportation and especially the air-borne lifeline depend on the daily weather as well as on the physical conditions of the land and the sea. Fog can isolate an entire community and, during freeze-up and breakup periods, a town that is dependent on a frozen sea or river for a landing field is often isolated during transition periods of climate when planes cannot land.

Alaskans also advise that the major industries—fishing, farming, lumbering, prospecting—are affected by climatic conditions, but they will argue, with reason, that most people hold false impressions about the "frozen" land and the great extremes of climate. It is true that the thermometer drops to seventy degrees below zero at some interior points, but the records also show one hundred degrees plus each summer. Eighty feet of snow falls in some mountain passes and the average rainfall in Anchorage exceeds thirteen feet and almost triples that amount in Valdez, less than two hundred miles to the east. But nature has provided enormous compensations in almost every area where the weather might seem "too wet," "too cold," "too stormy," or "too severe," and except for the Arctic, which is only one-quarter of the total land area of Alaska, the weather is comparable to many other states and Canada, because three-fourths of the forty-ninth state is in the North Temperate Zone.

The southeastern sections have a yearly average temperature comparable to the cities of Baltimore and Philadelphia. The temperature rarely goes to zero and, as a result, it is referred to as "the banana belt."

Predominant characteristics of this southeastern area are mild winters and cool summers, with moderate temperatures throughout the year, but there is rain during all seasons. In the capital city of Juneau for the past eleven years rain has fallen on the average 224 days out of every 365. In other sections the amount of rain measures from 26 inches to more than 13 feet a year, and as one southeasterner put it, "Our rainfall should be measured in fathoms, not inches."

In winter the snowfall is heavy in the mountain and inland areas, particularly at the heads of the fiords, but it is relatively light at sea level. No matter what the weather brings to southeastern Alaska, it is responsible for the magnificent scenery. The rain encourages the dense forest growth of Tongass National Forest and feeds the thousands of streams in which the salmon spawn. Because of heavy precipitation and warm temperatures, the spectacular glaciers have formed, grown, and moved across the land, carving the narrow fiords and towering cliffs of the impressive area.

The south central region enjoys the full flavor of four distinct seasons even though the moderate winters are as long as spring, summer, and fall combined.

Although snow is always visible clinging to the mountains, temperatures in the eighties are not uncommon during the warm summer months. The average is about ten degrees higher than in

Cheyenne, Wyoming, and Portland, Maine. Only three times in the past three years has the temperature at Seward fallen to 4 degrees below zero, and the average in winter is 25 degrees and 72 to 75 degrees in summer.

This mild climate of south-central Alaska and the entire southern coast results from the Japan Current, the Kuro Siwo, which has an average low of 38 degrees and a high of 57. Throughout the winter there are clear, sunny days tempered by warm winds from the Pacific Ocean.

The Aleutian Islands and the Alaska Peninsula in southwestern Alaska are known as "the birthplace of the violent storms" and "the weather kitchen of the North."

The climate of the Aleutians is rarely favorable and is usually cloudy, windy, foggy, and misty; there is usually heavy rain and a depressing "low ceiling." But there are days when everyone on the islands shares the exhilarating experience of sunshine.

Though the southwestern coastal regions of the Alaska Peninsula, the Aleutians, and Kodiak are the gathering areas of the natural forces that create the storms, there are large and beautiful sections entirely removed from the severe weather. In Kodiak the cold month of January averages 30.1 degrees and in August, the warmest month, 55; the year around, it is a perfect vacationland.

One interesting phenomenon in the region is the occasional "dust and snow fog" when the wild williwaws, the tricky winds blowing from the Aleutians, come sweeping down on Old Woman Mountain on Kodiak Island. For many minutes the loose snow falls from the mountain, while a stiff breeze below kicks up the summer dust and, in the foggy blindness, it seems as if the whole world has suddenly gone out of orbit.

The interior of Alaska has extremes of climate between the winter lows and summer highs. The rainfall is light over the great interior valleys of the Yukon and Fairbanks, and the weather is very much the same as in Montana, the Dakotas, and northern Michigan. The warm and usually dry summer in Fairbanks is from 66 degrees up to the 90's. The Yukon and Tanana valleys average around 60 and occasionally reach 100. The variable summers with considerable rain in McKinley National Park average from 50 to 54, with a daytime peak into the 80's.

In winter there is very little wind in the interior, the snowfall is light and powdery, and temperatures frequently fall below zero. It is the sub-Arctic and Arctic, the turbulent one-quarter of Alaska, which has helped to give the impression that all of the state is a frozen wasteland. At Nome, where the summer averages 50 degrees, residents organize midnight swimming parties. In winter it averages only 4 below, but there are winds and blizzards, and a year-round cool draft that seems to invade all the coastal areas along the Bering Sea.

North to Kotzebue to the northernmost tip of Point Barrow on the Arctic Ocean, the January averages are from 9 to 17 below zero to July highs of 40 to 52. The Arctic Ocean freezes solid, but the snowfall in the lowlands is less than in the state of Virginia. It is the winds and fogs of the far northern coast that are responsible for more discomfort than the cold, and there are times when it becomes a solid, thick, white wilderness as the snows blowing up from the ground and the snow falling horizontally on the cutting edge of the wind create a blinding "snow fog."

From one end of the massive land to the other, the temperature and turbulent climate, the unusual and sudden weather, require constant observation. It is recorded by practically every scientific measurement and device known to the meteorological world, and the United States Weather Bureau makes certain that the visitors, the residents, and the whole world can get up-to-the-minute information on the climate of Alaska.

The Weather Bureau Airport Station at Anchorage serves as the main meteorological office for international air carrier routes. The District and Airway Forecast Center issues basic aviation and general weather, seasonal fire weather, and marine forecasts for Alaska and adjacent waters. Local forecast services are provided by qualified meteorologists in the local weather bureau offices at Annette, Fairbanks, Juneau, and Nome to supplement those issued at Anchorage.

Throughout the year, direct radio broadcasts are made for the benefit of the general public from stations at Anchorage, Cordova, Fairbanks, Juneau, Ketchikan, Nome, Sitka, and Seward, and there are regular weather telecasts from TV stations in Anchorage, Fairbanks, Juneau, and Ketchikan.

Weather Bureau Airport stations are operated at various places, such as Barrow, Barter Island, Bethel, and Cold Bay, where a basic program of hourly weather, six-hourly summaries and six-hourly "winds aloft" observations are maintained by local residents in addition to their other occupations.

Typical of the spirit of the local observers is Arvid Hamberg, the postmaster at Angoon. "I record the current weather once an hour and transmit it to Sitka via radio telephone. Every hour, ten hours a day, Sundays, holidays, rain, snow, or shine, I check conditions. It gets mighty monotonous at times but I know my reports help keep a lot of people out of trouble. It's an important job that must be done." And Mr. Hamberg adds, "And it leaves me time to go fishing on summer nights."

In addition to all the reports, hourly aviation weather observations are available from twenty-five locations on a part-time basis, and fifteen other supplementary stations. In all, approximately 150 observations are made by individuals and government agencies throughout the state. This concentration on climate is one of the most valuable contributions to the safety and security of Alaskans and their visitors.

Many things may change in the great land. It is a richer and rougher land than the Wild West used to be. It is America's last frontier with more undeveloped natural resources and country than any other state of the Union, but there are "chechakhos" making their permanent homes in the state, investing their capital and taking part in the future, in the growing movement to develop Alaska's forest, oil, and mineral resources, fabricating timbers, furs and nonmetallic minerals, cultivating lands, building airports, roads, and homes, establishing businesses, developing hydroelectric power potentials, and building and maintaining a large tourist industry.

With all those prospects and plans many things will change. But not the people nor the climate, and because of them, Alaska will always be an exciting and friendly land to live in and a wonderland to visit.

CHAPTER II. KEYS TO ALASKA

When to Go

May through September is the ideal time of the year for travel to and from Alaska. Transportation by plane, boat, and bus runs on full schedules and travel by automobile is at its most enjoyable. All the elements are at their best for visiting and vacationing in all sections of the state. But most visitors go during the months of June and July, which are the peak summer months, creating a shortage of sleeping accommodations and filling the transportation facilities to capacity.

The summer season is shorter in Alaska because of its more northerly location, but three of the best months for travel are May, August, and September, the Alaskan spring and fall, when the air is crisp, the sun is warm, the hotels are less crowded, there are thrift rates on tours, and a vacationer's choice of things to see and do at a more leisurely pace.

The Alaska Visitors Association strongly recommends late summer and early autumn when the "long hours of daylight are still lingering with lovely midnight sunsets. Gardens are bright with flowers and lush with vegetables. Snows have receded up the lower mountain slopes. Animals such as moose, caribou and deer are polishing their antlers. There's a tang in the air." In winter the new state is just as the AVA describes: "Planes fly. Railroads run, taxis operate. Main roads, including the Alaska Highway, are kept clear. Heating bills go up. Fresh produce is flown in. Life goes on much the same as in Denver, Great Falls or Seattle." It all goes to prove that there is no special time to visit this vast wonderland but one thing is certain, all through the year tourists and settlers find some magic in this last great frontier which enchants them forever.

Lodgings and food costs hold to a fairly constant level throughout the year, usually about 25 per cent higher than in other states and Canada, because of the added expense involved in handling, transporting, and importing freight. Most food and all manufactured products are brought in from outside the state and must travel long distances to reach the Alaskan markets.

In the more isolated communities and in the Arctic, costs increase sharply, especially in winter months, and prices are proportionately higher.

During the winter months airplane service, Alaska's main line of transportation, operates on dependable and regular schedules, subject only to short delays because of local storm conditions, but other transportation facilities are curtailed. Boats operate less frequently and reach only the towns in southern Alaska where rivers and harbors are not frozen. Bus service operates at less than half of capacity because fewer passengers travel by bus in winter months. The Alaska Highway is not as popular as it is in summer, although the road is kept open the year around. Tours are not available in winter.

The cost of travel can be additionally expensive because of delays en route when weather closes in and the traveler is winterbound. Waiting for safe take-offs can result in additional hotel and food expenses. Such stopovers are considered to be "unexpected emergencies" when they happen to travelers in other states, but in Alaska they are considered "normal."

Reservations for Sleeping Accommodations

Regardless of the time of year, reservations must be made well in advance at hotels, lodges, motels, and other lodgings. Although Alaskans are anxious to welcome visitors and to make them comfortable, there are not enough places to meet the increasing demand for transient accommodations.

New accommodations and expanded facilities are mushrooming each summer and drafting boards are full of plans for larger hotels and motels. Even in the small villages ground is being broken to provide places for overnight visitors, but it is not likely that the supply will catch up with the demand.

Alaskans are great travelers not only abroad but within the

boundaries of their state and, in addition to their needs for overnight accommodations, there are migrations of "outside" businessmen, government workers, and industrial personnel putting a large burden on the already strained existing accommodations.

In the very small villages and at the outposts, sleeping facilities are practically nonexistent for transients. In rare instances it is possible to stay with schoolteachers, missionaries, or government personnel stationed at the settlements. They usually have an extra bed or space for transients but it is most always in use by "official" visitors. Invitations can be arranged through friends, acquaintances, by direct correspondence, or with the assistance of bush pilots servicing the village or outpost.

Overnight visitors in these isolated places will be treated more like guests than paying customers and, in some places, will not be asked to pay, but payment must be made. The minimum cost to the host for one guest staying one night and eating three meals at such places as Hooper Bay, Shungnak, King Cove, or similar settlements is $15. At more remote places the cost is even higher. Guests who might be in doubt about how much they should pay for the visit may ask the bush pilot who can always give a close estimate of the value of the food and shelter, and a suggestion of the price that should be paid for them.

New visitors to the state should plan ahead for lodgings in the cities and towns, requesting reservations by letter or booking space through a travel agent. A place will be found if a confirmed reservation has been made in advance. Sometimes in the smaller towns it will not be quite what the visitor expects, but it will always be clean and hospitable.

Clothing and Luggage

The advice of all seasoned travelers in Alaska is to "travel light." Regardless of the mode of transportation to the state, whether by water, highway, or by air, there is usually an air trip at some point during the visit. Light airplane luggage consisting of a Pullman case and Val-pack, and for women a hatbox which can be used for everything but hats, plastic containers for toilet articles or cosmetics, and a small sewing kit are recommended.

Clothing En Route

On the way to Alaska by plane, train, or any other means of transportation, light clothing should be worn to compensate for heated interiors, but a warm sweater or coat should be kept handy, especially on planes. When planes land at northern stops en route they become cold very quickly and passengers need an extra wrap until the plane takes off and warms up inside.

Clothing aboard tour ships is informal. Special formal clothes for any function or at mealtimes are unnecessary. Comfortable sportswear is the most popular apparel for ship travel.

Medium-weight topcoats should be included because it gets chilly in the evenings on deck, but fur coats are not necessary. Women should take sweaters, skirts, slacks, wool jackets, dresses, or sport suits, and one simple cocktail-dinner dress.

For men, one necktie might be worn for "dressing up" for the dances in the evenings, or for the captain's dinner party at the end of the trip. One or two wool sport coats, a sweater, and slacks provide adequate outer clothing.

Garments should be selected to weigh very much the same as those worn at home during the early spring and late fall. But the important raincoat and rain hat can be lightweight and preferably of plastic which is easy to carry and is most satisfactory for rainy days.

Clothing in Alaska

A woman of Nome replied to a question about clothing in Alaska, "There were times when I first moved here that I'd put on slacks, snowsuit pants, sealskin pants, sweater, jacket, parka, knit hood over my face, wool gloves and fur mittens, wool stockings, cotton anklets, sealskin socks, reindeer knee-high boots, and a couple of scarves, just to go across the street. I quickly learned that it isn't how much you wear when it's cold. A few loose-fitting clothes that protect you from the wind, don't weigh you down, and allow your blood to circulate, will keep you warmer. After all, who wants to look like a stuffed walrus when you don't have to?"

May through September—One dark business suit for men, and

a semiformal dress for women are completely adequate for all "formal" occasions in Alaska. The important wardrobe for summer should include sweaters, jackets, slacks, skirts, and medium-weight wool topcoats, a lightweight raincoat, rain hat, and overshoes, and wash-and-wear articles. If there is room in the luggage, an extra pair of walking shoes should be taken, even for nonwalkers who, like everyone else, will want to investigate the fullness and variety of Alaskan scenery and activity.

October through April—The same type of clothing is needed for these months, but all items, with the exception of the raincoat, should be heavyweight. A fur parka, or a wind-resistant, down-filled cloth Arctic parka gives the greatest protection in cold weather, but adequate substitutes are regular fur or winter-weight cloth coats, head coverings of wool scarves or winter hats with ear flaps, ear muffs, and gloves. And, as the woman in Nome suggested, loose-fitting clothes are the most comfortable and the warmest.

Baggage Allowance in Alaska

Planes allow 66 pounds on each ticket between Alaska and points outside the state. Fifty-five pounds are allowed on air-line scheduled flights and 30 pounds on bush flights between all points within the state.

The Alaska Railroad permits 150 pounds of checked baggage for each full-fare ticket and any amount of hand luggage carried aboard to seats or rooms.

Buses allow for 150 pounds of checked luggage and hand-carried luggage not exceeding 30 pounds.

Immigration and Customs Information

PERMANENT RESIDENTS OF THE UNITED STATES

Crossing the United States–Canadian border either way is usually made without difficulty or delay by permanent residents of the United States who plan to visit or pass through Canada. Passports are not required. To assist officers of both nations to speed the crossing, native-born United States citizens should carry identifying papers such as birth and baptismal records, voter's certificate, driver's license, or any other special document showing citizenship status. Naturalized citizens must produce their naturalization certificates. Alien residents of the United States must have their Alien Registration Receipt Cards and re-entry permits.

Baggage Entering Canada

Wearing apparel and personal effects are entered free of duty. Up to fifty cigars, two hundred cigarettes and two pounds of tobacco may be included, but only forty ounces of alcoholic beverages. This does not apply to merchandise or articles intended for other persons or for sale. All goods must be declared.

Sporting equipment for personal use is admitted duty-free. It can include fishing tackle, golf, tennis, and other game equipment, and fifty rounds of ammunition per person. Portable radios and television sets, musical instruments, typewriters, cameras, six rolls of film, and twelve flash bulbs per person are also admitted free.

Rifles and shotguns are permitted, but revolvers, pistols, and fully automatic firearms are prohibited unless boxed and sealed by customs and not opened or tampered with while in Canada.

Time will be saved at inspection points if each person has a handwritten or typed list of items in his baggage, and the serial numbers of such items as cameras, guns, and typewriters, and a brief description of each. The list need not include personal clothing, accessories, or toilet articles.

It is possible to transport sealed bonded baggage between one United States port and another, as well as between one Canadian port and another free of inspection, as long as the baggage and official cords and lead seals are not opened en route.

Dogs and Pets

Hunting and pet dogs may be taken into Canada free of duty under the following regulations:

Dogs from the United States must be accompanied by a certificate in one of the following forms: (1) A certificate signed by a licensed veterinarian of Canada or the United States certifying that the dog has been vaccinated against rabies during the preceding six months. Such a certificate must contain an adequate and legible description of the dog and the date of vaccination, and must be initialed by the inspecting official at the customs port of entry, then returned to the owner for future use. (2) A certificate signed or endorsed by an inspector of the United States Agricultural Research Service certifying that the dog has been inspected and found free of any symptoms of any contagious disease, that the dog has not been exposed to the infection of rabies, and that no case of rabies has occurred within a fifty-mile radius of the dog for six months immediately prior to the date of leaving for Canada. This certificate will be surrendered by the owner at the Canadian customs port of entry.

"Seeing Eye" and performing dogs entering Canada for a brief visit are exempt from the above regulations. All dogs transported by train must be either muzzled or crated.

Cats and bird pets may enter Canada when accompanied by owners, but the birds of the parrot family have to pass inspection by an inspector of the United States Department of Agriculture and must have been in the possession of the owner for sixty days prior to entry.

Plants and Tree Cuttings

Plants and cuttings cannot be taken into Canada without a certificate from the United States Department of Agriculture which indicates they are free of pests and disease.

Re-entering the United States

If a resident of the United States has complied with regulations of admittance to Canada, re-entry into the States is a matter of normal routine.

Articles Purchased in Canada

Once every thirty-one days, United States residents may transport merchandise to the States which is not intended for sale but for personal or household use up to the value of $200. It is duty- and tax-free, provided the resident has been in Canada at least forty-eight hours. An additional exemption of $300 is allowed once every six months for those who have been in Canada at least twelve days. Under either of these exemptions, but not both, up to one hundred cigars and one gallon of alcoholic beverages may be imported unless the laws of the resident's state prohibits the importation of alcohol.

To simplify entry to the United States, it is advisable to list purchases before reaching the border, keep sales receipts and invoices handy, and pack purchases separately for convenience during inspection. Gifts mailed to friends in the States are not included in these exemptions, and all articles shipped must be declared at customs.

Regulations governing travel by car through Canada are included in Chapter III.

CANADIAN RESIDENTS

Canadian citizens are not required to have specific documents as prerequisites of admission to the United States for visiting periods of less than six months, but it is advisable to carry papers which will establish citizenship status.

British subjects who have been admitted to Canada for residence and who reside there are not required to have specific documents for admission to the United States on visits which do not exceed twenty-nine days.

Baggage Entering the United States

The United States customs officials allow the traveler to bring personal clothing and effects, including cameras and similar personal equipment, and one quart of alcohol, duty-free. All goods must be declared. Regulations regarding all other items should be obtained from the United States consulate, or by writing to the Immigration and Customs Office, State Department, Washington 25, D.C.

Re-entering Canada

Personal clothing and effects are duty-free. Canadians who have been in the United States for more than forty-eight hours are allowed to return with one hundred dollars' worth of articles purchased in the United States, and may repeat this procedure once every four months, but the regulation excludes television sets, television tubes, and any item that cannot be hand-carried. Persons must accompany their purchases at ports of re-entry.

RESIDENTS OF OTHER COUNTRIES

Unexpired passports, visas, and special applications are required by the United States and Canadian immigration authorities. Specific inquiries should be made in advance to determine the current requirements by contacting any Canadian or United States consulate.

GIFTS

Gifts may be carried from one country to another by Canadian and United States residents. However, the limit is one gift per recipient and valued at no more than ten dollars, and it must be in the possession of the traveler at time of inspection. Gifts mailed ahead from one country to another must be declared, and receipts for all gifts sent must be shown for customs inspection.

CURRENCY

American currency may be converted into Canadian currency at any Canadian bank. There is no limit on the amount of American currency that can be taken into Canada. In most instances American currency is accepted as readily as Canadian in all the larger Canadian cities. However, when purchasing plane, rail, bus, and boat tickets, payment will be requested in the currency of the country in which the tickets are purchased. It is advisable to consult a United States bank for current rate of exchange.

For several years the Canadian dollar has been worth more than the American and, although Canadian shopkeepers accept the lower-valued American dollar, the reverse is not true in the United States.

Canadian residents traveling in the United States should have their funds converted to American dollars to avoid any problems. In Alaska, the tradespeople are familiar with handling Canadian currency, but there is always a chance that it might be refused.

Canadian residents planning to enter the United States should check the current Foreign Exchange Control Board regulations with their bank before leaving Canada.

Traveler's Checks

The most convenient way to carry money is in the form of traveler's checks. They are also a convenience and protection against theft, loss, destruction, and mutilation. The cost is $1 for each $100 worth of checks and these may be purchased at local banks. The banks can usually supply one or more kinds, including American Express, Bank of America, or National City Bank, which are recognized and accepted anywhere in the United States and Canada. It is preferable to obtain the checks in small denominations of $5, $10, and $20. When the checks are purchased, the purchaser receives a form on which he must list the number of each check and the denomination. This record should be kept separate from the checks as a protection in case of loss. If the checks are lost, stolen, destroyed, or damaged, the bank or office where they were purchased should be immediately informed and the missing numbers given. For additional safety, purchasers should carry their traveler's checks with them at all times and not pack them away in the baggage.

Personal Checks

There can be great difficulty in cashing personal checks, even with adequate identification, and there will be a fee for cashing the check if it is accepted. Traveler's checks are the best way to carry funds on the trip.

Letter of Credit and Bank Transfers

Travelers who are going to need large sums of money for business or personal reasons should make arrangements with their bank for a letter of credit which can be used at correspondent banks in Alaska or Canada, or for the transfer of funds direct to specific correspondent banks. It is necessary to carry a letter of introduction from the issuing bank to the correspondent banks which will serve as a means of identification.

Bank Fees

In Alaska bank fees are charged for cashing all checks including money orders, cashiers' checks, and certified checks other than those issued by local Alaskan banks. This fee pays the cost of transferring monies, and the cost of handling "outside" drafts. Check with any United States or Canadian bank for current charges and regulations regarding Alaskan bank charges.

Pets

In spite of the popularity of animals throughout the state, traveling in Alaska with pets is inconvenient unless owners are driving their own cars. There are some hotels and motels that do not allow animals and restrictions should be checked before making a reservation. In the large cities and towns there are always a few places that will take pets, but in the smaller and more isolated villages housing and facilities for caring for animals are extremely limited.

Limited veterinarian services are available in Anchorage and Fairbanks at private kennels and it is possible to arrange for medical attention at the large military installations located near these two cities. In other parts of the state there are practically no facilities except those maintained by individual pet owners and animal lovers.

The air lines and bush pilots transport crated animals accompanied or unaccompanied by owners. Motor buses have no facilities and special arrangements must be made in advance to take animals on the Alaska Railroad.

Photography and Equipment

Alaska presents many opportunities for amateur and professional photographers. The boundless scenery and the variety of wild animals provide memorable subjects for movie and still cameras.

Everyone should take a camera and photo equipment on the trip. Color slides of the state, picture post cards, and souvenir photos are available, but they are limited in subject matter and are surprisingly conventional considering the vast photographic potential.

The best kinds of cameras or special equipment are a matter of personal choice, but a good, weatherproof camera case is a necessary piece of equipment.

Conditions of climate and light during the summer months are similar to those in Washington, North Dakota, Michigan, and Maine. Photographing some areas in winter, especially in the interior and the Arctic, is a risk unless cameras and equipment have been checked, serviced, and adjustments made for protection against freezing or inferior performance as a result of exposure to severe cold climate.

Standard film equipment and accessories for still cameras are available in cities, towns, and even in many of the trading posts in the small villages. However, it is best to carry an auxiliary supply to cover any local shortages. Movie film and equipment are available only in the larger cities.

Black-and-white film is developed and printed in the cities and towns, but there are only limited facilities for having color or movie film processed. Most Alaskans send theirs outside the state for processing.

The two places for camera repairs and service are located in Anchorage, at Stewart's Photo Shop or Mac's Foto Service. Both firms feature a large stock of equipment, cameras, and accessories, and provide expert advice on the use of cameras in all areas of the state.

Throughout Alaska, even in the smallest communities, the local film supplier is a well-informed and helpful source of photographic information about the area.

State Symbols

Alaska's flag, the state flower, the official bird, and the song are in evidence everywhere in the state. They are used as designs on everything from manufactured souvenirs to handmade jewelry, and even the words to the state song appear on scarves, tiles, and other giftware.

The state flower is the forget-me-not. The official bird is the willow ptarmigan. Alaska's flag, the Big Dipper and the North Star in gold on a blue background, was designed by Benny Benson, a thirteen-year-old orphan boy who was attending school at the Jesse Lee Home in Seward. He explained his design in this way:

"The blue is for the Alaska sky and the forget-me-not, the Alaska flower. The Big Dipper is for the great bear, a symbol of strength. The North Star is for the future State of Alaska, the greatest State in the Union."

Alaska's official song, "Alaska's Flag," is from a poem by Miss Marie Drake, written to acquaint school children with the meaning of the flag. She wrote:

> Eight stars of gold on a field of blue—
> Alaska's flag. May it mean to you
> The blue of the sea, the evening sky,
> The mountains, lakes, and the flow'rs nearby;
> The gold of the early sourdough's dreams,
> The precious gold of the hills and streams;
> The brilliant stars in the northern sky,
> The "Bear"—the "Dipper"—and, shining high,
> The great North Star with its steady light,
> Over land and sea a beacon bright.
> Alaska's flag—to Alaskans dear,
> The simple flag of the last frontier.

Some Alaskan Words and Phrases

English is spoken throughout the state. In some of the remote native villages Aleut, Eskimo, and Indian predominate, but there are always local residents who speak English. If desired, interpreters may be hired by contacting the head of the village council or inquiring at the trading posts, stores, or schools, but "chechakhos" may get a flavor of the language of the "last frontier" from the Aleut, Eskimo, Indian, and Alaskan words and phrases listed below:

ALASKAN MALEMUTE: A famous breed of working dogs used to pull sleds in the north country. It is a breed separate from the Siberian Husky which is also a noted sled dog. Malemute is also known as Malemuit and the name Alaskan Malemute is registered by the American Kennel Club.

ALCAN: Another name for the Alaska Highway derived from ALaska and CANada which begins at Mile 0 in Dawson Creek,

British Columbia, and officially ends at Mile 1428, Big Delta Junction, Alaska, ninety-seven miles southeast of Fairbanks.

BALEEN: The stiff flexible growth extending from the roof of a whale's mouth in long strands and forming a giant sieve. Shiny black baleen is used for inlay on ivory carvings, contrasting with the ivory surface. It is also woven into baskets by Eskimo men, a feat requiring skill, strength, and patience because this tough material is difficult to work with. Baleen is also commonly referred to as whalebone.

BANANA BELT: Words used to describe the "tropical" areas of Alaska, notably the warmer southeastern region with its lush forests, heavy undergrowth, rapid-growing vegetation, and moist climate.

BINGLES: Imitation or phony money. Originally aluminum tokens or "chits" used for money by the Matanuska Valley settlers during the winter of 1935-36. The $5 and $10 bingles were gold in color and all lesser denominations were silver in color.

BLACK DIAMONDS: Local iron ore which is brilliant jet when cut and polished, and is popularly used as settings for rings, bracelets, and other types of jewelry.

BREAKUP: Time of the year when there is much mud, slush, and flooding as the ice begins to thaw and the snow melts. The water pressure swells under the ice in rivers and streams, forcing the ice to crumble and quake; blocks of ice flow swiftly downstream to the icebound sea, pushing, grinding, and breaking the icy barrier.

THE BUSH: A term borrowed from Africa, Australia, and Canada which is used to designate the remote areas that are sparsely settled. Commonly used in referring to "wide-open spaces" but more specifically applied to the Arctic tundra and river valleys where there are few trees and all vegetation grows close to the earth.

CABIN FEVER: Words used to describe a kind of claustrophobia, melancholy, and hypertension resulting from too many hours of darkness and too much time spent in isolated areas by trappers, prospectors, and residents of the sub-Arctic and Arctic during the long winter months.

CACHE: Log huts on tin-wrapped stilts used to store food and supplies out of the reach of animals. "Wet" caches, used in summer by homesteaders, trappers, and prospectors to keep foods cool, consist of a screened box-frame suspended from a rafter or tree limb and kept covered with a damp cloth.

THE CHAIN: Another name for the Aleutian Islands, the long broken tail of islands that extend from the Alaska Peninsula westward to Attu Island in the North Pacific Ocean.

CHINOOK: Refers to salmon, and also to the warm southwest wind blowing from the sea to the mainland.

CHECHAKHO: Also appears as "cheechahko" or "cheechako." A Chinook Indian word adopted by Alaskans which means "just arrived" and is currently used in good humor and not as an insult.

CHUCK: A term applied to any body of water, large or small.

CLEANUP: The amount of gold accumulated at the end of a season regardless of the method used to extract the ore.

DERBY: A term usually applied to fishing, sled-dog racing, and deer-hunting and whale-hunting contests.

FOUR-FIVE-SIX: A popular but illegal gambling game. Though it is played with three numbered dice it is similar to the card game "Twenty-One." The first roll of dice is for high man who is designated Banker. The game proceeds with all players competing against the Banker. Bets are placed and the Banker rolls. If he rolls the sequence 4-5-6 or 6-6-6, he collects all bets. If a 1-2-3 or a pair and an ace comes up, the Banker pays off. When he throws a pair and any number other than an ace, the dice are then passed to the next player to the left, eventually continuing around the circle of players. Each player rolls until he has a pair and one odd number. The pair can be higher or lower than the Banker's, but the odd number must be higher to win. Three of a kind and 4-5-6 are always winning throws and allow the player to become Banker if he desires. The player loses if the odd number is lower than that of the Banker, if he throws a pair and an ace, or if the dice come up in a 1-2-3 sequence. The Banker is not allowed to remove any money from the bank until he loses the bank to another player.

FREEZE-UP: The time of the year when sea ports are icebound and all bodies of water are frozen. This condition does not exist in most coastal ports of southeastern and south central Alaska which are open the year around.

HOOTCH: Any hard liquor but specifically that which is home-made. This slang word is said to have originated in Sitka during the early days when the Indians distilled a volatile molasses mixture known as "hootchenoo." Hootchenoo is the American spelling for the southeastern Alaska Indian word, "khutzn'hu," designating an archipelago, inlet, and village on Admiralty Island. Illicit liquor manufacturing at the village brought federal disapproval and the United States Navy guns shelled the village.

ICE WORM: The "ice worm" began as a great fictional joke during the gold-rush days and was a source of many tall stories. Newcomers were treated to drinks with a bit of spaghetti in them and for many years the ice-worm legend was popular. During the settling of the Matanuska Valley the ice worm was revived and an organization known as the Ancient Order of Ice Worms spear-headed a campaign against the local governing agencies, creating great controversy. Real ice worms do exist and specimens may be seen in the Territorial Museum in Juneau.

IGLOO: Also spelled "iglu," an Eskimo word meaning house or hut, but in Alaska they are built neither of snow nor of ice blocks, except in extreme emergencies, for temporary shelter when no other building material is available. An igloo is commonly built partially of wood logs, boards, driftwood, or scrap lumber, occasionally combined with whalebone, metal sheathing obtained from discarded oil cans, or other scrap metals. Sod blocks are banked around the outside to provide additional insulation and in some cases the blocks enclose the structure. In summer the sod has a tendency to send out sprouts and wild flowers. Eskimos build ice-block windbreakers for protection when fishing through holes in

the ice in open areas. They have the appearance of partially finished igloos, but that is the extent of ice-block construction in
Alaska. On the other hand, the Eskimos of northern Canada do
construct homes of ice and snow.

IRON CHINK: An automatic device for splitting and cleaning
fish which may be seen when visiting the canneries; it is an expres-
sion coined as a result of automation when the machines replaced
the Chinese workers and made the "China gang" obsolete in
Alaska.

KAYAK: A small, lightweight, Eskimo skin boat which has a
single small opening in the top where one person can sit while
propelling the boat with a two-bladed paddle. The rim of the
kayak opening has a wooden hoop attached on which the Eskimo
secures his waterproof parka, literally sealing himself in the kayak
so that water cannot penetrate. So efficient is this method that the
kayak and passenger may roll completely over in the water and
return upright without being swamped. The Eskimos have developed an extraordinary skill in handling these boats and navi-
gating them in the open seas. A similar skin-covered boat is the
"bidarka," also referred to as the "bidar" or "bidarkee," from the
Russian word meaning canoe.

KUPIAK: The Eskimo word for coffee.

MUKLUK: A fur boot made by the Eskimo women skin sewers
which has soles made of tough sealskin or sea-lion skin curled up
at the edges and shaped to fit at the heels and toes by crimping
the hide. It is still the custom for some Eskimo women to fashion
the soles in the old way by biting the leather with their teeth to
form it into the proper shape, but many of the younger Eskimo
women now use pliers to do the job. The upper part of the boot is
made of reindeer hide and other hardy furs. The top portions are
decorated in patchwork style, using colored furs, wool yarns, or
grass to achieve geometric designs. Reindeer sinew is the thread
used for sewing together the various parts of the boot, which is
always designed with the fur side of the hides on the outside. A
removable inner sole of dried grass or baleen shavings is added

for comfort, as well as for absorption, so no freezing moisture collects.

MUKTUK: The rubbery outer layer of black or white whale skin and fat, usually two to three inches thick, is a popular Eskimo food. This chewy substance, similar to gristle, is cut into slabs or served in small squares which are chewed raw or served pickled.

MUSH: The command to a sled-dog team which means "go" or "go faster." The term is also used to describe traveling on foot over snow.

MUSKEG: Swampy areas formed by the deposit of layers of water-soaked and decayed vegetation with a covering of moss and scrub growth, forming a deceptively solid-looking surface.

OOMIAK: Also umiak, the large Eskimo walrus-skin boats used for hunting and transportation. They are frequently outfitted with modern outboard motors.

OOGRUK: Also ugrook and ugruk. The sealskin or sea-lion skin used for making mukluks and moccasins. It is also an Eskimo food.

OUTSIDE: Means anywhere except Alaska and usually refers to any of the other states.

PANHANDLE: A word used to describe the southeastern section of Alaska.

PARKA: Pronounced "parky." A jacket or full-length garment made of fur, windproof and waterproof fabrics, or a combination of both, with an attached hood for protecting the head from the cold and a fur ruff encircling the face for protection. Fur parkas of high quality have a body, sleeves, and hood of seal, squirrel, or raccoon skins with the fur side out, a wide band of decoration on the bottom, and cuffs consisting of geometric designs patched together from various colored fur pieces. The hood has a ruff of long-haired fur, usually wolf or wolverine and sometimes a combination of both. Eskimo women wear the full-length "fancy dress" parkas which slip on over the head. The men wear the jacket type. Special raincoat parkas are made from cured seal gut sewn together with sinew which are lightweight, waterproof, windproof, and translucent. A parka cover of bright-colored cotton print fabric is worn over the fur parkas to protect them and to keep them clean.

PERMAFROST: The name given to the condition of the earth in most areas of the Arctic and sub-Arctic above the Alaska Range where the soil remains frozen all year around except for a thin layer on the surface which thaws during the summer.

SKOOKUM-HOUSE: A jail or prison, derived from the Chinook Indian word "skookum," which means strong, big, or great.

SOURDOUGH: The mixture of water, sugar, yeast, and flour which is allowed to age and ferment before being used to make bread or hot cakes. Only a portion is used at a time and that is replaced by adding a little more flour and water to the original. The more frequently the sourdough is used and replenished, the more it improves in quality. A sourdough is an old-timer, and, as the saying goes, "The first twenty years in Alaska you are Chechakho, the next twenty you become a sourdough, and after forty you are a pioneer."

STATESIDE: A word for the continental United States.

TILLICUM: A friend or partner, usually of long association.

TUNDRA: The vast, grassy, treeless, and swampy Arctic plains areas that cover about 30 per cent of Alaska's land area. It is the natural range for herds of caribou on which a large part of the native population depends for its livelihood.

ULU: Also umak, a homemade, very sharp knife shaped like a small single-blade vegetable chopper. It is used by the Eskimo women to cut skins and blubber and is an important tool in making mukluks, parkas, and other garments.

WANIGAN: A small building, hut, or shack, mounted on large skids which can be easily moved from one place to another.

Yo-Yo: An Eskimo game played with two small fur balls, each attached to a leather string. The object of the game is to hold the leather strings in one hand and make the two balls on the other end revolve in opposite directions for a prolonged period of time. It requires a type of co-ordination like rubbing the head and patting the stomach at the same time.

Legal Holidays

Government agencies, banks, and most business firms observe the following legal holidays: January 1, February 12, February 22, March 30 (date of Alaska Purchase, called Seward's Day), May 30, July 4, the first Monday of September, October 18 (Alaska Day), November 11, Thanksgiving Day, Christmas Day, and every general election day. If a holiday falls on Sunday, the following Monday is treated as a legal holiday.

Time Zones

Alaska has four time zones; going from east to west, they include: Pacific Standard Time, Yukon Standard Time, Alaska Standard Time, and Bering Standard Time.

When it is 9:00 A.M. at Seattle, Washington, it is:

9:00 A.M. at Ketchikan and Juneau (P.S.T.)

8:00 A.M. at Yakutat and Skagway (Y.S.T.)

7:00 A.M. at Cordova, Valdez, Seward, Anchorage, and Fairbanks (A.S.T.)

6:00 A.M. at Nome (B.S.T.)

The Aleutians and Little Diomede are in the Bering Time Zone, and southeastern Alaskan towns north to and including Juneau use Pacific Standard Time.

Travelers using the Alaska Highway through Canada will encounter the following time zones:

Alberta Province—Mountain Standard Time

British Columbia—Pacific Standard Time

Yukon Territory—Yukon Standard Time

In May and through August British Columbia is on Daylight Saving Time.

Bush Pilots and Plane Service

The average Alaskan uses airplanes thirty-five to forty-five times more than other Americans and many own their own planes.

Air transportation is the lifeline of the state, and it started with bush pilots who have played a key role in the development of the state ever since the early 1920's.

They are highly skilled men who carry supplies and passengers, deliver medicine, and transport the sick and injured. Everything from dog teams to heavy mining and construction equipment is carried in their planes. Bush pilots maintain the only transportation link with the remote areas of the state and where there are no landing fields, they bring their planes down on river sand bars or any available clearing. With their pontoon planes they land on isolated lakes and waterways to service the people living in the bush country. In winter the pontoons or wheels are changed to skis so that only a patch of snow is needed for landing.

Individual bush pilots fly their own planes or work for air-line companies providing scheduled service between the cities and the bush. As part of their routine duties they deliver groceries, serve as shopping experts and shoppers for the bush people, and are called upon to drop newspapers, magazines, messages, and parcels to prospectors and trappers who are alone in a wilderness area where landing is impossible.

For the isolated customers in the bush, these pilots not only provide transportation; they are also close friends of their customers who consider them as part of an enormous family, a family that is linked together by the men and their planes.

Everything from single-engine planes to two-engine DC-3 air liners are used by these pilots for bush flights. The planes are operated the year around and only the severest weather interrupts the scheduled services.

The planes are comfortable but passengers are frequently surrounded by mounds of cargo. The interiors of the larger planes are constructed for multiple service and quick conversion to carry passengers or accommodate freight. The seating arrangement is the same as on any air liner; however, unoccupied seats are folded up and locked in the walls to make room for a kitchen stove, refrigerator, sled, or any other large item to be delivered.

Hostess or steward service is provided on the air liners between larger communities and meals are served aboard free of charge. Ticket sales are handled at the airport, but in the cities the air lines and charter bush pilots maintain downtown ticket counters in hotels and office buildings.

Highways

In 1905 the Alaska highway system consisted of 2,200 miles of very poor roads with less than 500 miles of improved gravel surface and 10,000 miles of trails and sled roads used by the miners, fishermen, and the military. Today the highway system totals 5,153 miles, with 1,959 miles of year-round paved roads connecting the cities of Anchorage, Valdez, Fairbanks, and Seward with the Alaska Highway. The secondary roads are paved in the immediate vicinity of the cities and towns, and the rest are gravel surfaced. Approximately 1,500 miles of secondary roads are connected to the paved highways and open to traffic all year; the rest connect isolated communities with rail, water, or air transportation facilities.

At present, southeastern Alaska cities are not connected to the Alaska highway system although there are roadways leading short distances out of the towns to industrial sites or near-by villages.

In addition to the Alaska Highway #2, the principal highways in Alaska are: Richardson Highway #1 which begins with Mile 0 at Valdez and goes due north, joins Glenn Highway at Glennallen Junction, Mile 115, then proceeds north, connecting with the Alaska Highway at Big Delta, and continues on to Fairbanks, a distance of 365 miles. Glenn Highway #3 begins at Mile 0 at Anchorage and goes northeast, crossing the Richardson Highway at Glennallen Junction at Mile 189 and continues to the Alaska Highway where it ends at Tok Junction, a distance of 328 miles.

The secondary highways are: Denali Highway #8 which begins with Mile 0 at Paxson on the Richardson Highway, travels 160 miles westward to Mount McKinley National Park entrance, and continues through the park an additional 89 miles to Kantishna.

Steese Highway #6 begins with Mile 0 at Fairbanks and goes northeast to Circle on the Yukon River, a distance of 164 miles. This highway is open the year around from Fairbanks to Chatanika at Mile 31 and is open over the entire length from mid-May through November.

Sterling Highway #5 begins with Mile 0 at Seward, follows the

Seward-Anchorage Highway north to Mile 38, turns west to Kenai, then south to Homer, a distance of about 175 miles.

Seward-Anchorage Highway #4 begins with Mile 0 in Anchorage, and is paved the entire length south to Seward, a distance of 131 miles.

Taylor Highway #3 goes north at Tetlin Junction, Mile 1301 on the Alaska Highway to Eagle, a distance of about 160 miles; this highway also has a fork turning off before Eagle that runs across the Canadian border to Dawson, Yukon Territory. This highway is open to travel from June through November.

Haines Highway #9 begins with Mile 0 in Haines and runs northwest to meet the Alaska Highway, a distance of 154 miles. The first 41 miles are paved to the Canadian border.

Communications

Communications in Alaska are extensive. Every city and town has telephone and telegraph services, and long-distance calls are handled quickly and easily. Small villages and communities all have some form of radio communication, using either the "White Alice" network or individual ham operators who are part of the "Sourdough Net," which handles communications traffic five nights a week on the seventy-five-meter band and includes women ham operators who have a special club of their own called "PARKA" (Polar Amateur Radio Klub of Alaska), with headquarters in Anchorage, which also handles messages and other communications. Mukluk Telegraph, a commercially sponsored radio program, broadcasts messages to the bush at nine-thirty every evening six nights a week from Anchorage. Communications are also handled by ship-to-shore phone service and "bush phone" facilities in hospitals, schools, or other government installations.

The "White Alice" communication system is unique to Alaska. It uses ultra-high-frequency radio relays to transmit telephone conversations and telegraph messages between the remote villages, cities, and towns. As recently as 1956, it was extremely difficult to place a call from the capital city of Juneau to places like Nome without long delays and interrupted conversations. Today, however, many communities are receiving their first reliable, full-time long-distance telephone facilities through "White Alice."

In this system, radio relays are used because of the difficulty of building and maintaining wire circuits across the state's inaccessible regions and servicing them during extreme weather conditions. The radio relay also minimizes interference from atmospheric and meteorological conditions which previously hampered communications in Alaska.

"Beyond-horizon" radio uses huge antennas of distinctive shapes. Some, resembling outdoor movie screens, weigh one hundred tons, are sixty feet high, and are aimed at the horizon, facing each other, about two hundred miles apart.

At the transmitting point, scores of separate telephone conversations and telegraph messages are combined into a single radio signal. A "feed horn" on a tower in front of the big antenna sprays the signal against the face of the antenna, which beams it out toward the horizon like a huge searchlight. The deflected signal is received by another movie-screen type antenna where it is amplified and sent on its way to the person on the other end of the circuit.

"White Alice" is the largest "beyond-horizon" communications network to be built. The 33 relay stations cover a telephone circuit totaling 170,000 miles and a telegraph circuit of 50,000 miles.

These circuits are made available to the public through the Alaska Communications System which has been in existence since 1900 and is operated by the United States Army, providing communications between Alaska and the rest of the world. It serves the general public, ships at sea, governmental agencies, the Department of Defense, press services to newspapers and radio broadcast stations, and exchanges all classes of commercial and government traffic with connecting lines in Seattle. It is directly responsible for 40,362 miles of radio circuits, 6,800 miles of open-wire lines, and 1,400 miles of submarine cable.

Telephone and Telegraph Rates and Services—Telephone and telegraph rates are moderate; as an example, the three-minute night telephone rate to Seattle from Anchorage is $5.25, and

$4.50 from Juneau. Telegraph rates for a fifty-word night letter to Seattle from Anchorage is $2.35, and $1.85 from Juneau.

Telegrams for people en route will be held at the local Alaska communications office if marked "hold for call" by sender. In smaller towns and villages a list of undelivered telegraph and telephone messages is posted daily in the post offices.

Mail Service

The airplane has gradually replaced the dog teams and power boats on Alaska's mail routes, carrying the majority of mail between points in Alaska, as well as between Alaska and the rest of the world. The last scheduled dog-team mail route now operates between Gambell and Savoonga on the St. Lawrence Island. Today the service between all points is substantially accelerated by air lines, nonscheduled carriers, and bush pilots.

All mail should be sent by air. Regular mail is slow; it goes by boat to southeastern and south central Alaska and is transferred to the Alaska Railroad for delivery to the interior and communities along the rail line. Regular mail to Nome, northwestern Alaska, and other remote points, goes by boat to Anchorage or by train to Fairbanks, and is carried from these cities by air to the final destination. Lengthy delays of several weeks are not uncommon for this kind of mail service.

Anchorage, Ketchikan, Juneau, and Fairbanks are the only cities with house-to-house delivery service. In all other communities, residents rent boxes at the post office or receive mail in care of General Delivery.

For travelers

Canadian postage stamps must be used on mail posted in Canada. Packages sent from Alaskan cities to Canadian cities will be subject to duty and customs regulations the same as all packages from Canadian cities to points in the United States.

Trips should be planned so that mail can be picked up en route. Letters may be sent in care of General Delivery at known stopovers in Canada, as well as in the United States.

For Ships' Passengers—All mail sent to passengers in care of steamship lines is delivered to the ship before departure. Round-trip passengers may collect additional mail that has accumulated after departure at the ship's ticket office on return to Vancouver.

Mail should be addressed with passenger's name, ship's tour number, and departure date. Passengers on the S.S. *Glacier Queen* or the S.S. *Yukon Star* should have mail sent in care of the Arctic Alaska Tours in Seattle.

Mail may be forwarded to Skagway at passenger's request; however, advance arrangements must be made and funds advanced to cover air-mail forwarding charges. It is not recommended that mail be forwarded to passengers on round-trip tours because it may be delayed in transit. If it is necessary to receive important mail in Skagway from people in the United States or Canada, the sender may address the mail direct to General Delivery, Skagway, Alaska, or in care of the ship's agents in Skagway.

There are mailboxes aboard ship for outgoing mail which is processed and forwarded by ship's personnel so that it travels the most direct route to its destination. However, American postage stamps must be used for mail that is going ashore at Alaskan ports, and Canadian postage stamps at Canadian ports.

Shopping

Most small towns and villages have at least one general store to supply the local needs. Although there is little variety, the stock of foods is almost always of high quality, especially the canned products, because they are mostly all shipped in from outside the state and storekeepers discovered long ago that it is more economical to ship in the best products. Little-known brands are seldom seen on the shelves and there are never special sales of inferior products to entice new customers. The same situation is true of clothing, household equipment, and supplies.

In the larger cities, specialty shops for men and women carry the most fashionable clothing, but never in large quantities and not in all sizes. Most of the clothing is the outdoor type, practical and long-wearing, and the shops carry a time-tested variety from world markets. Salespeople are well informed and helpful to customers in choosing the right items to suit local conditions.

The quality and variety of hunting, fishing, and outdoor equipment is excellent and shopkeepers can be relied on for advice.

There is a noticeable absence of luxury items in the shops because there is very little demand for them, but, compared with conditions in other states, shoppers may feel that everything is a luxury because of the prices. That is a situation brought about by the high cost of shipping items into the state.

Shopping for gifts, souvenirs, and arts and crafts is easy and productive; even in the most remote villages native stores carry a good supply for visitors. There are many souvenirs and gift items from manufacturers, some of high quality and many inferior. Choosing authentic indigenous arts and crafts, especially native-made products, can be difficult without some advance knowledge of the differences that exist between partially or wholly manufactured items which seem to be handmade.

There are items which are not produced in Alaska but are so Alaskan in appearance that it is almost impossible to know what is real and what is not. The authentic native arts and crafts made exclusively by Aleut, Indian, or Eskimo people almost always have the Alaska Native Arts and Crafts label. The trademark is an Eskimo hunter in a kayak, superimposed on an Indian totemic eye design, with the letters ANAC at the top.

Alaska Native Arts and Crafts

ANAC is the name of Alaska Native Arts and Crafts Cooperative Association, Inc., a clearing house organized as a private business, a nonprofit co-operative engaged in the procurement and marketing of Aleut, Eskimo, and Indian craft products. It is a wholesale supplier for all Alaskan native crafts produced by its members, and the main offices are located in Juneau.

Eighteen village groups are members of the organization, as well as many individual native craftsmen.

For many years, the Aleuts, Eskimos, and Indians supplemented their meager incomes through the home manufacture and sale of such handicraft as ivory carvings, mukluks, baskets, totems, and moccasins. However, selling their handicrafts was by trial and error. Unable to find or reach suitable markets, craft producers were faced with a huge surplus of articles.

In 1937, teachers at the government school in Nome were encouraging a group of Eskimo skin sewers, who, through organization, good management, progressive designing, and adapting to current market demands, were attracting much favorable attention. The Nome Skin Sewers, as they are called, took on the work of providing arctic clothing for Admiral Byrd's expeditions and the success of this project led to the formation of a co-operative skin sewing business owned and operated by over one hundred Eskimo women.

Other teachers were stimulating a revival of native crafts in the schools and villages, such as at Kotzebue, one hundred miles north of Nome, and as a result, a clearing house was established by the government to handle the sales of native products.

From the beginning, the value of the clearing house was apparent. It was a service organization procuring stock for consumers, as well as finding markets for craftsmen. It stabilized prices, encouraged pride of workmanship, and stimulated the crafting of objects which were useful and still kept the decorative old art forms.

Soon after the inauguration of the new program, the Indian Service teachers were enlisted in its promotion and urged to set up active crafts programs wherever possible. This impetus alone gave Alaska's native craftsmanship an enormous lift. During the first few years of growth under the Bureau of Indian Affairs, master craftsmen and craftswomen were employed as part of the school programs to instruct. Over fifty native instructors in skin sewing, ivory carving, Chilkat blanketry, kayak-, snowshoe-, and boat-making perpetuated and revived the native heritage.

As a result of the program, lasting influences were established and forgotten arts were revitalized. In some villages entirely new crafts were introduced as a result of the growing importance and demand for the better-styled, functional native crafts.

The development of the trade-mark and the certification of merchandise sold by ANAC aided prospective buyers in selecting authentic work from among the many imported imitations and falsifications of the art of Alaska's natives.

From the $29,000 in sales of the first year of operation, ANAC gradually increased its services so that the net sales in recent years have averaged close to $150,000 annually and, since 1937, well over two and a half million dollars' worth of arts and crafts products have been sold.

A large percentage of the money is distributed among the native craftsmen who would be in need without this market outlet. In addition to the products sold through ANAC, the craftsmen have developed additional markets through local traders, as well as utilizing many of the products themselves.

Many native villages list the production of arts and crafts as one of the two basic occupations in their trade economy. In localities not offering the advantage of a store or trading post, individual craftsmen mail their handiwork direct to ANAC in Juneau.

Not only is the present production of arts and crafts filling a vital need in supplying part-time and seasonal employment to the native hunters, trappers, and fishermen, but the industry provides many Alaskan shops with attractive and appealing merchandise. To keep up with the demand for authentic crafts, remote and isolated Alaskan villages are visited by ANAC personnel to evaluate, purchase, place orders, and suggest adaptations which would improve sales.

To allow the native producers a fair price as well as to keep prices at reasonable levels for the purchasers, ANAC operates on a small profit margin.

The major articles made by the natives and carrying the ANAC trade-mark are both useful and decorative. They are made of superior materials which are associated with the craftsmen's immediate environment. Skin sewing, which includes moccasins, mukluks, parkas, jackets, fur mittens, gloves, and bags, are made from seal, oogruk, reindeer, moose, deer, caribou, and wolf skin, and represent over half of the craft production. Ivory figures carved from the tusks of the walrus make up close to one-fourth the total. Basketry is the next highest in production, with wood carvings and totems closely following. They are the four major crafts of Alaska, but along with them are such diverse and intriguing examples of native handiwork as the Chilkat blanket, jade jewelry, wood and bone ceremonial masks, model dog sleds, kayaks, bidarkas, and snowshoes, full-size seal harpoons, silver bracelets, baleen toboggans, ink drawings on reindeer skin, snow glasses, and jewelry made of caribou hoof, Eskimo yo-yos, baleen baskets, and totems ranging from four inches to five feet tall.

It has been assumed by some that, as the Eskimo, Indian, and Aleut integrates his life activities with those of the white population, he will abandon his traditional craftsmanship. No doubt this will be true in some cases. The qualities of a superior craftsman have made the native efficient in the skilled occupations of the white man. But home industry and the creative drive are factors which help to influence the continued productivity of native arts and crafts.

Indian Arts and Crafts Board

Another important influence on the craftsmen and craftsmanship is the vital and active Indian Arts and Crafts Board, a branch of the Department of Interior, which has a year-round field representative in Alaska to aid in the marketing, production, and promotion of native-owned projects, and to give advice and assistance in forming new projects. Many of the products of the groups sponsored by the Indian Arts and Crafts Board are sold in the native villages and in stores and shops throughout the state. The board also co-operates with ANAC in the promotion and sale of authentic native crafts to world-wide markets.

Special Health Hints and Foods

Hospitals and medical assistance are available throughout the state except in extremely remote villages where minor accidents and sicknesses are diagnosed and treated via the bush radio network between the villages and the nearest medical installations. When serious illness or injury occurs in a remote area, the patient is flown out by bush plane to the nearest doctor or hospital.

Drugstores and prescription counters have sufficient medical supplies in all the large cities and towns. Smaller communities and villages have limited supplies at local trading posts or general stores. Any special medication should be carried by travelers going to remote areas.

In isolated places where there are water shortages, keeping

clean can be a minor problem. A package of Wash n' Dri, cleansing lotion, dry shampoo, and witch hazel will help to make the trip more enjoyable.

Food and drinking water served in public restaurants and cafés are clean and should not present any health problems. Native foods are a tempting curiosity, but they should be avoided. Occasionally visitors receive invitations to dinner in native homes. While visiting Eskimo families, the meal may consist of reindeer stew, dried or smoked fish, and canned or fresh berries, depending on the time of year.

Some of the more unusual foods served in the Eskimo country are muktuk, a dish of whale skin and blubber, oogruk, or seal, which has been cooked, dried, soaked in seal oil, and then stored in sealskin pokes until served. A recipe for bear feet indicates that "most people like the bear feet better than the meat. Cook them well and add salt. Four feet would take about one teaspoon of salt. Take them out of the pot and let them cool. Eat them with seal oil."

That recipe comes from the perfect book on Eskimo cookery and ingredients, *The Eskimo Cook Book*, written by Eskimo students at the Shishmaref Day School who share profits from the book with the Alaska Crippled Children's Association. Copies may be purchased for 50 cents at the Gilded Cage, the Alaska Crippled Children's store in Anchorage at 225 E Street. Or they will mail copies for 60 cents prepaid.

One of the other noted recipes in the book is Lincod Eskimo Ice Cream which is prepared in two parts: "Grate reindeer tallow in small pieces. Add seal oil slowly while beating with hand. After some seal oil has been used, then add a little water while whipping. Continue adding seal oil and water while whipping. Then prepare the Lincod. First cook and boil the Lincod with water in the pot and no salt. Remove all the bones from the fish and break the fish into small pieces. Dry the pieces for a while and mix these with Eskimo Ice-cream. Add seal oil once in a while and as much water as you need."

Tipping

The procedure for tipping in Alaska is much the same as in any other state. In restaurants, bars, and other eating and drinking establishments tips are given at the rate of 15 per cent of the total check. It is not necessary to tip at soda fountains, coffee shops, or cafés except for complete meals.

Entertainers in bars, night clubs, and restaurants are given tips by those requesting special numbers at the rate of $1 or more per request.

Hotel bellboys receive tips of 25 cents per bag and the same amount for each room-service delivery. It isn't necessary to tip for maid service unless the stay is a week or longer and then it is entirely optional, depending on extra service received.

At the small roadhouses and family-owned lodgings no one tips owners of the establishments.

Alaska Railroad porters are tipped 25 cents for each bag carried and the car porter should be tipped at the termination of the trip for any special services rendered en route. Dining-room porters receive 15 per cent of the total meal or refreshment check.

Bush pilots, air-line hostesses and personnel, bus drivers, and the United States-Canadian immigration and customs officials should not be tipped.

It is optional whether or not to tip professional hunting and fishing guides at the end of their services.

It is not polite to give money to individual performers at Indian or Eskimo dances or games, but money may be given to the group. It is not customary to tip natives who permit photographs to be taken of themselves, their homes, or their families.

At dinners and socials given by business, civic, or social organizations there are no tips unless the chairman of the event specifically requests it.

On package tours by boat, an amount equal to 15 per cent of the fare should be allowed for tipping ship's personnel. Choice of how tips should be distributed depends largely on individual attention and service received. Tipping is usually done just prior to the end of the voyage and is presented in lump sums rather

than in small amounts given each time a service is performed.
The ship's purser and officers should not be tipped.

Insects and Allergies

Except for the mosquito, Alaska is almost free of the insect
nuisance. Poisonous snakes haven't yet discovered the state, and
ragweed and other high-irritation pollen are almost unknown. But
mosquitos are subjects for discussion second only to the "weather
talk."

There are hundreds of stories about mosquitoes and many of
them have become a part of Alaskan lore, like the one told by a
sourdough about the two mosquitoes who "lifted a man right out
of his bed and dragged him outdoors. Then one of them decided
to go back in and get the man's wife."

"What?" asked the other mosquito. "And take a chance of
leaving him out here for the big ones to get?"

Stories like that contribute to the Alaskan mosquito legend,
but they are not as much of a menace as some sourdoughs would
like outsiders to believe. However, it is a good idea to take along
a repellent and keep it available especially in June to mid-July.

Children's Activities

Some of Alaska's most enthusiastic visitors are children. In
Alaska children go everywhere, on camping trips, fishing, hiking,
swimming, and rock hunting. Up to sixteen years of age they are
allowed to fish without licenses.

Teen-agers will find their counterparts in Alaska playing the
same jukebox records, going to socials, dances, basketball games,
and congregating in the corner drugstores for cokes. Traveling in
Alaska gives young visitors an opportunity to experience some-
thing of the frontier country and a hint of what the pioneer days
were like in their own home states.

Parents traveling with small children will find nursery schools
in the larger Alaskan cities and towns offering services by the
hour and day, or for longer periods of time.

Warning to Hikers

Because Alaska is truly a big land, hikers should not set out on trips before investigating the trail conditions, terrain, and local weather peculiarities. Forest rangers, the police, and local residents are always helpful, and the personnel at lodges, hotels, and other commercial establishments are most always aware of local conditions.

Those who want to explore the remote areas, or hike on trails that are not well marked, should take the precaution of notifying a responsible person of the plan, the direction, and proposed destination of the trip.

The scenery is so tempting that many people are inclined to stop their cars along the highways and take a side trip on foot. It is a very dangerous thing to do unless the area is well known or the hiker has been briefed in advance. The chance of getting lost is only part of the danger; the more serious problem is that of wild animals, especially in areas of large bear and moose populations.

Films on Alaska

For a preview of Alaska it is fun to see a few of the many adult and children's motion pictures available at nominal rental fees. These films are distributed to organizations, clubs, schools, or any interested group. For information about showings write to the following distributors:

American Museum of Natural History, Film Library, 79th Street and Central Park West, New York 24, New York. The museum has a comprehensive film library with several films on Alaska including "Eskimo Children," a single reel which rents for $2; "Alaska's Silver Millions," three reels and renting for $2; and "Nanook of the North," six reels renting for $10.

Ideal Pictures, 58 East South Water Street, Chicago 1, Illinois, has distributing offices in Portland, Oregon, Los Angeles, California, New York City, and twenty-two cities throughout the country. Their films include "Alaska—Modern Frontier," single reel, rental $2.50; "Alaska," 1½ reels, rental $3.50; and all of Walt Disney's short subjects on Alaska.

Northern Films, 1947 14th Avenue North, Seattle, Washington, specializes in Alaska films and has many excellent ones available.

Outdoor Films, Box A 848, Kodiak, Alaska, offers films of Kodiak bears and other wildlife in and around Kodiak.

Encyclopaedia Britannica Films, Inc., 1150 Wilmette Avenue, Wilmette, Illinois; The Museum of Modern Art, 11 West 53rd Street, New York 19, New York; and Association Films, Inc., 347 Madison Avenue, New York 17, New York, all have large film libraries with Alaskan subjects.

Pan-American World Airways has a feature film on Alaska which may be requested at any of their offices throughout the country. The Audio Visual Center, Inc., 1205 North 45th Street, Seattle 3, Washington, is the distributor of the film produced by the University of Alaska showing the campus life, activities, and facilities of the university.

CHAPTER III. HOW TO GO

There is transportation to Alaska from any city in the United States or Canada, traveling many exciting routes, with stopovers en route for visits to the beautiful and interesting places, or traveling directly and quickly to the forty-ninth state.

The major form of transportation to consider is air travel, especially if you have limited time in which to make the trip. Alternate choices include traveling by automobile, which may be accomplished from any point in the United States and Canada on highways leading to the heart of Alaska. One can go by boat from the West Coast or may choose any number of "mixed" forms of transportation, in part on trains, boats, airplanes, motor coaches, or automobiles, with innumerable combinations of each depending on the length of time one can devote to travel en route, as well as the amount of money budgeted for the trip and the individual's personal preferences.

By Air

Speed, accessibility, and convenience are major factors of the air travel to and from Alaska, and within the new state the airplane is the primary means of transportation from place to place. In many instances, it is the only way.

Seattle, Washington, is the main departure point in continental United States because of the frequency of service and the greater choice of routes.

Canadian passengers may fly from Seattle, Vancouver, or Prince Rupert, B.C., depending on which is the most convenient. Ellis Air Lines runs a scheduled flight service from Prince Rupert, B.C., to the cities of southeastern Alaska connecting with flights to all other points in Alaska.

Passengers leaving from Vancouver, B.C., may fly to Seattle

via United Airlines or Trans-Canada Airlines to make connections for Alaska. Alternate routes from Vancouver include the Canadian Pacific Airlines to Whitehorse in the Yukon Territory in Canada, then by the White Pass and Yukon Route train to Skagway, or the Canadian Pacific Airlines flight to Fairbanks. But the plane schedule should be confirmed because the service is not always in operation.

Generally speaking, Alaskans do not favor one air-line service over another, nor are there great variations in service between the major air lines. Choice depends more on the time you want to travel, your destination, and the availability of space.

All points in the United States and Canada are within twenty-four hours or less from Alaska.

TYPICAL ROUND-TRIP AIR FARES*

	First Class	Air Coach
New York/Anchorage, Alaska	$540.40	$373.00
Chicago/Seattle	228.70	160.10
Chicago/Vancouver, B.C.	244.50	176.70
Denver/Seattle	148.90	114.40
Los Angeles/Seattle	129.50	96.70
Minneapolis/Seattle	196.10	151.50
Winnipeg, Manitoba/Seattle	186.00	149.40
Winnipeg/Vancouver	165.00	132.80
Montreal, Quebec/Vancouver, B.C.	333.00	246.00
Seattle/Anchorage, Alaska	202.50	(None avail.)
Seattle/Fairbanks	178.20	" "
Seattle/Nome	226.80	" "
Seattle/Juneau	108.00	" "

* U.S. dollars quoted, tax not included.

Air lines serving the "gateway cities" include: Alaska Air-lines, Canadian Pacific Airlines, Northwest Orient Airlines, Pacific Northern Airlines, Pan-American World Airways, Trans-Canada Airlines, United Air Lines, and Western Airlines.

Plane Reservations

Reservations may be made directly with the air lines whose representatives are located in most of the major cities. Many people prefer to make arrangements with their local travel agents and it is recommended that a travel agent make the plans for the trip to Alaska, particularly one who is a member of the American Society of Travel Agents (ASTA). These agents not only assist in securing reservations, but also provide excellent assistance in planning the entire Alaskan trip. ASTA members are familiar with all travel to and from Alaska and within the state. They have more complete travel information than most any other service you might consult, primarily because the majority of services in Alaska are also members of this international organization.

Reconfirmation of Reservations—To avoid any complications, it is advisable to reconfirm reservations at least six hours in advance of departure and give the air-line ticket agent your full name, your local address, and the telephone number where you can be reached. At stopover points en route, it is an excellent idea to check in at the ticket counter before leaving the airport to reconfirm the next part of your trip. If you don't know where you will be staying locally, let the air lines know by telephone, wire, cable, radio, or mail as soon as you are located. This precautionary measure may save an unnecessary trip to the airport should it become necessary for the air lines to change the flight because of weather conditions, changes in equipment, mechanical repairs, and other emergency situations.

Baggage

Travelers en route to Seattle with tickets that combine several classes of service may be limited to 44 pounds, depending on the type of ticket purchased. It is advisable to check exactly how many pounds of baggage are allowed to avoid extra charges for overweight.

All air lines have a baggage allowance of 66 pounds for travelers entering Alaska from points outside the state, and the same allowance applies on the return trip. However, when traveling from one

city to another in Alaska, baggage allowance between points is
30 to 55 pounds, an important point in planning and packing so
that extra expense may be avoided.

If you know in advance that your baggage will be overweight,
it will save money to ship part of it a few days early by air freight.

All baggage is weighed in before boarding the plane, including
brief cases, typewriters, large cameras, guns, and fishing tackle,
whether you plan to carry them aboard or have them checked to
the plane. Normally, the only exceptions are a lady's handbag or
pocketbook, an overcoat or wrap, a foot rug, an umbrella or
walking stick, a small camera, a pair of binoculars, and a reasonable amount of reading matter. For infants, food to be consumed
en route, and a carrying basket or small bassinet will be allowed
on board. A fully collapsible wheel chair will be carried free of
charge, as well as crutches or other necessary equipment aids for
passengers.

Ski equipment and other oversized sports equipment are subject
to special additional carrying charges on some air lines.

Baggage Insurance—Most air lines assume an insurance liability not exceeding $250 value per adult ticket. Additional insur-
ance may be secured at a nominal fee and it is a recommended
precaution.

Check-in Time

The air lines request that passengers report to the ticket counter
twenty to thirty minutes before flight departure. Reservations are
subject to cancellation if passengers do not appear at least ten
minutes before departure.

Personal Travel Insurance

Air-line trip insurance may be purchased to cover the trip.
Maximum insurance is $62,500, obtainable in units of $6,250 at
a cost of $.25 per unit. This may be arranged at the airport where
the insurance companies maintain booths staffed with trained
personnel. There are also insurance coin machines located in the
airport terminals. In all events, passengers should not carry the
trip-insurance policy with them; it should be mailed to a respon-

sible person who will not be on the same flight and who will place it in safekeeping.

Before starting out on the trip, it is a good idea to check over your current insurance policies to determine the amount of coverage you have in the event your personal belongings are lost, damaged, or stolen while traveling. If you are not adequately insured, a "floater" policy may be obtained to assure complete coverage.

Children's Fares

One child under the age of two accompanied by an adult is carried free of charge, providing the child does not occupy a seat. Additional children under twelve years, accompanied by adults, are charged half the normal adult fare. Air lines or travel agents should be consulted for fares, services, and requirements for children traveling unaccompanied.

Pets

Consult each individual air line or your travel agent in reference to regulations for carrying animals, birds, live fish, or reptiles. Each air line has its own regulations and services concerning the handling of pets, and a little planning in advance guarantees greater comfort and convenience for you and the pets. Also check customs requirements in Chapter II.

Meals

Well-prepared complimentary meals are served aloft at conventional mealtimes on all flights between Seattle and Alaska. Snacks are provided between meals and usually include light sandwiches, fresh fruit, cookies, pastries, and a hot or cold drink.

Stopovers

Arrangements may be made for stopovers at any scheduled stop on the trip. These arrangements should be made prior to departure from the last destination. Sudden decisions to stop over should be avoided unless they have been confirmed with the air line. It is also necessary to have confirmed reservations for hotel or other sleeping accommodations before making the stopover visit. The air-line ticket agents make every effort to assist in obtaining lodgings in advance.

Airport Services

Taxi, bus, or limousine service at the Seattle and Vancouver airports is available for use when there is a lay-over between flights before continuing to Alaska. This service is recommended for shopping, visiting, or sight-seeing in the area. Before leaving the airport, be sure to check with the ticket agent for the correct departure time of your next flight. Make certain there is plenty of time to leave the airport and return. If there is any doubt about the time of departure, you are asked to check with the air line by telephone during the interval in which you are away from the airport. You may wish to check into one of the local hotels or motels near the airport to freshen up or catch some sleep. The air-line ticket agent can assist in making reservations and obtaining transportation to the lodgings. Eating, cleaning, and shopping facilities are located at the air terminals.

Car rental—Car rental services are available at both airports for the convenience of passengers en route. These services are perfect for sight-seeing, shopping, visiting, or business purposes. Arrangements may be made in advance of arrival through the airline ticket agents or at the airports on arrival. The car rental services maintain air terminal offices and personnel to assist you. The rates are $10 per day plus 10 cents per mile and a minimum deposit of $25 to $30 for each day the car is going to be used. Identification will be requested in the form of an air-line, rail, or bank credit card or papers that establish financial responsibility. Gasoline credit cards are not accepted as sufficient identification.

Credit Cards and Pay-When-You-Return Plans

All major air lines, some banks, credit organizations, and many travel services, such as American Express, issue credit cards upon personal application and some banks, credit organizations, and air lines will handle your travel expenses on a monthly installment basis.

A credit card has many noteworthy conveniences, not only as a means of deferred payment, but also as a means of identification and establishing credit along the way. Applications for credit should be made well in advance of your trip. Travel agents will assist you with this matter.

Immigration and Customs

Passengers on flights originating in the United States who plan to leave the plane at Canadian points and passengers on flights originating in Canada getting off in the United States will be checked by immigration and customs officials. Passports are not required, but the traveler must carry proof of citizenship status for officials at the ports of entry. For complete details consult immigration and customs in Chapter II.

Plane Services En Route

All flights carry a good supply of current magazines, brochures about air travel, informative leaflets of Alaska, and newspapers. A few toilet articles are available, such as soap, cleansing cloths, and disposable tissues. There are playing cards and games on most flights, although the magnificent scenery en route will keep you occupied most of the flight.

Seats are not reserved on the majority of the planes. It is best to choose one that gives the most unobstructed view, especially when traveling during the daylight hours. There are many beautiful panoramas to be seen from the windows of the plane; the mountains, glaciers, fiords, and waterfalls of southeastern Alaska will seem close enough to touch during a great part of the flight.

Smoking of cigarettes is permitted, except during take-offs and landings and on the ground, but they cannot be purchased on the plane. Be certain to carry enough cigarettes to satisfy your needs between airports. Pipes and cigars are forbidden at all times. Liquor is sold in limited quantities aboard some air liners; however, sales are "confined to aircraft in flight."

If you want any additional services, you may ring for the flight hostess or cabin attendant. At your request they will bring blankets, pillows, and refreshments to your seat. Free gum is given at take-off and landing as a matter of flight routine.

Should you not feel well during the flight, by all means let the attendant know and you will receive the benefit of experienced attention. If you have any doubts about how you are going to react physically to air travel, or if you know that you are prone to airsickness or nervousness in flight, consult your local doctor before the trip for a prescribed supply of special medication to take along.

Ditching Orientation

After take-off from Seattle, the flight attendants give a demonstration of the correct procedures to follow in the event of an emergency should it become necessary for the plane to land at sea. The demonstration of this "ditching" operation is the equivalent of lifeboat drill on a ship, except that it only takes a few brief moments and the passengers do not participate in the demonstration except as observers.

By Ship

There is excellent passenger-boat service in summer, primarily devoted to round-trip tours, although arrangements can also be made for regular travel and one-way transportation.

The passenger service to Alaska on Canadian and American ships operates from late spring through early fall, approximately from May to September. The main line of travel is the famed Inside Passage from Vancouver, B.C., to the cities of southeastern Alaska—Ketchikan, Wrangell, Juneau, and Skagway.

Traveling by ship is not a case of just "getting to Alaska." It is one of the most enjoyable and leisurely ways to enter and visit the new state. The Inside Passage is as calm as it is beautiful. The stars seem brighter and farther away, and in summer there is a mild glow in the sky reflected by the midnight sun which is far to the north but is a constant reminder that the ship is sailing into its domain. Life aboard ship is informal and there is always a pleasantly balanced schedule of recreation. The organized activities will not intrude on your enjoyment and are available when and if you feel the need for them.

From Seattle to Vancouver

All ships sail from Vancouver, B.C., which is a short and beautiful steamer or plane trip from Seattle.

By steamer you cross Puget Sound, stopping in colorful and historic Victoria, B.C., and continue through the Straits of Juan de Fuca to Vancouver. The one-way trip takes approximately seven hours' travel time, not including the hour and twenty minutes spent in Victoria. It is so pleasant that it should be a serious consideration for those travelers who have extra time.

Steamer service is operated by Canadian Pacific and there are two air lines carrying pasengers between the two cities, United Airlines and Trans-Canada Airlines. The one-way fare by plane is $8 tourist or $11 first class. The boat trip costs $6.50.

AMERICAN SHIPS

The minimum cost for a seven-day, round-trip tour between Vancouver and Skagway is $205 to $305 during the May, June, late August, and September thrift season. The same accommodations during the remainder of the summer season vary from $225 to $355 on the American cruise ships operated by the Alaska Cruises, Inc., and Arctic Alaska Tours, both at 420 Joseph Vance Building, Seattle, Washington. Round-trip fares apply only to passengers traveling and returning on the same voyage, or to those passengers laying over between sailings for the special tours operated by these companies. In all other cases, one-way rates apply, and they vary from $110 to $170 at thrift rates, or from $155 to $215 at regular rates. Sailings are scheduled to depart every fifth day from Vancouver, B.C., and Skagway, Alaska, via the S.S. *Glacier Queen* or the S.S. *Yukon Star*. Passengers desiring accommodations with private shower and toilet facilities may obtain them at the additional price of $31.20 per person one way. All other rates include a berth in an outside cabin, with hot and cold running water and all meals aboard ship.

CANADIAN SHIPS

Steamship tour service is offered by the Canadian National Steamships and Canadian Pacific Princess Lines from late May to early September, with sailings departing from Vancouver and Prince Rupert, B.C.

The Canadian National's S.S. *Prince George* offers a round-trip, nine-day luxury tour between Vancouver, B.C., and Skagway,

Alaska. Sailings are scheduled every ninth day. All-expense tours range in price from $245 to $540, with special rates for children accompanied by adults. One-way space is not available. The steamship stops at Prince Rupert, B.C., Wrangell, Ketchikan, Juneau, and Skagway. At Skagway time is allowed for round-trippers to take a side trip via the White Pass and Yukon narrow-gauge railway to Carcross, Yukon Territory, Canada, and return to the ship.

The Canadian Pacific's seven-and-a-half-day cruise aboard the S.S. *Princess Louise* travels round trip between Vancouver or Prince Rupert, B.C., and Skagway, Alaska. The passenger capac-ity is for 214 persons, with sailings scheduled every eighth day. The all-expense tour minimum is $225. It is also possible to go one way to Skagway and return to Vancouver via Canadian Pacific Airlines at a minimum round-trip rate of $210. Special children's rates are available. One-way space is extremely limited and not always available. The round-trip fares are the same whether you choose to begin your trip in Vancouver or Prince Rupert, B.C.

Canadian Pacific also operates weekly summer service on the S.S. *Queen of the North,* stopping en route at numerous Canadian communities along the Inside Passage and arriving in Ketchikan on the third day out of Vancouver. The one-way fare is $62.50, berth with meals included.

Reservations

Reservations may be made directly with the steamship com-panies or through your local travel agent. All advance reservations require a deposit which varies in amount with each company and the type of service you request. If you must cancel your reserva-tions, the deposit will be returned when the space has been sold again. The chances of recovering your deposit are greater if you notify the company of your cancellation as soon as possible. The demand for space during the summer season is great and the num-ber of accommodations is limited. It is advisable to plan and make reservations at least four months in advance. Your travel agent will be of great assistance to you in planning the trip by ship and making all preparations.

Baggage

Each adult ticket allows free transportation of 150 pounds of baggage and 75 pounds for children. Charges are made for overweight at a nominal rate. Individual items weighing in excess of 250 pounds may require special handling and special permits from the steamship company. If you are traveling round trip, you may store baggage not needed for your trip with the steamship company at Vancouver if you make arrangements in advance. Free storage is permitted for thirty days, then storage charges will be made.

Bonded Baggage—You may check in bond any sealed baggage not needed during the voyage between Seattle and Skagway, thereby avoiding customs examination. All other baggage will be inspected by Canadian and United States customs officials.

Immigration and Customs

Inspection of the credentials and baggage of passengers voyaging between Seattle and Vancouver is made at Victoria or Vancouver, B.C., for those entering Canada. Southbound passengers entering the United States are inspected at Seattle. For complete immigration and customs regulations consult Chapter II.

Travelers on Canadian ships—For customs, immigration, and compliance with United States shipping regulations, you are required to fill out a questionnaire giving personal statistics and listing contents of baggage. This questionnaire, which accompanies your ticket, is submitted to the purser's office either before you sail or immediately after you board ship.

The purser's office issues you a numbered identification card which you retain and present to the United States immigration officer, who will either board the ship an hour before arrival at Ketchikan or immediately on arrival at that Alaskan port.

After having your identification card stamped by the immigration officer, you may go ashore at any Alaskan port without further formality, except that the card must be retained and shown to the ship's officer when you return to the ship, as proof of having passed through immigration.

Customs inspection in Alaska takes place only when you intend to go ashore with baggage. The examination is made as you leave the gangplank. One-way northbound passengers, terminating at an Alaskan port, will be subject to examination of all baggage (except bonded baggage) before leaving the ship or on the dock immediately upon arrival at the destination. Arrangements should be discussed in advance of departure with the purser's office.

Southbound customs and immigration inspection from Alaska is held on arrival at Prince Rupert or Vancouver. Passengers are issued Canadian immigration cards which must be stamped and initialed by the Canadian immigration office and shown to the ship's officer before going ashore at any Canadian port.

Special Regulation—The United States shipping regulations do not allow foreign vessels to transport passengers between two American ports, where the ports of departure and destination are American. This regulation applies whether passengers leave the vessel accidentally or for any reason, and only affects southbound passengers from Alaska on a round-trip tour aboard a Canadian ship.

You can stop off for sight-seeing visits at Alaskan ports, but you are checked off the ship and must return before the sailing and surrender the numbered identification card that has been issued for this purpose. Failure to do so is a contravention of the American Coasting Regulations and can cause serious difficulties for the shipping line and individuals involved. This regulation does not affect passengers traveling on American ships sailing from Canadian ports.

Pets

Facilities are not provided for carrying pets on the ships. However, in special instances, arrangements may be made with the steamship line and they should be consulted long in advance of the trip for the rules and regulations for transporting pets.

Dining Facilities

The food is excellent and bountiful, including in-between meal snacks. The service is good and there are lengthy menus to choose from. On most voyages there are the usual first and second sittings for meals, with an hour allowed for each sitting. You may choose the sitting you prefer. If your seating arrangement or hours do not prove satisfactory, notify the steward and changes will be made depending on the availability of space. Every effort will be made to accommodate you.

Mealtimes are announced by bugle, chimes, or over the public address system a half hour before each serving and at the meal hour. The sound of the signal is always welcome because a healthy appetite goes with travel by boat on the Inside Passage. The trip is extremely calm because you travel only on the sheltered seas and the fresh sea air is always invigorating.

Ship and Shore Time

Pacific Standard Time is maintained aboard ship for the entire voyage but ships stop at ports of call which are on Alaska Standard Time. Therefore, before leaving the ship for sight-seeing trips or lay-overs en route, the differences in time should be checked with the ship's bulletin board or one of the officers.

Activities and Services Aboard Ship

Sitting rooms, library facilities, clubrooms, and observation lounges are conveniently located. The ship's bulletin boards are well posted with all services and daily activities. Bar service is available at specified hours in the cocktail lounges. On deck and indoors there are games such as shuffleboard, quoits, ping-pong, or bingo. Tournaments are easily arranged through the deck steward. Music is piped over the public address system and each evening there is dancing and "horse races" or movies. Deck chairs, robes, and pillows are available, and a newsstand sells photo supplies, playing cards, cigarettes, cigars, soft drinks, candy, gifts, magazines, toilet articles, and various sundry items.

Valet service is available for pressing clothes. There is an interroom telephone service, and messages may be sent and received via the radio ship-to-shore service. There is a lost and found service department. Arrangements to store currency and valuables in safekeeping are handled through the purser's office.

Barbershop and beauty parlor facilities are available on the Canadian ships. It is especially recommended that women make their appointments as early as possible; the schedule rapidly fills up and appointments during the choice hours are difficult to obtain as you near your destination.

Baths may be scheduled for those without a private bath in the stateroom by ringing room service for an appointment.

By Train

There is no way to reach Alaska by railroad from the continental United States and only one route from Canada, traveling between Whitehorse in the Yukon Territory to Skagway, Alaska. In spite of the lack of any other form of rail transportation entering Alaska, the Whitehorse to Skagway, 110-mile railroad trip via the White Pass and Yukon Route is one of the most historically and scenically beautiful train trips in all of Canada and the United States.

The train follows the same exciting route as the old trail traveled by the gold prospectors in '98 from the Klondike region, along the Yukon; then it climbs up and over the 2,885-foot White Pass and sweeps down abruptly to sea level at Skagway.

Because of the popularity of this short-line railroad, nearly all important tours of Alaska either include it in the itinerary or make provisions for tour members to take a side trip over this historic route.

The White Pass and Yukon Route may be reached by bus, ship, auto, and plane routes from the United States and Canada. The round-trip fare between Whitehorse and Skagway is $34, one-way transportation costs $18.50. The railroad operates on a five-day-a-week schedule from late May through September, with one train daily each way. The one-way trip takes approximately five hours. Parlor-car accommodations and lunch are included in the fare. The train makes many stops en route for passengers to get off, look at the magnificent scenery, visit historic landmarks, and make a photographic record of the trip. On a round-trip tour it is necessary to stay overnight in either Whitehorse or Skagway and to make the return trip the following day. Overnight expenses are not included in the fare.

Train Service in the United States and Canada

If you are considering going to Seattle or Vancouver, B.C., by train to make connections with ships, plane, or bus to Alaska, you have a wide selection of trains, routes, and schedules to choose from. Excellent service from the east and south is offered by Canadian National, Canadian Pacific, Great Northern, Northern Pacific, Union Pacific, and Southern Pacific railways. Your travel agent will be able to assist you in planning the train trip so that you have the best connection with the transportation to Alaska.

TYPICAL ROUND-TRIP RAILROAD FARES *

	First Class	Coach
New York/Seattle	$224.75	$150.95
New York/Vancouver, B.C.	218.83	152.45
Denver/Seattle	85.20	63.90
Denver/Vancouver	113.55	81.55
Los Angeles/Seattle	99.00	56.70
Los Angeles/Vancouver	110.20	63.90
Minneapolis/Seattle	106.35	79.65
Minneapolis/Vancouver	106.35	79.65
Winnipeg/Seattle	97.95	76.79
Winnipeg/Vancouver	97.95	76.79
Montreal/Vancouver or Seattle	196.32	145.49

* U.S. dollars quoted, tax not included.

Rates on Canadian and United States trains traveling cross-country from one coast to the other are identical and, if time permits, a traveler may go from New York to Seattle through the United States and return through Canada and the cost will be no greater than going and returning the same route. Such a trip requires at least two weeks' travel time, preferably more because it is an excellent way to visit a variety of resort areas, national parks, and cities, and to enjoy a wide variety of scenery and interesting sights in both countries on the way.

Baggage

With your full-fare ticket, you are allowed to check 150 pounds of baggage. You may also take as much additional baggage as you can carry aboard the train. However, because you will be transferring to another form of transportation before reaching Alaska, the baggage limitations on connecting transportation services should be considered in planning your baggage for the complete trip.

By Bus

Transportation by bus during the summer months may be arranged from any community in the United States and most communities in Canada. The main line of travel direct to Alaska by bus will be on the Alaska Highway.

Travel by bus can be a very pleasant experience, especially during the summer months. It is a leisurely way to become acquainted with the people, sights, and communities en route to Alaska.

Seattle, Washington, and Great Falls, Montana, are two of the major cities in the United States from which bus travelers depart for connections with bus services in Vancouver, B.C., or Edmonton, Alberta, Canada, and on the Alaska Highway.

If one does not want to make the entire trip by bus from his home, there are excellent rail and air-line connections to Edmonton from all Canadian and United States points with convenient and frequent service.

From Edmonton to Whitehorse

Canadian Coachways, Ltd., operates between Edmonton and Whitehorse on a schedule of three trips a week, all year around. This is an express service leaving Edmonton at 12:15 A.M. every Tuesday, Thursday, and Saturday and arriving in Dawson Creek at 10:35 A.M. the same day. You change in Dawson Creek to the Whitehorse bus at one thirty the same day, with time to eat a good meal and to stretch your legs before the trip north over the Alaska Highway.

As an alternate, more relaxed schedule, you can leave on

Canadian Coachways, Ltd., on the morning bus which leaves Edmonton at 9:15 A.M. on Mondays, Wednesday, and Fridays and arrives that evening at 7:35 P.M. This gives you a better opportunity to see the beautiful Peace River Country in daylight and, by arriving in Dawson Creek the night before, you can get a good night's sleep before leaving for Whitehorse.

It takes approximately eighteen hours to travel between Dawson Creek and Whitehorse. This is a continuous trip with no stopovers along the way except for rest and mealtime stops. The one-way fare from Edmonton to Whitehorse is $50.75. There is a change in time from Mountain Standard in Dawson Creek to Pacific Standard Time, and to Yukon Time at Whitehorse, so you gain three hours en route.

From Whitehorse to Fairbanks

The White Pass and Yukon Route Bus Service, in connection with Alaska HYway Tours, Inc., operates between Whitehorse and Fairbanks. It is a two-day trip by bus, starting at 8:00 A.M. from Whitehorse every fourth day during June, July, August, and September, stopping en route at 6:00 P.M. the same day for an overnight lay-over at Scottie Creek, Alaska, leaving the following morning at eight thirty and arriving in Fairbanks at six thirty that evening. Buses depart from Fairbanks en route to Whitehorse on a similar schedule with the same stopover.

The one-way fare between Whitehorse and Fairbanks is $43.08. This does not include the overnight stop, which costs approximately $12 to $14 per person for meals and lodging. Frequent rest stops are made en route, as well as regular stops for lunch.

The baggage allowance is 65 pounds and there is a nominal charge for excess baggage.

Transportation by bus from the United States may be arranged through the Greyhound Bus Lines or National Trailways Bus System, whichever is more convenient for you. From Canada the bus services include the Canadian Coachways, Ltd., Northern Stages, Ltd., White Pass and Yukon Route Bus Service, and Western Canadian Greyhound Lines.

TYPICAL ONE-WAY BUS FARES FROM THE UNITED STATES AND CANADA *

Seattle/Fairbanks via Prince George, B.C.	$139.12
New York/Fairbanks via Great Falls, Montana	167.38
Great Falls/Fairbanks	111.13
Los Angeles/Fairbanks via Seattle	163.02
Denver/Fairbanks via Great Falls	136.33
Minneapolis/Fairbanks via Great Falls	134.53
Dallas/Fairbanks via Great Falls	153.98
Montreal/Fairbanks via Edmonton	168.22
Winnipeg/Fairbanks via Edmonton	136.67
Vancouver/Fairbanks via Prince George	135.32

* U.S. dollars quoted, tax not included.

Baggage Allowances

Your regular fare adult ticket allows for 150 pounds of baggage on the bus to your destination and you may carry an additional 30 pounds of hand luggage aboard. However, because the baggage allowance on the portion of the trip between Whitehorse and Fairbanks is only 65 pounds, you should consider this when planning what you will take with you.

Stopovers En Route

If you want to stop over and spend the night in any United States or Canadian communities, you should allow at least $10 extra per overnight stop for lodgings. Plans to make stopovers should be discussed with the bus-ticket agents in advance to determine what connections you will be able to make in order to continue the trip without lengthy delays.

Services En Route

Most of the larger cities and some smaller communities in the United States and Canada, with the exception of the Alaska Highway, have overnight cleaning and laundry services at the larger hotels, and there are laundromats and other private concerns offering quick cleaning service. There is a good selection of restaurants, hotels, motels, lodges, movie theaters, drugstores, doctors, dentists, and all necessary services.

Along the Alaska Highway, from Dawson Creek to Whitehorse, a distance of 917 miles, stops are made in very small communities, at roadhouses, lodges, trading posts, or hotels where there are good but simple meals, and gift counters, with limited shopping facilities for stationery supplies, magazines and newspapers, toiletries, clothing, and accessories.

There are telephone, telegraph, and post-office services the entire length of the trip.

Your bus driver and the ticket agents at the bus depots can direct you to the various local business concerns, amusements, and points of interest.

Highway Conditions

Buses travel over many miles of gravel road on the trip to Alaska. Beginning approximately 400 miles north of Vancouver, B.C., from the west coast, and approximately 100 miles northwest from Edmonton, Alberta, there are stretches of road that are predominately gravel surfacing up to within 150 miles of Fairbanks, Alaska. Passengers are not likely to be inconvenienced by these conditions, although in some areas there are very dusty conditions. The buses are all modern but not all air-conditioned. The bus drivers are experienced in driving these highways for the maximum safety and comfort of the passengers.

Special Items to Carry

Tissue cleansing cloths, disposable washcloths, skin lotions, and astringents can add to the comfort of the trip, but a large supply is unnecessary because these items can be purchased along the way. Always carry mosquito repellent, especially during June through mid-July. A supply of candy bars, cookies, crackers, or fresh fruit is good to carry with you on the bus or between stops. For women who use a special brand of cosmetics, an extra supply is helpful, as some brands are not sold along the way.

Mail

You should be well acquainted with your itinerary before you leave home, and know which cities and communities you will be visiting long enough to pick up mail. It is suggested that you have mail sent to you, care of General Delivery, to post offices at scheduled stops or stopovers. Mail should not be sent in care of the bus lines or bus stations because the bus companies do not provide a mail service for passengers. All mail should be sent by air mail to avoid delays. Letters mailed in Canada must be posted with Canadian postage stamps.

By Automobile

You can drive to Alaska direct from your home in comfort. The main route of travel will take you over the famed Alaska Highway which begins at Dawson Creek, B.C., and takes you through a magnificent wilderness country direct to Fairbanks, Alaska. Of the entire trip, the Alaska Highway represents 1,523 miles, of which 1,221 are in Canada and 302 are in Alaska.

The Alaska Highway is twenty-six feet wide and has a well-graded gravel surface built for heavy-duty service. It is excellently maintained. It is a well-posted highway with directional and safety signs, and is well patrolled by highway maintenance crews and the Canadian Mounted Police.

The countryside is an exciting, rugged land, rich in scenic beauty with dense forests, mountains, and tree-lined lakes, and along the highway there are places to stop at intervals of approximately every twenty-five miles for gas, food, lodging, and supplies.

Except for these stopping-off places and a few mining and construction camps, you are remote from civilization and in a sportsman's paradise of hunting and fishing.

APPROACH ROADS TO THE ALASKA HIGHWAY

The Alaska Highway is generally approached from the United States on major highways leading north from Seattle, Washington, Spokane, Washington, or Great Falls, Montana. The major connecting highway in Canada is the Trans-Canada Highway, which stretches from eastern Canada at Ottawa, Ontario, to Vancouver, B.C.

West Coast drivers from Seattle travel U.S. Highway #99 which becomes Canadian Highway #1, and continue to Hope, B.C., taking the Fraser Canyon Highway from Hope to Prince George. From there, the Hart Highway goes to the beginning of the Alaska Highway, which starts at Dawson Creek at Mile 0. From Seattle to Dawson Creek is a total of approximately 840 miles. The highways are paved up to within approximately 400 miles of Vancouver, and the remainder of the trip to Prince George has sections of gravel. The highway is predominately gravel from Prince George to Dawson Creek.

Drivers from Spokane, Washington, travel U.S. Highway #95, which becomes Canadian Highway #3 and continues to Fort Macleod, Alberta. There, a turn north on Highway #2 goes through to Edmonton. The route from Edmonton to Dawson Creek is via Canadian highways #16, #43, #34, and #2. From Spokane to Dawson Creek is a total of approximately a thousand miles.

From Great Falls, Montana, U.S. Highway #91 heads north to the border, becoming Highway #4 in Canada. Drivers continue on #4 to Lethbridge, Alberta, then turn west on #3 at Fort Macleod with the remainder of the trip exactly as it is from Spokane, Washington. The distance between Great Falls and Dawson Creek is approximately 900 miles.

The highways from Spokane and Great Falls are paved all the way to Edmonton, and highways beyond to Dawson Creek are partially paved, but there are many gravel sections.

TYPICAL MINIMUM COST AND TRAVEL TIME

New York/Fairbanks
         13 days, averaging 350 miles per day
Great Falls/Fairbanks
         8 days, averaging 300 miles per day
Seattle/Fairbanks
         8 days, averaging 300 miles per day
Minimum daily cost per person for lodging, meals, gas, and oil: $15.00

All the gravel highways are kept in good condition in all seasons of the year. Advance reports on road conditions are available from the Alberta Travel Bureau in Edmonton, Alberta, and from the British Columbia Travel Bureau at Victoria, B.C. Current reports are also available at the border entry points and highway stops along the way.

Gasoline Credit Cards

Standard Oil, Esso, and Chevron credit cards offer services the entire length of the trip. Other credit cards may be used intermittently at stops on the approach roads, along the Alaska Highway, and in Alaska.

Insurance and Accident Coverage

Before starting on the trip, have your local insurance agent issue a "nonresident insurance card," listing your coverage for public liability and property damage. There is no difficulty or expense in obtaining this card and it will assist in a settlement if there is an accident or incident involving bodily injury or property damage in excess of a hundred dollars while traveling in Canada. If you travel without the card and have an accident, your car will be impounded.

Dogs and Pets

Hunting or pet dogs and other animals may be taken into Canada. Consult the customs regulations in Chapter II.

Personal Supplies and Auto Equipment

For your own comfort carry an insect bomb or mosquito repellent. The mosquito population is active from June to mid-July.

Plastic or canvas clothing bags that can be closed securely are needed to protect clothing from dust. If you use zippered bags, masking tape placed over the zipper will keep out any fine dust.

Carry sunglasses and take a camera, film, and photo accessories. Film is available in all popular standard sizes but an extra supply of six rolls is a worth-while precaution. Camera accessories are not always available and are more costly as you travel north; therefore, filters, light meter, bulbs, etc., should be included on your packing lists.

Carry a flashlight in your car, preferably a lantern model that has a built-in red signal light or blinker. Have on hand a fire extinguisher and a first-aid kit, as well as a towrope, pick and shovel, tire and tube repair kit (cold patch), and a basic set of car tools.

The car should have a heater because of the cool early morning and late evening hours. For maximum comfort it should be equipped with an air-ventilation system permitting you to drive with the windows closed in the dusty areas. It is recommended that you have a guaranteed spare tire and that all tires be six-ply or nylon for summer travel. The exterior of the gasoline tank should be covered over with rubber padding to protect it against flying gravel.

Auto Maintenance and Repairs

Minor repairs and limited maintenance service are available at frequent intervals throughout the trip. Service for foreign-made cars, except British and Canadian, is rarely available outside of the larger cities.

Tubeless Tires—Repairs for tubeless tires may not be available at some of the small establishments along the way, particularly on the northern approach roads and the Alaska Highway. It is advisable to carry spare inner tubes so, if damage occurs to your wheel rims or you have air leakage, the inner tube can be used for driving to the next service stop.

Accommodations and Service on the Alaska Highway

The cost of gasoline on the Alaska Highway ranges from fifty to seventy-five cents per gallon. In Canada the imperial gallon is the authorized measure in which five Canadian gallons are equal to six United States gallons. It is not necessary, and can be dangerous, to carry extra gasoline in your car.

Prices of accommodations and food compare with those in the northern tier of states and southern Canada. In the smaller lodges there are rooms for from $3.50 to $5 per person per night, and up to $10 and $12 for a double room at the larger inns and hotels. Breakfast, lunch, and dinner prices range from 75 cents to $3. The accommodations are not scarce but they are rustic-looking and some are rather primitive, especially the plumbing.

When stopping for the night at small places, it is advisable to inquire about the hours when the electricity and water are on. Some places generate their own and do not operate on a twenty-four-hour basis. The hours of operation are usually from seven in the morning until ten at night.

Outward appearances are not indicative of the accommodations or food along the Alaska Highway. For the most part, food is plain but good and accommodations are modest but comfortable. You won't find swank hotels or motels, except in or near the larger cities; however, improvements are being made at a fast pace, accommodations are becoming more plentiful each year, and there is less distance between them.

Accommodations and food are not available at the highway maintenance, construction, or mining camps en route.

During the summer months the next stopover should be planned each morning and reservations made in advance each day by telephone or telegraph to the lodging you have chosen. Give your name, approximate arrival time, and the amount of space you need.

There is only one section of the highway where you must drive more than seventy miles before reaching a place to eat and sleep. All others are less than fifty-five miles apart, averaging about twenty-five miles' distance between stops.

Dry-cleaning facilities do not exist along the Alaska Highway, except at Dawson Creek, Whitehorse, and Fairbanks. There are, however, laundry facilities at almost every community along the way.

Telephone and Telegraph—The Northwest Communication System, operated by Canadian National Telegraph, provides facilities for public long-distance telephone and commercial telegraph services. These facilities are located at repeater stations and stops approximately every twenty-five miles along the route. Connections can be arranged for telephone and telegraph messages direct to Alaska and, via Edmonton, to any destination.

Camping—The Canadian government has provided ten free campgrounds and seven lunch stops along the Alaska Highway.

These facilities are for the convenience of travelers who carry their food and supplies. Parking areas are convenient to cooking and kitchen shelters.

Each location has a fireplace, tables, good water, and toilets. Firewood is available. The campgrounds have indoor cooking ranges. You need a tent or other shelter for sleeping out, in addition to camping equipment, including mosquito netting, lanterns, dishes, pots, and cooking and eating utensils.

When camping in the woods at other than organized sites, it is necessary to get a permit from local fire or game wardens before entering the bush.

Fire Hazards

Be extremely careful about dropping lighted cigarettes and matches, or any inflammable material.

Fire-fighting equipment and personnel are very limited in the miles of wilderness. The undergrowth is dangerously dry because of the low humidity in the north and even the rain does not penetrate into the ground far enough to give protection. All these areas are vulnerable to forest, brush, moss, and undergrowth fires, as evidenced by the many "burned out" or fire-damaged places.

If you should see a fire, report it immediately over the nearest telephone to the Royal Canadian Mounted Police or game warden.

Make sure your campfires are out, and take extreme caution to see that all sparks, flame or hot ashes, and coals are completely extinguished.

It is necessary to have permits for campfires in British Columbia and may be necessary in the Yukon Territory and Alberta at the time of your trip. You should check and, where necessary, get your permits from the police or forest ranger stations conveniently located in the larger towns en route.

Speed, Courtesy, and Caution

The most economical, comfortable, and practical speed is 40 miles an hour. However, the maximum speed limits on the Alaska Highway are:

Passenger vehicles	50 miles per hour
Trucks	50 miles per hour except in the Yukon Territory where it is 40 miles per hour
In camp areas	30 miles per hour
When passing road maintenance equipment and crews	30 miles per hour

Excessive speed on gravel roads is dangerous and costly. It is harder on tires and flying gravel can cause considerable damage. For additional safety for your own car and others traveling on the gravel roads, it is advisable to slow down when passing and when dust is encountered.

Along the highway you are likely to meet up with your fellow drivers more than once on the trip, so that normal courtesies of driving become all important.

It is a rule of the road to stop when hailed for help by another car.

During daylight hours in summer, cars are traveling the highway at intervals of about every fifteen minutes, so there is little chance of getting stranded. The Canadian approach roads and the Alaska Highway are being improved every year, and the only real hazards of the journey are those created by careless and thoughtless drivers.

The Year-Round Highway Conditions

The trip on the Alaska Highway is a long one and weather has a great influence on the traveling conditions. The preferred travel season is from June through September; however, the highway is open all year round. As a summer bonus, the extra-long days provide more hours of daylight to enjoy the trip.

December-January-February—During these months, snowfall usually averages from ten to fifteen inches a month and the highway is generally in good condition. The hard-packed snow provides smooth driving. Below-zero weather prevails and precautions should be taken to have the necessary clothing for protection against such weather. Automobiles should be completely winterized to withstand sixty-degree-below-zero temperatures. Tire chains, towrope, pick and shovel, and a means to produce fire should be carried in the car. A sleeping bag should be taken for additional protection in case of car trouble so you can keep warm while waiting for assistance.

Winter Driving—Motorists have special conditions to face when a car gets the full effect of extremely low temperatures in winter. Warnings to "keep the gas tank full or moisture will condense and freeze the fuel pump and line," and "don't put all your faith along with anti-freeze in the radiator—it's the oil jelling on the engine that'll give you trouble" is sound advice given by Alaskan motorists along the highway. It's all a matter of know-how and experience, plus paying close attention to helpful suggestions, doing some special investigation on your own before attempting winter driving, and knowing how the car will react and what to do about it in an emergency. If you are not experienced in winter driving, you should obtain instructions or information from your automobile club or your local state motor vehicle offices, or write to the manufacturer of your car for details before driving to Alaska in winter.

March-April-May—Melting snows create icy conditions during March. Throughout the months of April and May travel along the highway is usually slow owing to spring thaws with flooding, slush, and mud conditions. During this period there is likely to be restricted travel in certain sections to allow maintenance crews to make repairs for summer travel. This may involve short delays until the work is completed. In such cases warning signs are prominently displayed. Drivers are advised to use extra caution during these months and to carry tire chains, towrope, pick, and shovel.

June-July-August-September—These months are the most favorable for motoring. The days are warm and evenings are cool. The road is well graded, although a long dry spell makes it dusty. It is suggested that you carry a good spare tire, preferably six-ply or nylon, as well as a basic set of car tools and insect repellent. It is also advisable that the underpart of the gasoline tank be protected with a piece of rubber tire or inner tube against flying gravel. When heavy dust conditions are encountered, head-lights should be used, and tail lights should be kept dirt-free for better visibility. The best way to avoid most of the dust is to keep a reasonable distance behind the car ahead.

October-November—During October and November rain, light snowstorms, and frost make the road slippery. Drivers should keep informed about current highway conditions before proceeding from point to point. This information is usually posted at the telephone repeater stations, or may be obtained at the highway maintenance camps en route. Chains, a container of sand, a pick and shovel should be carried.

THE HAINES ROAD

The Haines Road, connecting the port of Haines, Alaska, with the Alaska Highway, is at a turnoff point, approximately ninety-nine miles west of Whitehorse, Yukon Territory. The Haines Road is open to traffic during the summer period from June through October, and Haines is the only city in the southeastern section of Alaska that can be reached directly by automobile. The road is paved from the Canadian border to Haines.

How to Reach Various Cities in Alaska

The cities of Juneau, Sitka, Skagway, Ketchikan, Wrangell, and Petersburg cannot be reached directly by car; however, during the summer months, steamship transportation is available for shipping cars from Vancouver or Prince Rupert, B.C., to Ketchi-kan, Wrangell, Juneau, and Skagway. The cost one way from Vancouver is $49.50 to Ketchikan, $60.50 to Wrangell, $71.50 to Juneau, $82.50 to Skagway, and $99 to Whitehorse.

Skagway or Juneau can also be reached by driving to Haines and taking the M. V. *Chilkat* Car and Passenger Ferry boats which transport autos. The fares are $25 one way from Haines to Juneau and $17.50 from Haines to Skagway. Passenger fares are $5 per person to Juneau and $2.00 to Skagway.

Another way to reach Skagway is to drive to Carcross or White-horse from the Alaska Highway, then ship the car via the White Pass and Yukon Route railway south to Skagway. Arrangements may also be made with the railway to ship cars direct from Skagway to Vancouver. This arrangement is useful for travelers wishing to continue their trip from Skagway by other means of transportation.

The Ritchie Transportation Company ships autos by barge via Dease Lake and the Stikine River to Wrangell, providing another service from the Alaska Highway beginning at Watson Lake Junction, Mile 635. Reservations must be made in advance with the Ritchie Transportation Company at Wrangell.

The combined travel by car, sea, or rail gives an excellent opportunity to enjoy a more comprehensive trip.

There are direct roads from the Alaska Highway to many Alaskan cities and towns in the interior and south central section of the state, including Anchorage, Fairbanks, Palmer, Valdez, Seward, Homer, and Mount McKinley National Park.

There is no way at present to drive to Barrow, Nome, Kodiak, Kotzebue, or any of the towns and communities on the Aleutians west of the Alaska Mountain Range or above the Arctic Circle.

Canadian Regulations, Customs, and Immigration for Motorists

Every person entering Canada, either from Alaska or from any other part of the United States, who intends to drive over the Alaska Highway should have in his possession at the time of entry into Canada a sufficient sum of money for the trip, or should be able to prove to the satisfaction of frontier officers that he can obtain in Canada any additional funds required. The sufficient sum can be estimated by figuring the total mileage to be driven from point of entry to point of exit. This will indicate the amount of gas and oil required for the trip and the approximate number of days en route in Canada. In the same way, the number of people in the party multiplied by number of days and average daily cost of food and lodging will indicate a total expenditure. A reasonable sum should be included in the estimate for possible road emergencies.

Drivers must carry the car registration certificate and a driver's license. All passengers will need proof of identity and citizenship status. If you are not the legal owner of the car, you must have notarized written permission from the owner authorizing you to take the car out of the country. Failure to do so means that you will not be able to enter Canada at the border.

Motorcars in poor condition or cars that are more than ten years old must be entered on a commercial vehicle permit, with either cash or guarantee bond for export at the rate of approximately one-half of 1 per cent of the value.

Furniture, Equipment, and Baggage—Household effects, tools of trade, or any items of merchandise not ordinarily classifiable as normal baggage, carried in passenger vehicles driven by the owners or in small personally owned trailers, may be entered on a tourist permit and released without security. Regulations governing other personal baggage are the same as for any person entering Canada; however, in addition, a two days' food supply per person (excepting pork and pork products), and gasoline and oil for three hundred miles of motoring, may be taken into Canada free of duty or deposit.

Prepare a complete list, in triplicate, of items to be taken across the border and keep it up to date if purchases are made during the trip. This will be a great help at customs inspection and will speed the entire operation, especially for those who are transporting household equipment or extras other than personal clothing, toiletry articles, and a small quantity of personal effects.

Larger quantities of goods or materials and personal baggage may be transported "in bond" under seal between the borders.

Trailers and House Trailers—House trailers up to fifteen feet long will be permitted entry when towed by any four-wheeled automotive vehicle, unless the customs officer at port of entry decides that the vehicle used for tractive purposes is not equal to the task. House trailers sixteen to thirty feet in length will be admitted when pulled by any standard American make of automobile not lighter than the Ford-Plymouth-Chevrolet class. Any trailer larger than thirty feet will be admitted only when towed by a vehicle of at least three-quarter ton rating. All such motor vehicle-trailer combinations must be covered by a commercial vehicle permit, with cash deposit or guarantee bond as security for export. The Canadian customs officer at the frontier port of arrival will determine, by inspection, the amount of cash deposit or bond to be taken out. Agents for government-approved bonding companies are located in close proximity to principal ports of entry into Canada. Cost of such guarantee bonds is reasonable.

British Columbia Trailer Restrictions—Between Yale and Lytton, B.C., on Highway #1, the over-all length of the automobile and the trailer must not exceed thirty feet; the gross weight of the automobile and trailer with load must not exceed 35,000 pounds; the width must not be greater than eight feet. Motorists pulling trailers exceeding these measurements may by-pass the Yale-Lytton Highway by driving via Hope, Princeton, Merritt, and Spences Bridge.

Loading and Clearance Regulations—The gross weight of vehicle and load traveling the Alaska Highway shall not exceed six hundred pounds per inch width of pneumatic tire, inside diameter, fully inflated. The over-all width of vehicle and load shall not exceed eight feet. The over-all height of vehicle and load shall not exceed twelve feet six inches.

The over-all length of any single vehicle shall not exceed thirty-five feet with or without load. The over-all length of any combination of vehicles shall not exceed sixty feet. Semitrailers shall not exceed forty feet. Not more than one trailing vehicle can be attached to any towing unit.

If any of these weights or measurements are exceeded, a permit to travel over the Alaska Highway must be obtained from Headquarters, Northwest Highway System, Whitehorse, Yukon Territory, or from the Garrison Commander, Dawson Creek, B.C. A detailed loading chart may be obtained by writing to the Canadian Government Travel Bureau, Ottawa, Ontario.

Firearms and Fishing Tackle—If you carry rifles and shotguns in transit, they must be registered immediately on entry with the game or police authorities. Fifty rounds of ammunition per person may be taken into Canada free of duty.

The admission through customs of rifles, guns, and fishing tackle is not the same as a permit to hunt or fish. Firearms and fishing tackle which are not to be used while traveling through British Columbia must be sealed, and a permit to carry such equipment must be obtained without charge from any game warden. In Alberta and Yukon Territory, rifles and shotguns carried in transit must be broken down or encased, and kept in the car at all times.

Revolvers, pistols, or other automatic weapons which are the personal property of persons traveling by highway to and from Alaska through Canada can be transported in your car without special firearm import permits, under the following regulations: (1) the firearm must be placed in a separate container and sealed by Canadian Customs. (2) At the port of exit the seal will be removed by the customs officer. If there is indication that it has been tampered with, the firearm will be seized.

Canadian Hunting and Fishing Regulations—The open seasons and limits in Canada are often changed. To get current information before planning a trip, write to the game departments of the provinces in Canada. As an example of typical costs for licenses, British Columbia nonresident fishing licenses are $7, in Alberta $1, and in the Yukon Territory $2. Big-game licenses are $50 in British Columbia, $100 in Alberta, and $150 in the Yukon Territory. Hunting and shooting are prohibited within one mile of the highways, with or without a license.

Drive-and-Get-a-Free-Trip Plans

You may earn a paid trip to Alaska by taking delivery on a new car in Seattle, Portland, or Detroit, and driving the car to Alaska where automobile prices are considerably higher than in the other states due to shipping costs. Arrangements may be made with auto dealers in Alaska by writing to: Northwest Auto Sales, Inc., 420 East 5th Avenue, Anchorage.

Summer Tours

During the tourist season, from May to September, many visitors travel to Alaska on package tours, either escorted or unescorted. The tours are planned on time schedules suitable to the comfort, interest, entertainment, and convenience of the group. The tours to Alaska are well organized and managed and, as a result, they effectively save time and money and provide the tourist with a satisfying coverage of the major activities and sights of the season.

In Alaska, as elsewhere during the tourist season, there are limited accommodations and travel facilities, but tour members have the advantage of co-ordinated services by the tour operators, and each member is guaranteed the best service available for the money.

In keeping with the informal way of doing almost everything in Alaska, the package tours are predominantly unescorted in the sense of having a full-time guide leading the traveler by the hand. Tours are met at their destination by tour agents who assist with the transfer of luggage and the transportation to lodgings. Additional guidance is available if desired, but it is not imposed on the group. There is a noticeable lack of commercialism and hurry which are sometimes associated with package tours.

Tours to Alaska are excellent for the traveler who dislikes planning travel details and who prefers the company of a group.

Leaving from Seattle, the prices of tours range from $205 for a seven-day trip during the thrift season to $759 for an eighteen-day de luxe vacation during the busy summer season. Bookings for all tours are not difficult to obtain if arrangements are made at least four months in advance, and it is advisable to consult a travel agent for assistance in arranging the most suitable tour for your tastes, in reserving space, and in handling details.

A substantial advance deposit is required at the time reservations are made and the balance is due sixty days before the tour begins. Deposits are returnable only if the reservation can be resold.

Arctic Alaska Tours in Seattle, the largest touring service for the state of Alaska, offers the most comprehensive selection to choose from. Greyhound Highway Tours, Inc., offers many escorted and unescorted tours. American Express, American Youth Hostels, Thomas Cook and Son, and Scenery Unlimited Tours, Inc., are excellent sources of escorted tours. There are special tours for hunters, fishermen, photographers, skiers, campers, honeymooners, educators, and students. Most of the major tour services will arrange tailor-made tours for groups with special interests.

Chartering Boats

Boats may be chartered from the West Coast ports of the United States and Canada for trips to Alaska by individuals or groups. For details and costs, write to the Chamber of Commerce in Seattle, Washington; Portland, Oregon; San Francisco, California; or Vancouver or Prince Rupert, B.C.

Chartering Planes

All major commercial air lines have chartering services available the year round, and charter planes for group travel is a worth-while consideration, particularly during the off-season. The larger air lines, such as Pan-American, Northwest Orient, and Canadian Pacific, are mainly equipped to handle only groups of fifty or more. Arrangements should be made with their charter representatives located at ticket offices and airports in the major cities.

Air lines with smaller planes handle smaller groups and individual charters. These services are also available at the larger airports in the United States and Canada.

During the off season from October through May, groups of twenty-one or more can usually charter a plane at considerable savings of time and money. For business firms and groups chartered planes are great conveniences for quick travel to Alaska, but for the individual they are costly.

The cost depends on the services required, but there is no one prevailing price. It is dependent on the kind and size of the plane, whether or not it is hired for one way or round trip, the distance it will travel, the number of personnel needed for the trip, the time of year, the route flown, and the cost of any additional services, such as lay-overs, side trips, and other special requests.

As an example of the cost during the off season, a DC-3 may be chartered at a flat rate of $1 per mile and will accommodate twenty-one people. DC-6B's or DC-7B's accommodate from seventy-five to one hundred passengers at a cost of approximately $4.50 per mile on a round-trip flight with minimum personnel and no special services included.

Hiring a Pilot—At major airports there are charter service companies, as well as individual pilots for hire. Individual pilots flying private aircraft must be commercially licensed to fly for hire. If they are not licensed, then passengers are not protected in the event of an accident or incident involving the plane or the pilot. For your own safety and protection, hire only pilots who hold a commercial pilot's certificate.

Fly Your Own Plane to Alaska

Plane trips by pilot-owners are a very popular means of travel and Alaska is well equipped to handle all types of aircraft entering the state.

There are approximately four hundred airports in Alaska which have services for small-plane owners flying aircraft with wheels. Of these, thirty-seven are Civil Aeronautics Administration intermediate fields on the Alaskan mainland, open the year around, with runways of four thousand feet or longer. All are served with communications as well as navigation aids, and instrument approach procedures are always in effect.

Alaska has 7,915 miles of civil airways. Seventy-four hundred of them are equipped with air traffic control, radio ranges, radio beacons, and homing markers. Nearly all the principal communities are linked by networks of intermediate fields and communications networks.

Seaplane facilities in Alaska vary from poor to excellent. Lake Hood, ten minutes from downtown Anchorage, has all facilities required and the largest concentration of seaplane activity in the world, with some 275 seaplanes based there the year around, converting to skis in winter. Fairbanks has limited seaplane anchoring facilities on the Chena River, but no docking or commercial refueling facilities.

Many CAA intermediate field locations are adjacent to rivers, so that aviation fuel is available, with many roadhouses or general stores at towns or settlements along the rivers and highways which carry supplies of aviation gas in five-gallon cans, and aviation oils.

Southeastern Alaska, including Ketchikan, Juneau, and Skagway, is essentially a seaplane operating area, but private facilities are scarce. Transients are served by Alaska Coastal Airlines and Ellis Air Lines at their docking facilities which are located at most of the towns in the area.

Although the seaplane is the most practical airplane to use in southeastern Alaska, its private use is very limited because of the scarcity of fresh-water operations. Continued operation in salt water is extremely expensive because of high maintenance costs.

The Northwest Staging Route, from Edmonton through Northwest Canada, is under the control of the Royal Canadian Air Force, RCAF, and pilots flying through the area are required to fly exactly according to flight plan, or return to their starting point. They are not allowed to alter flight plans by "re-filing" in the air. Each plan must be specifically approved by the RCAF prior to departure. If the RCAF does not approve of weather conditions, they will not approve the flight.

The inside route is strongly recommended for all landplanes in summer and winter. From a weather point of view, the coastal route is hazardous throughout most of the year with frequent low ceilings and visibility. For a landplane, the coastal route offers no practical forced landing opportunities except in the tall trees or water. It is a long hop between airports and coastal weather can close in from all directions while the airplane is en route.

Average weather over the greater part of Alaska, except for the coastal regions, is surprisingly good all year. The usual precautions must be observed in flying through mountain passes because of the turbulence in the strong winds and the danger of getting caught by the weather. There is a prevalence of false passes which look navigable but are really dead ends. These passes frequently extend many miles before becoming dead ends, and there is a chance of running out of gas before pilots can retrace the course.

The vacation pilot should always allow for better-than-normal weather conditions so he can fly higher and with better than legal minimum visibility.

Tremendous improvements are being made each year in Alaska. Every phase of aircraft facilities and operation, including control, safety, and communications, is being enlarged, extended, and improved. Alaska is a leader in the field of aeronautics and offers excellent vacation opportunities for pilot-owners of planes.

International Airports of Entry—The only international airports of entry for Alaska are the Juneau Municipal Airport and Juneau Seaplane Airport, the Ketchikan Airport and Seaplane Base, and Wrangell Seaplane Base. These are ports where planes may land at any time without giving advance notice of arrival.

Other airports in Alaska which have been granted landing-rights-only are Anchorage, Fairbanks, Skagway, Adak, Fort Yukon, Northway, and Shemya. For all of these airports pilots should give advance notice of arrival to the United States customs officer who will notify immigration and public health so that necessary inspection may be made. Advance notice of arrival should be given at least two hours prior to expected time of arrival.

There is a penalty of $500 for failure to give advance notice which may be levied against the pilot or the owner of the plane. Under ordinary circumstances the pilot may send his request to the CAA at the expected port of arrival, asking them to notify both customs and immigration to prevent any undue delay.

Additional Information—Anyone planning a private plane flight to Alaska should study the Civil Aeronautics Administration's *Flight Information Manual,* the *Airman's Guide,* the *Alaskan Flight Information Manual,* and the requirements of the Royal Canadian Air Force. A handy and valuable booklet called *Terrain Flying* may also be ordered from the CAA. It contains a special chapter on flying in Alaska and gives many practical aids and suggestions for flying over the various types of country.

CHAPTER IV. PANORAMA OF CELEBRATIONS AND EVENTS

The majestic 584,000 miles of Alaska are so enriched with monumental mountains, unfathomed lakes and waterways, and such vast panoramas that the entire territory can appear to be overwhelming and frightening. But the comparatively small and friendly population makes the gigantic country seem like a familiar and small community.

The warmth and helpfulness of the population are extended to everyone traveling or settling in the unusual country, giving the very welcome impression that they are old acquaintances. This impression is exemplified during the special Alaskan events which are part of the year-round scene in the "last frontier."

From the villages in the Arctic to the cities on the southeastern coast, many people leave their homes and congregate for the colorful and traditional celebrations and, before long, a new person feels the unity of the small population and becomes a part of it at the winter carnivals at the beginning of the New Year, the festivals at the end of winter, the beginning of spring and the ice breakup, the opening of the fishing and hunting seasons, the summer, fall, and year-end native events. The list of celebrations is long and varied, and each one captures the great and friendly spirit of Alaska.

Fairbanks Ice Carnival

The first months of the new year are the occasions for many winter carnivals, but the largest of them all is the Fairbanks Ice Carnival in mid-March. This great celebration, heralding the end of winter and the approach of spring, includes the famous North American Championship Dog-team Races.

Alaskans look forward to this event with great anticipation

during the winter and, arriving at Fairbanks for the ten-day carnival, everyone is immediately caught up in the spirit of expectancy and fun on every street and corner of the crowded interior city.

Following the vigorous greetings and the sharing of recent winter experiences, the talk turns to animated discussions and anticipations of the crowds, the dog races, the Eskimo dancers, the queen, and the weather with its promise of longer and brighter days ahead. Darkness continues through most of the daylight hours, but it never darkens the spirit of the carnival, and the decorative lights along the streets are reflected in snow, illuminating each event in brilliant reflected light.

A whirlwind of events compete for attention, including the Fairbanks torchlight parade, which is romantically beautiful in its winter setting, the fast and thrilling sled-dog races, the bowling matches, ski-sailing, and a variety show staged by local talent. There may be a sleeping-bag contest at the racing field where many couples compete in a typically Alaskan contest. A man bundled in one bag and a woman in another stretch out beside their dog team and sled waiting for the signal to wiggle free of the bags so they can hitch the dogs to the sled and race to the field goal. Another special event is performed by the parajumpers from the Sky-Divers Club who add to the thrills as they drop from planes and perform some air-borne magic. Eskimos please tourists and old-timers alike with exhibitions of native dances, games, and the spectacular leaping and bounding from a trampoline of stretched skin, manipulated by a circle of Eskimos who hold the skin taut, then slack, tossing their companion to unbelievable heights. There are contests and exhibitions of all kinds: photography, auto ice-racing, the world's championship Eskimo yo-yo competitions, skiing, ice hockey, figure skating, skijoring behind teams of racing sled dogs, art exhibitions featuring nationally known artists alongside local housewives and miners, and the notable paintings of the Farthest North Art Guild. And there are the age-old curling competitions on the ice rink, presented in the royal Scottish tradition.

Curling teams from Canada compete regularly with the teams from Fairbanks in gala bonspiels. There is great pageantry accompanying this event, which was first played in Fairbanks during the winter of 1905-06, when it was brought in by the stampeders from Dawson, Yukon Territory, where it had been a favorite camp game. This sport has a long tradition in the north country. It originated in Scotland about the sixteenth century and was played with naturally rounded stones. Now the polished stones are imported from Scotland, and in this game, which is compared to bowling, the stones slide on an ice rink with players wielding brooms trying to speed or retard the progress of the stone as it moves into scoring position.

The Craft Show is a colorful collection of authentic Alaskan crafts, displaying a variety of weavings, jewelry, carvings, and the ceramic products of the Fairbanks Mud-nesters. Additional products of Eskimo craftsmanship can be seen and purchased at the Eskimo bazaar.

The University of Alaska students and members of the faculty are active participants in the carnival, adding their talents and youth, and holding campus activities. Local and state-wide social, fraternal, civic, and business organizations join in the holiday spirit and hospitality that make the winter Ice Carnival a festival of fun and excitement.

The Coronation Ball, a salute to the new Miss Alaska, queen of the carnival, is a gala spectacle that features the loveliest girls in Fairbanks and brings out the finest dress parade of the new year. In attendance on the queen and her court are some of the old prospectors from the bush, spruced up in their best, and cavorting with society matrons, city merchants, Eskimos, Indians, and other citizens representing the many facets of Alaskan life.

Throughout the Ice Carnival there are varied activities for children, teen-agers, and grown folk that amaze and delight one. Tired spectators may take a breather and enjoy a dog-sled ride, or attend the Snowshoe Baseball game, a hilarious contest of wit and burlesque which draws large crowds to enjoy the tumbling on snowshoes and to cheer favorite native sons. At the Eielson Air Base indoor pool there are special events, such as water ballets and diving exhibitions.

Camera enthusiasts are everywhere and flashbulbs are in evidence at every event. There is so much going on that photographers have a field day exposing miles and miles of film.

And Saturday night before the Ice Carnival draws to a close, tribute is paid Old Man Winter in one of the biggest and most colorful parades in Alaska, with bands accompanying the marching and drilling units from many other states. Beautiful, imaginative, and humorous floats of every description feature the renowned celebrities of Alaska and the carnival passing in review.

The Ice Carnival is sponsored by the action-minded Fairbanks Junior Chamber of Commerce and the Alaska Dog Mushers Association. Their co-operative efforts are at peak performance during the three days of competition when the North American Championship Dog-team Races take over carnival and the minds and hearts of everyone there.

Most Alaskans agree that these three days are the most exciting, and a love for the dogs, plus some knowledge of the sport of sled-dog racing, is vital to the fullest enjoyment, the fun, and the excitement of these championship races.

North American Championship Dog-team Races

Long before carnival, preparations are made and competitions are held locally throughout the state for this big event. Some of the finest teams in Alaska, as well as a few from other states, arrive in Fairbanks to participate in the exciting three-day contest.

The Fairbanks Ice Carnival Dog-team Races have events for men and women "mushers." Women's races are two twenty-mile heats, which are run on consecutive days, and the men race an extra thirty-mile stretch. For the winners of all three heats there are prize purses amounting to $2,500.

Dog fever touches everyone in Fairbanks and spreads to all corners of the state as speculation runs high. Those who cannot come to Fairbanks for the races keep close contact by radio to hear the latest results.

Contrary to any belief, the sled dog is not a remnant of the past. This breed is still a vital part of today's living in Alaska. Most important is the racing dog, followed closely by the working dog who still provides transportation and fulfills emergency missions when needed. Many hundreds are still used by doctors, missionaries, Eskimos, Indians, and trappers, and the mail route on St. Lawrence Island, even today, is a sled-dog operation. Even the airplane, which replaced the great need for vast numbers of sled-dog teams, cannot perform the individual missions when weather conditions are impossible. Then only a team and musher can do the important work. This is especially true in the sub-Arctic interior and Arctic regions.

Many Alaskans own, train, and race a dog team and most of them hope to win the Fairbanks races. They keep their dogs in condition for recreation and show, but also in readiness to work when needed.

Old-timers complain, "The dogs aren't what they used to be," "The new breed can't stand up under the strain of a long haul," "These mushers don't have the old drive." But the fact is, there are still amazing things being performed by today's mushers and dogs. In a weight-pulling contest, for instance, one sled dog showed his prowess by pulling a load of 900 pounds. On another occasion, two dogs traveled seventy-five miles in two days pulling half a ton of supplies and the added weight of the musher.

Experiments are under way by the military to develop cross breeds of Siberian Husky, Alaskan Malemute, Eskimo, and Mackenzie Husky strains that will be capable of traveling thirty miles a day, to survive on two pounds of food daily, and to haul from 100 to 120 pounds' pay load.

It takes careful breeding and training to develop animals possessing the speed, the strength, and the endurance to travel extended periods of time and remain healthy in severe cold and gale winds.

Sled dogs are in evidence all winter in Alaska. Teams can be seen pulling stalled cars out of snowbanks on the downtown streets of Fairbanks. In Nome, Kotzebue, Wales, Barrow, Shishmaref, or any other Arctic village, the sled dogs work the freight runs, towing water or wood supplies and filling the needs of everyday living.

At the Fairbanks races, spectators can get close to the dogs at the starting chutes before the races to watch as harnesses are adjusted and teams are formed in readiness. They are the first-class dogs with first-class mushers. In the lead of the team will be one of the outstanding performers, the lead dog. The teams are bunched close and seemingly calm, but they anxiously await the signal that begins the first of the three heats in the three-day, seventy-mile race.

Looking at a lead dog spectators can see the dignity, courage, and unusual qualities of a dog holding a high position. Lead dogs may be male or female, and they must be capable of sparking the team to peak performance, and possess intelligence and an uncanny sense of direction. The dog should be the fastest and the toughest, and have the greatest courage and self-confidence for the race ahead. Lead dogs must be peaceful and know how to avoid trouble among the teammates. They are expected to know how to demand and get speed from the team and inspire an additional spurt of speed when conditions on the trail demand it. If need be, they must continue a race on nerve alone and know how to stave off exhaustion. Initiative and feeling of responsibility must rank above that of all the other dogs. There are many demands on the brave lead dog, exceeded only by those of the musher who does not use a bridle and rarely a whip, controlling the sled and issuing commands: "gee," turn right; "haw," turn left; "whoa," meaning stop, and "mush," to send the team flying off to the races.

During the three days of the North American Championship Dog-team Races, the trail is well patrolled and progress is reported from aircraft which flies over the racers and reports, via radio, every detail of the thrilling event. Homes, restaurants, hotel lobbies, bowling alleys, and every conceivable place in Fairbanks have receivers tuned in to catch the on-the-spot broadcasts originating from the plane, as well as from ground stations strategically placed along the trail of the race.

Watching the dogs and the musher, one can almost see the bond of confidence that exists, particularly between the lead dog and his master. Each seems to know the other's shortcomings and needs, and they achieve a co-ordinated chain of command.

There are tension and anticipation in the crowd of thousands who gather at Creamer's Field, a mile from the center of Fairbanks, the site of the start and finish of the races. Speculation runs high around the hospitable bonfires and coffee shacks where crowds gather to ward off the thirty- to forty-degree chill in the air. There is much talk of last year's race and racers, and experiences and memories of dog racing; there is speculation about the possibility of accident or other misfortune in the day's race because almost everyone there knows the rule that requires all dogs starting the race to finish that race in order for the team to qualify. When a dog is sick or injured and unable to continue, it must be carried in the sled for the remaining distance. Another rule states that the same dogs must be used on successive days, so that there are usually seven to nine dogs in each team although only five are required by the regulations.

At the finish of a day's heat, there are high spirits among those who can boast that they backed a winner and much partisan enthusiasm by the backers of each team. Some of the spectators at lookout points along the trail come in bursting with news and details of what they've seen. And as the last sled teams arrive, the crowd breaks up and returns to the festivities in the city.

The sled dogs are returned to their kennels; though the race has excited great interest about them, little is known of the origin of the Husky and Malemute. Ages ago they may have been a cross between domestic dogs and wild wolves. What is more important, the Alaskan Malemute and Siberian Husky are recognized by the American Kennel Club and around the world as thoroughbred breeds of their own. The Husky is a lighter dog, weighing up to about seventy pounds and the Malemute is some twenty to thirty pounds heavier. All manner of cross breeds are used as sled dogs. The Husky is as closely identified with Alaska as the St. Bernard is with Switzerland and the Lion Dog with China. These animals make good house dogs and pets and, though they have a heavy coat of hair which protects them from extreme cold, they are able to adjust rapidly to warmer surroundings.

Litters are large, averaging from six to seven puppies, and the dogs begin harness training when six months old, the time to learn manners and teamwork. But actual work and serious racing do not begin until they are about a year and a half old. The dogs are fed dried salmon and commercial mixtures, although some dog owners feed them horse meat, tallow, and meal when it's available. The diet is well balanced and produces extremely healthy specimens. Sled dogs are not fighting dogs and give battle only when there is good reason.

They will always be a vital part of the Alaskan scene and the fastest and best-trained of the sled dogs continue to be the high lights of the Fairbanks Ice Carnival.

Anchorage Fur Rendezvous

If one can plan time for vacation earlier in the year, every effort should be made to attend the Annual Fur Rendezvous in Anchorage, which is held one month earlier than the Fairbanks Ice Carnival. Those fortunate enough to be able to include both will enjoy some rare experiences.

In February of each year the city of Anchorage turns out in all its gala holiday finery to present a celebration equal to Fairbanks in many respects and superior in others, climaxed by an Alaskan spectacle, the fur auction.

The Anchorage Fur Rendezvous is popularly known as the "Mardi Gras of the North," with one week of revelry and merrymaking and business activity. The fur business is the focal point of the serious side of the occasion because furs are still an important product of export from the northern state. Professional fur buyers come to Anchorage from New York, California, England, France, and other important areas to buy trappers' wares for shipment to the world's markets where they will be processed and fashioned by experts who convert the raw hides into a wealth of the finest muffs, stoles, collars, capes, jackets, and coats. Scraps are used as trimmings for everything from bottle openers to dog collars.

Anchorage is one of the prime sources for the best furs, and this annual auction is open for bids from all who attend the Rendezvous. The auction is held in front of City Hall in the early afternoon each day. Prices are lower than one would expect in the market, but risks are higher for inexperienced buyers. Visitors often compete with the pros and excitement mounts to a high peak as bids are made for the magnificent array of pelts—ermine, wolf, wolverine, seal, squirrel, and a complete assemblage of the fur wealth of Alaska.

The Fur Rendezvous features events and exhibitions that amaze, amuse, and excite, and there is one in particular that could be considered as a shocking high light. The shocker is presented by the Eskimos and is billed as a "seal hunt pageant," in which seals are butchered in front of the spectators to show a facet of everyday life in the Arctic. A performance of this pageant is usually held every afternoon and evening in the Municipal Auditorium. Other phases of the Eskimo exhibition, the folklore and story dances with ceremonial masks and mitts, the games, and skin-tossing are choice attractions.

Visitors and residents of Anchorage "live it up" day and night during this week-long celebration, taking full advantage of the large and varied entertainments.

The Rendezvous' All-Alaska Dog Sled Races, known as "the richest race of its kind in the world," attract great attention because, not only are they a preview of some of the great teams that will compete at the Fairbanks championship races, but because the outcome can be decisive for many hopeful runners. The high point is a seventy-five-mile race and the stakes total over $6,500 in prize money. Additional races are held by women mushers who compete over a ten-mile course with ten or more teams trained and driven by women. Even children's teams have their own races during the week and, although sled-dog racing for all ages is a high light of Fur Rendezvous, it by no means dominates the festivities, and presents a problem or two to the organizers of these events who are not always certain that the weather will cooperate and keep snow on the streets for the racing. With daytime temperatures in the high fifties and a bright sun cheerfully adding to the brilliant festivities, scores of trucks are often pressed into service to scurry back and forth throughout the still long nights, hauling fresh snow from the near-by mountains to cover the streets of downtown Anchorage where the dog teams streak with their sleds, into the heart of the city to the finish line.

Fur Rendezvous also features skin-diving exhibitions, a curling bonspiel, ice hockey games, figure skating, and a variety of championship ski events held in Anchorage's Arctic Valley, including downhill slalom and cross-country contests attracting a stellar field of skiers from all over the United States, as well as competitors from Europe. There are additional thrills as the stock-car races are run off on a track of treacherous ice.

It is easy to make friends and find plenty to do during this week. Anchorage's famed Community Chorus and Symphony Orchestra are on hand for concerts; the Little Theater offers talented productions, sometimes with big-name stars; musicians and performers from Hollywood and New York bring a special enthusiasm to the audiences at this Rendezvous.

There is time for leisurely feasts of Chinese, Italian, Mexican, and Scandinavian delicacies, or native Eskimo and Indian cookery. And for those in a hurry, there are barbecued "mooseburgers" to eat along the way.

Tickets are on sale for votes to elect the queen of Rendezvous who will be crowned at the Coronation Ball which climaxes the entire week. And for a "warm up" to the coronation, there is the Miner's and Trapper's Ball featuring beard-growing contests, costume parades, excellent music, and a variety of entertainment along with an evening of dancing. There are square and folk dances, there is dancing in the streets, and for those who would rather watch others, the Copper River Indian or the Diomede and King Island Eskimo dancers should be seen.

As a guarantee of more than enough for all visitors and residents at the Rendezvous, special professional boxing and wrestling matches are presented along with the Alaska Association Bowling Tournament. The "consumers' carnival" is a sale of the latest merchandise, and the fur style show features the newest of next year's models.

From year to year the events grow in interest and pleasure. Those that don't, quickly fall by the wayside, so that only the best remain to make the Anchorage Fur Rendezvous one of the biggest and brightest of Alaska's many celebrations.

Other Winter Carnivals and Sled-dog Races

Every community, large or small, has its own local celebration. Winter carnivals are held at Homer during February or March and Tanana in April. Cordova gets an early start on the others with its big Annual Masquerade Ball in January. At Tok, Big

Delta, Nenana, Kotzebue, and many other communities, the concentration is on sled-dog races. From January through March, visitors and prospective settlers can help Alaskans sweep out the winter gloom and welcome the approaching spring.

Nenana Ice Classic

The Ice Classic can be experienced only in Alaska. It is a very special event involving many thousands of people. It does not bring forth any large communal festivities, but there is much excitement and suspense across the state, and the preparations for this event on the part of man and nature are major attractions of each year.

The Ice Classic is Alaska's biggest "guessing game" with the pay-off date sometime in April or May. Naming the exact date in advance is impossible and even the lucky ones don't know until the last minute. That is the big game.

Anyone can participate, according to the rules, if they live in Alaska and are considered a resident, but there are others who have found ways and means to get in on the game. Business firms in other states with offices or affiliates in Alaska have been known to juggle their personnel on paper so that the New York or California employees are briefly eligible to take a guess, either in their own name or through the office pool. Then there are people who have relatives and friends in Alaska and they somehow get in under the barrier. But these exceptions are few and the best way to participate is to be in Alaska for an extended visit, or become a resident.

The object of this game is for the participant to guess the month, the day, the hour, and the minute that the ice breaks on the Tanana River at the town of Nenana. A tripod is frozen into the ice; a wire goes from the tripod to a tower on the shore and is connected with an electric clock that stops when the ice sheet on the river lifts and begins to move downstream. When it has gone about one hundred feet the clock stops and records the winning time of the Ice Classic, designating the official winner of more than $100,000.

Gambling is illegal in Alaska so the "guess" tickets are handled by express and air freight for distribution from headquarters to all Alaskan communities; then they are returned with each of the participants' selected date-hour-minute, name, and address. Bars, restaurants, stores, and chosen persons handle the tickets in the towns. The cost is, and has been for many years, $1 per ticket. Many groups get together and buy blocks of tickets and share their guesses. Many individuals buy a handful on their own.

Closing date on the sale of tickets is well in advance of the breakup, and tickets are then forwarded in five-gallon gasoline cans to Nenana where they are sorted into pigeonholes according to the date and time of each guess. In Nenana, giant books are prepared, listing everybody's guess and name. The books are then distributed to the various cities and towns so that everyone can check to see that they are properly listed, and also to have a look at what their neighbors guessed.

Some of the lucky times guessed in the past have been May 15 at 1:32 P.M., April 26 at 4:03 P.M., and April 29 at 1:26 P.M. May 14 has been a good date a number of times and so has April 30. The first few weeks in May, and times after noon, seem to have been more consistent winners. It is all hit or miss, but people try working out formulas in higher mathematics. Some begin in the fall of the previous year and measure the ice crust when it forms on the rivers, checking how rapidly it forms and how rapidly the water level drops. This kind of figuring sometimes includes the angle and intensity of the sun when it hits the high mountain peaks and starts to melt the snow in late winter, and also checking the speed of water flow moving in the streams from the distant mountains. The success of the formula depends upon keeping an accurate record of weather conditions during the winter months—snowfall, precipitation, winds, and temperatures. Such a formula could reveal the exact winning minute of the breakup at Nenana and whoever tries this method of calculation will be following the footsteps of others who have gone to even greater lengths to predict the winning time. Some try astronomy, others consult fortunetellers, collect "hot tips," "dope" nature's phenomena in scientific journals, or just make wild guesses.

Somehow it seems that the legal residents have the best chance of winning. It must add luck, because so far no outsider has found himself in the position of holding a ticket and not being able to collect because of the residence rules.

The true prophets are those old-timers who have known the river intimately over a period of years and have a "feel" for its idiosyncrasies. They know how it is affected by weather conditions, its grinding power, and its potential. And they will share this information with the newly landed "chechakkos." On the day the ticket sales close, there is much discussion between old-timers and short-termers, visitors and newcomers, as the last-minute effort is made to put the right guess in the can. A dozen times during the day a person is reminded by friends, shopkeepers, casual acquaintances, and even strangers that midnight is the deadline for the Ice Classic. From that time on, the participants play a waiting game.

The breakup itself is spectacular, especially at places like the Ramparts on the Yukon, where the ice goes through the big canyon and there are some blocks as big as houses, tumbling and crashing along. When the breakup seems imminent at Nenana, radio, television, and newspaper people are usually on hand to relay the news to their papers and stations because all Alaska is on the alert, waiting for the breakup. The instant it happens, everyone in Alaska is a winner because it is the official beginning of spring and from that moment on the state begins to feel the warmer winds, the migratory birds are on their way, gardens will soon bloom, fishing season is getting in stride, bathing suits and water skis come out of closets, clamdiggers hit the beaches, the boat shows begin, the animals stretch and shake off their winter drowsiness, and the state prepares for the spring and summer celebrations.

Gold Medal Basketball Tournament

The Gold Medal Basketball Tournament takes place during February of each year in Juneau, climaxing an exciting winter season for this extremely popular sport.

Basketball is the number-one sport in Alaska, drawing crowds of spectators who cheer the local teams to state-wide victories. The games also bring enjoyment to many in every corner of the state, including the isolated families and trappers who follow this intramural event via radio. In addition to the school teams, there are games between city businessmen's leagues, the Alaska National Guard and other military personnel, and the University of Alaska; for several years, international exhibition teams like the Globetrotters have gone to Alaska and played to enthusiastic crowds all the way from Nome to Juneau.

The local teams travel considerable distances to participate in varsity exchange games. Seward sends its team to Fairbanks for two games in the series and the Fairbanks team flies to Seward for two return visits. Nome sends its team flying around the state to compete with teams of other cities. These trips are expensive, costing a minimum of $500 to send a team from Seward to Fairbanks for one game, but it is worth it to the local people and they give their wholehearted support.

It's high-flying basketball at its best and the competitive spirit is at a peak during the season. Some of the greatest rivalry centers around the Fairbanks High School Malemutes, whose arch enemy is Anchorage, and when they clash it's a serious and thrilling business for all concerned.

Basketball is held in high regard by Alaskans. The town hero is the season's basketball star, not only because of his local conquests but by state-wide standards and approval. His fame is the town's fame, and he is a high-ranking personality in the state. Every indoor court in Alaska is jammed from the converted quonset hut in Barrow to the most modernly equipped gyms in the Anchorage schools, and even in the bush basketball hoops are set up behind the cabins or tacked on trees for the children and adults to sharpen their hoop technics.

Visitors can see many of the top-ranking teams and Alaskan cage stars by attending the annual Gold Medal Tournament in Juneau. It is the "big time" in Alaskan sports.

Midnight Sun Baseball Game

One of the oldest classic events in Alaska is the Fairbanks Midnight Sun Baseball Game, starting at 10:30 P.M. on June 21 of each year, saluting the longest day of the year. This annual sport event dates back almost to the birth of the city of Fairbanks during the great gold-rush days of the early 1900's. Artificial lighting, in spite of all the modern improvements, is unnecessary because the midnight sun gives full illumination to the ballgame in Griffin Ball Park in downtown Fairbanks.

The players are a cross section of the best baseball talent in the state, including members of the armed forces, many of whom are on leave from the national professional leagues, colleges, and sandlots, combined with their counterparts from the civilian ranks.

Alaska's baseball season is short because winter crowds it and so it is played with added zest, getting off to a rapid start and whipping through to a lively finale. The high light of the season for Alaskans, as well as for some fervent fans in other states, is the Midnight Sun game. It is a battle extraordinary with Fairbanks providing all the additional festivities expected of a big sporting event.

Southeastern Alaska Ski Championship

Ski enthusiasts should be in Juneau the last week of March for the annual Southeastern Alaska Ski Championship which takes place at the Douglas Ski Bowl, less than five miles from the center of Juneau. A popular means of transportation to the scene of these activities is provided by Sno-cats, which carry spectators and skiers up the three-mile trail, picking them up at a point on the Douglas Highway just ten minutes' drive from town. There are also flights by helicopter which operate from downtown Juneau, making an easy journey to the Bowl where outstanding skiers compete for top honors on the unsurpassed slopes and ski terrains.

Skiing is a favored winter sport in Alaska and there are ski clubs in many of the larger communities where competitions are scheduled irregularly throughout the winter, roughly from early November to the last of April, at ski areas such as Ester Dome or Cleary Summit Ski resort, near Fairbanks, where the John McCall Ski Tourney is held. Homer has the Kachemak Ski Club and ski tow on Ohlson Mountain Road, the Arctic Valley Ski Bowl is just outside of Anchorage, Cordova has one on Mount Eccles, Sitka on Harbor Mountain; among the many others is the military-civilian run on Kodiak Island. Practically every community in Alaska has ski activity with the exception of the far southeastern areas where snow and ice are rare even in the winter months.

Facilities for skiing are great and there is widespread interest and keen competition on all slopes, with skiers coming to Alaska from all over the world.

Arctic Valley is located ten miles from Anchorage and draws over twenty thousand skiers on each week end and holiday. The Valley is in operation five days a week under joint operation of the military and the Anchorage Ski Club. It has six tows of the Pomo-lift variety ranging in length from 900 to 1,700 feet. The slopes are noted for dry powder snow; temperatures seldom drop below zero and almost never rise above freezing. Hot food and warming shelters are available at the resort.

Cleary Summit at Fairbanks has three tows rising a maximum of 3,300 feet above the 280 acres of dry powder snow. The tows operate in any temperature, as the slopes are protected from the prevailing winds. The lodge at Cleary is built of wood and native stone, and has been cited as the finest ski lodge in the state.

Many plans are under way to expand the present facilities in all the ski areas in the state. New areas are being opened yearly as, for instance, at Mount Alyeska in the Girdwood Valley, 38 miles from Anchorage on the Sterling Highway. It has two rope tows with a combined length of 3,000 feet and a vertical drop of 900 feet. The Mount Alyeska ski area covers 160 acres, with a recently installed 4,000-foot chair lift and the newest ski lodge facilities.

Douglas Ski Bowl has a tow, and overnight facilities for members and guests of the Juneau Ski Club. There are also two warming huts on the trail and the three-mile downhill run from the Bowl to the highway is one of the spectacular features of this beautiful area. The nearby Juneau ice fields are not as well developed as the Bowl but they provide hundreds of downhill runs. Though there are no lifts as yet, there is helicopter service to the big runs and, for the skier willing to climb, this is one of the biggest ski adventures in the world.

Events at the Southeastern Ski Championship are varied from

year to year but always include slalom, downhill, and cross-country competitions. Additional thrills occur when the combined sport of dog racing and skiing, skijoring, is on the schedule. This method of cross-country running behind a team of dogs is fast becoming a popular event.

Fairbanks-Nenana Boat Races

Alaska's sheltered harbors, inland waterways, and a coast line of 26,000 miles, longer than the coast of the entire continental United States, inspire a lot of water-sport activity for residents of the state.

The Fairbanks-Nenana Boat Marathon in July is one of the biggest not only in Alaska, but in all northwestern United States as well. Inboard and outboard motor champions by the dozens compete on the sixty-mile stretch of the Chena and Tanana rivers to win top-money prizes and valued trophies.

Seward Fourth of July Marathon

The Fourth of July is celebrated in every village, hamlet, town, and city in Alaska, and in each it is like a kaleidoscopic view of all the events of the year. It is as though it were a matter of personal pride for each community to have the best celebration in the state.

Seward features a race to end all races on the Fourth. It is called the Mount Marathon Race and any mountain climber with or without experience may enter. Those out of practice can arrive in Seward a few days early and try the mountain to become familiar with the terrain, or they can practice on some other peaks in Alaska to get into condition. It is recommended.

Mount Marathon juts up 3,022 feet from Seward and the big race begins in the heart of the downtown area at sea level. The object of the race is to climb the slope to the peak and return, choosing any route that seems best, but all routes feature forty-five-degree angles and hair-raising cliffs along the way to the top.

Contestants are not allowed to use any equipment and the feat requires the utmost in strength, stamina, and courage.

Judges are stationed at the summit where the racers must check in before they descend. The round trip must be accomplished within ninety minutes or the racer does not qualify for the awards which consist of cash prizes and trophies.

For the spectators, the streets of downtown Seward offer an excellent view of the racers as they climb the mountain. Thousands throng the flag-festooned streets, perching on every available ledge for an hour and a half of breathless excitement, which takes place yearly in the afternoon hours of the Fourth.

Mount Marathon offers a special challenge not only to climbers that are eager to prove that they can complete the trip, but also to those who want to chop down the established fifty-two-minute record.

Valdez Truck Road-eo

In Valdez there is a "Truck Road-eo" in August for the best and safest truck drivers in the nation. Trucks parade and forty-foot vans compete with tractors in truck driving feats. The winner receives $50 monthly for a year and runners-up receive cups and belt buckles. There are street dances, complex and demanding field tests, softball games, teen-age road-eo events, and a *smörgåsbord* feast.

Arts and Crafts Shows

Juneau is the scene of the Annual Arts and Crafts Show in mid-March. For everyone interested in the creative arts and crafts, this is a superior exhibition of the most current works by Alaskan artisans, writers, and painters, including the finest from the guilds in Fairbanks, Anchorage, Haines, Skagway, Sitka, Wrangell, Ketchikan, and Juneau.

This well-organized and colorful exhibition shows enameling, sculpture, paintings, silk screen, woodworking, weaving, jewelry, native Eskimo and Indian crafts, ceramics, creative writing, music, photography, driftwood, lapidary, mosaics, needlework, and "live" demonstrations by leading craftsmen, achieving a representative cross section of the creative talents in Alaska. The show is not a sales exhibit but arrangements can be made to buy direct from the artists.

During the year many one-man shows are held, even in the

smallest villages, and in the larger cities they can be seen in banks, restaurants, hotels, airports, airplanes, trains, ships, museums, and in just about every conceivable place including clotheslines and back-yard fences. The annual exhibition in Sitka of the Baranof Island Arts and Crafts Association is in November and includes the works of twenty or more artists and craftsmen with holders of national prizes among them.

Petersburg's Spring Festival

On May 17, for three days, Petersburg, Alaska, might well be matched with any Norwegian community of equal size. Actually Petersburg is like a year-round part of Scandinavia transplanted to southeastern Alaska.

The Spring Festival brings a surge of color and added flavor when visitors, as well as residents, join in a delightful round of merry activity which is unique and exciting.

During the days of festival, and particularly on the seventeenth of May, the citizens of Petersburg observe customs of the old country with traditional dances and Norwegian costumes. Picture weavings, carvings of trolls and witches, enamelwork, silverwork, and many of the handicrafts of Norway are featured in homes and public decorations. Eiler Wikan's extraordinary collection of original "early-day" Norwegian clothes is on display. The halibut fleet is in and boat crews are on hand with their pockets jingling with coin from the first catches.

Petersburg puts out the welcome mat, inviting all to participate in a wealth of civic, social, and organizational programs, varying from exhibitions of hand arts both old and new, to singing, folk dancing, *smörgåsbord* feasts, salmon barbecues, and fish fries, and the official ceremonies that are held in observance of the Norwegian Independence Day. There are dozens of events during Spring Festival in May, and one month later the community celebrates Saint Hans Day in a midsummer celebration with all the friendly spirit of the Spring Festival but with the added high lights of bonfires and picnics.

It is a joy to be one of the participants at either of these intimate, colorful, and entertaining celebrations in Petersburg.

Salmon Derby Days

Two to three days during the last week of May or the first week of June in Ketchikan are set aside for the special King Salmon Derby for all fishermen or nonfishermen who want a unique fishing experience.

In early March, Ketchikan opens the fishing derby celebrations with a season-long contest, giving prizes for the largest fish caught weekly, and grand prizes at the end of the five-month season. The special days in late May or June are a derby within a derby known as Ketchikan King Salmon Derby Days. For this special prizes are awarded totaling more than $10,000 for the "big ones." King salmon weighing up to seventy-nine pounds have been caught during these contests, and hundreds are brought in that exceed fifty pounds.

Alaska has many of these salmon derbies throughout the salmon-fishing season. Juneau's Golden North Salmon Derby takes place in July and prizes there have a value greater than $15,000. In all the derbies, prizes are mainly donations from local business firms and sponsoring organizations, and they include everything from new cars, round trips to Hawaii, Seattle, or the Pasadena Rose Bowl games, sixteen-foot boats with motors and trailers, outboard motors, and freezing units to television sets.

Juneau's Golden North Salmon Derby is sponsored by the Territorial Sportsmen, Inc., and proceeds from the sale of fish entered in the contest are used to support scholarship funds for local youths, as well as conservation projects.

There is a general closing down of business activities in Juneau for this fishing holiday celebration, and the streets become deserted ghost walks down to the water fronts. Almost everyone who has been able to arrange for boat transportation is out on the waters in boats of all sizes, shapes, and conditions. Riding herd over this large fleet is the United States Coast Guard, keeping close watch to see that overly enthusiastic fishermen don't get carried away in their efforts to land the biggest fish of the derby.

At the Valdez Silver Salmon Derby during the month of August, and during the "Fish-for-Fun" season which lasts from May through August, fishing may also be done from the shore, giving everyone a chance whether there is a boat available or not.

The Seward Silver Salmon Derby attracts between 2,500 and 3,000 sports fishermen during its August event and here, too, prizes valued at $10,000 or more are distributed to the winners.

Cordova's derby is Labor Day week end and, like the others, is open to all visitors with special events for children. Sitka's derby is in July. They are all traditional annual events in Alaska, and anyone who can arrange to be in one of the communities during the local event is assured of good fishing and excellent Alaskan hospitality.

Skagway Summer Celebrations

Skagway's hospitality is wide open to everyone seeking a hearty celebration and a view of what it was really like in the fabulous days of the gold stampede—"the Klondikers," "the Yukon Trail and Chilkoot Pass," "Soapy Smith," the gamblers, dance-hall girls and the "golden dreams."

During the summer months the Days of '98 celebration is in full swing every night when the boat comes in and citizens in gala frontier costumes of 1898 celebrate as they did in the old days. The doors of the Golden Nugget Saloon are thrown open so that visitors can crowd around the gambling tables, see the can-can girls, and soak up the raucous, rich atmosphere of the early times.

Kangaroo courts are in session, "The Shooting of Dan McGrew" is re-enacted in all its glory, old-time dances are in progress, serenaders are in the streets, and the water front of Skagway is once again a gold-rush mecca.

Fairbanks Golden Days

When Felix Pedro struck gold in 1902, he set off a gold rush in the Fairbanks area which is still being celebrated. Discovery Day, on July 22, marks the founding of the second largest city in the new state.

The wondrous days of the stampede and the fateful sour-doughs who turned an uncharted wilderness into a thriving metropolis and tramped the mountains and waterways of the heart of Alaska in a never-ending search for the riches of the land, all are commemorated in the Midsummer Golden Days at Fairbanks.

This celebration is lavish in its displays honoring the recent past with re-enactments of the pioneer landing by riverboat on the banks of the Chena River, special ceremonies for Felix Pedro at the monument erected in his memory, and the public displays of relics from Fairbanks' golden history.

Lively events fill every hour of the long summer days with visitors panning gold in the streets and competing in the World's Championship Gold Panning Contest. All the dazzle of a booming gold-mining camp passes in review, with bearded sourdoughs and their ladies in turn-of-the-century fashions.

Every male resident must wear a beard or display his shaving permit to keep out of the kangaroo courts and to avoid a fine or serve a sentence in the jail. Beards are the fashion of the day, gaining added importance in the beard contests when the groomed and pampered "bushes" win prizes for best of show, best color, best length, strongest when wet, curliest when dry, fanciest to the eye, most golden, and even a prize to the fellow who can't raise more than a wisp, as long as it's the smallest wisp.

For many visitors and residents the high light of Golden Days is the Old Timers' Baseball Classic, which is played more for humor than sport. The champions of this classic go on to play other teams in other towns during the whirlwind baseball season. Those who miss the classic in Fairbanks may catch up with the hilarious team as it travels around the state.

Fairbanks is well experienced in being host for festivals whether it is the Ice Carnival or Golden Days or the dozens of other local celebrations held throughout the year when guests receive the royal Alaskan welcome.

Alaska Day Festival

October 18 is Alaska Day and in Sitka the annual celebration is the high light of this significant event—the historical United States purchase of Alaska in 1867 from Russia. Sitka was the old Russian capital and remained the capital city of Alaska until the early 1900's. Every year the residents re-enact the rais-

ing of the American flag, with special official ceremonies commemorating the event during a three-day celebration which
features period costumes, beards, mug-up and fashion shows,
dances, tours, exhibitions of antique and modern-day artifacts,
luncheons and dinners, and the Alaska Day Pageant. There is a
Days of '67 dance, children's costume parties, band concerts, and
a costume ball in a genial atmosphere, reflecting the holiday
spirit of the entire city.

Eskimo Spring and Summer Celebrations

The short summer season and an even briefer spring in the
northern areas of the state crowd the playtime and festivals
together. In most villages and towns that are predominantly
Eskimo, including Kotzebue, Nome, Barrow, Savoonga, Gambell,
and Hooper Bay, the activities center around Eskimo life and
Eskimo customs, with two important events focused on the
activity of whales.

Kotzebue has the Beluga Whale Derby as soon as the ice goes
out. Barrow has a whale feast in July after the first whale is
caught. Exact timing of these events is very much dependent on
the weather, but, when it begins to look hopeful, word is passed
along and a date is announced. This is true also of the celebrations in the other villages, and it would be difficult to visit anywhere in the villages of the Arctic or near-Arctic regions during
any week of summer without being able to participate in one or
more of the local celebrations, particularly on the Fourth of
July, when a celebration is assured.

In the Arctic regions activities are varied. At larger celebrations the Eskimo drummers and chanters give a native rhythmi-
cal background to a chorus of dancers in nonceremonial, as well
as ceremonial, dances and costumes. There are sled-dog races,
snow conditions permitting, and kayak and skin boat races,
spear-throwing contests, foot races of all kinds, Eskimo games,
and blanket tossing. The women have parka races to see who
can race the fastest to a set goal, carrying a baby pickaback
inside the parka hood. First one to the goal is not the winner, but
she will have a head start on the fast manipulations required
to flip her baby around inside her loose-fitting parka, into her

arms, then with a few wiggles, shakes, and a jerk—a trick requiring unique co-ordination—the baby is brought forth from the parka. The first one to accomplish this feat wins the prize.

Feasting is an important part of these events, with muktuk to chew on, whale steaks, smoked fish, Eskimo ice cream, fresh and preserved berries served with sugar and canned milk, or with seal oil or plain. Additional delicacies to select from are the more conventional reindeer or caribou steaks and imported staples from the cities.

At Kotzebue in early March reindeer races are sometimes featured, along with a tomcod race between Eskimo couples. The couples race out on the sea ice, set up camp and equipment, dig a hole in the ice, which may well be five feet deep, and start fishing for tomcod. Everyone participating is well experienced, and it is a close and unbelievably fast contest to see which pair will bring in the first fish and win.

The Kotzebue Beluga Whale Derby is open to everyone who will participate in this sport when the ice goes out. But anyone who is worried about disposing of the whale they catch needn't worry because all the whale meat caught belongs to the Eskimos. To be a winner in this derby means catching the longest whale; landing one of about fifteen to seventeen feet, and weighing approximately one hundred pounds per foot, is not unusual. Winners collect their prizes at the Fourth of July festivities and become celebrated personalities in the town, along with Miss Arctic Circle, the Eskimo queen chosen during this July holiday.

Miss Arctic Circle reigns supreme until Barrow's Labor Day celebration when Miss Top o' the World is chosen. Then it is difficult for nonpartisans to decide which one represents the most beautiful Eskimo girl in the northland.

The towns and villages on the sea coast and waterways feature boat rides for visitors in umiaks, the walrus-skin boats outfitted with modern outboard motors, sled-dog rides on snow if it exists, or on sleds fitted with wheels giving the passenger the effect of being in a dog race. There are always superior displays of ivory, jade, or skin products, handmade by the Eskimo men or women. Baseball games are held between the natives, military personnel, construction workers, and other civilian workers of the community, or even visitors if they want to participate. Thoughout these festivals the spirit of friendliness and warmth prevails and all join in turning each hour of sunshine into double-time fun.

Strawberry Festival

Haines celebrates its gigantic and famous strawberry crops with a festival which takes place during late June and early July. Strawberries are the size of a measuring cup and visitors will not only be able to see them but may take a pail and collect these giants and eat them to the heart's content. The date of this celebration in Haines is planned to coincide with the ripening of the berries.

There are many holiday events taking place during this celebration and most are planned to take advantage of outdoor living, including picnics on a pay-as-you-go or potluck basis for everyone, adventure tours of the sights, beach parties, arts and crafts exhibits, and exhibition dances by the Chilkat Indian tribe in ceremonial masks and costumes. As souvenirs of this event, a wide variety of preserved delicacies are on sale, prepared by the local housewives who have captured the splendor of these kings by creating tempting recipes that do full justice to the size, quality and taste of the Haines strawberries.

Music Festival

The Anchorage Annual Music Festival is entirely a community project for musicians and singers, with guest artists and composers invited to attend from all over Alaska and the other states. It is sponsored by the Anchorage Community Chorus, Anchorage Community College, and the Anchorage Symphony. The guest conductor for the event is Robert Shaw and, under his baton, the combined groups give inspired performances.

The Music Festival is not devoted exclusively to performances and the listening pleasures; it also includes lectures, round-table discussions, master classes, and concerts, as well as recitals and private instruction for those seeking college credit which may be obtained from the Anchorage Community College.

The Festival runs for a period of ten days in the summer or fall, and an example of its enormous popularity is the growth in attendance from 1956, when it began with an audience of five thousand, to 1959, when approximately ten thousand people attended. The major concerts include a chorus of over one hundred, a symphony orchestra numbering over sixty-five, with more than five hundred active participants in all the other festival activities. Supplementing this large assemblage are ten or more professional artists brought to Anchorage by the sponsoring organizations.

Almost everything about this festival of music has a typical Alaskan touch, from the wild-game dinner at the opening of the Festival to the concerts which feature the works of Alaskan composers. It is one of the goals of the Music Festival to encourage more state composers to write and, because the Festival concerns itself with new works, it even goes outside the state to commission music for its concerts. Critical attention from other cities of the nation has given the highest praise to this "most remarkable music festival in the Western Hemisphere."

It is all the more remarkable considering that this project, involving 750 people and drawing audiences of 10,000, takes place in a city of 31,000 people, in a state with a civilian population of less than half the population of Denver, Indianapolis, or St. Paul.

Fairs and Expositions

Alaskans are rightfully proud of their agricultural, homemaking, and homesteading accomplishments. The giant heads of cabbage bring cash rewards to every entry exceeding fifty pounds, and there are always a few with many runners-up in the forty-pound bracket. Jams, jellies, needlework, arts and crafts, canned wild game and other products, baked goods and specialty sourdough creations, flower exhibits from gardens that produce beautiful diminutive dwarfs to gigantic blossoms are exhibited in great abundance.

Visitors are aware of the fantastic strides being taken to improve and develop a highly productive agricultural supply which is one of the important needs in the new state. Each of the fairs provides a panoramic view of the efforts being made by Alaskans to reduce the margin between supply and demand locally to avoid the costly importing of food products which has always been responsible for the high cost of living.

The Tanana Valley Fair at Fairbanks, the Matanuska Valley Fair at Palmer, and the Harvest Fair in Skagway in August are representative of the many fairs and agricultural expositions held during the summer months; the 4-H fairs during September in a dozen and more communities are climaxed by the All-Alaska 4-H Fair in Anchorage late in that month. And with all the serious importance of these events, there is a background of festivities for the participants and spectators at the colorful and vital harvest celebrations.

Calendar of Other Events

June and July

Auto Races—Races are held in Anchorage's Alaska Speedway, a $50,000 modern racing bowl with paved track. Fairbanks has jalopy racing and stock-car races at both the Tanana Valley Fairgrounds and the Rendezvous Speedway, which draw large crowds on summer Sundays and holidays, and for children there are soapbox derbies in most of the larger communities, along with the teen-age drag races in Nome.

Golf—Championship matches are held at Anchorage and Fairbanks golf courses. There are many long hours in the summer day to enjoy the popular game.

Indian Dances—At Copper Center on the Richardson Highway, performances are given by the Copper River Indians in colorful costumes every night during the summer season. Easy to reach from Anchorage or Valdez.

"Workshop on Alaska"—An annual five-day workshop is presented at the close of the University of Alaska's summer school for those seeking an intensified orientation in Alaskan

wildlife, history, anthropology, education, literature, and art. This workshop is included in some package tour trips, but it is open to everyone.

Prospecting—Organized field trips are planned by prospecting clubs in all the larger cities for those who want to "prospect" for gold, uranium, oil, and other precious minerals and stones, or merely for the enjoyment of the scenery.

Boat Races—Southeastern Alaska's harbors and inland waters, as well as the lake and river runways in the interior, feature a multitude of races and regattas in conjunction with other major events and special racing competitions.

Swimming Meets—King's Lake in Matanuska Valley, Lake Spenard near Anchorage, and dozens of other locations, feature water-sport competitions and games both local and state-wide. Juneau has a heated pool and others vary from "the ol' swimming hole" to abandoned gravel pits.

August, September, and October

Wild-Game Dinner—An annual Alaskan treat sponsored by the Matanuska Valley Sportsmen which usually takes place sometime in October.

Deer Derby—A feature in Sitka during hunting season. There are prizes for the hunters.

Halloween Dance—Recognized throughout the state as an outstanding event, the big dance is held at Bethel in October.

November, December, January, and February

Philippine Festival—The celebration of the Filipino people at Juneau who honor their great patriot José Rizal on December 30.

Concert Series—Alaska Music Trail concerts with special children's performances. In all large cities and many small communities. Internationally known artists are heard at these concerts, which are scheduled throughout the fall, winter, and spring seasons.

Concerts—The University of Alaska Madrigal Singers and student chorus groups make frequent appearances during the winter season in Fairbanks and College.

Nome Roof Garden Party—In November the lucky ticket holder attending this event will be the winner of the largest gold nugget found in Alaska during the current year. There are many "door" prizes for this pre-Thanksgiving celebration.

Theater—The Kodiactors at Kodiak and theater groups in Anchorage, Fairbanks, the University Drama Department, Juneau, and groups in other cities are highly rated in lists of entertainment in the state.

Valley Homesteaders Achievement Day—This typically friendly and inviting occasion is scheduled annually in November at Palmer and features the homemakers' displays and a winter-time "country fair."

Dances—Almost every Saturday night there is a dance in the towns. Some have as their theme "Sadie Hawkins," "Hard Times," "March of Dimes," or local and national celebrations, and are held in local gyms, restaurants, bars, hotels, recreation halls, quonset huts, lodges, roadhouses, or wherever there is space. Folk-dance clubs in Fairbanks and other cities have special events and everyone is invited. The Alaska Native Brotherhood gives an Annual Ceremonial Costume Dance about November 1 in Fairbanks.

Christmas Contests—The contest each year in Fairbanks for the best displays of outdoor Christmas decorations is for all residents who do their best to compete with the aurora borealis.

Bowling Contests—Every night, in every town with a bowling alley, there are local competitions and frequent meets with out-of-town challengers which draw heavy attendance.

Hockey Matches—Most rinks are outdoors. Games are fast and furious and sometimes feature contests between local Alaskan champions and Canadians, who were largely responsible for introducing this sport in the far north.

Armed Forces Day—Always a big celebration for cities and towns near military installations. In the Arctic areas the famed Alaska Scouts National Guard units participate.

Yulefest—Scandinavian celebration in Petersburg in December with the folklore, dances, music, arts and crafts, and Christmas ceremonies of the "old country."

March, April, and May

Indian Potlatch—After the trapping season there are sled-dog races, games, and dances in Indian villages and towns.

Music Festival—Students at Mount Edgecumbe School, Sheldon Jackson Junior College, and Sitka Public Schools schedule a conference and feature local musicians, singers, and entertainers.

Hiking and Mountain-Climbing Clubs—Clubs organize special trips to conquer trails and peaks beginning in spring and continuing through the summer and into fall. In winter the hikers take to snowshoes.

Colony Day—At Matanuska, this tribute to the famous settling of the valley is held the latter part of May. Displays, entertainment, official ceremonies, and competitions are a part of the festivities.

Blessing the Fleet—Sitka has a special "Blessing of the Fleet" the Sunday before the fishing season opens. It is an impressive and significant event.

All Year Around

Sportsmen's Clubs—Alaska's Sportsmen's Clubs hold rifle meets, shows, and fishing derbies, sponsor educational programs and maintain lodges and facilities for indoor events as well. Kodiak, Matanuska, Tanana, Fairbanks, Anchorage, Juneau, and Ketchikan are only a few of the many clubs.

Archery Contests—The Alaskan Bowmen, the Blacksheep Bowmen of Anchorage, and the Tanana Valley Archers in Fairbanks are among the many archers' clubs holding competitions.

The timing of events in Alaska is as informal as the atmosphere of the celebrations. Dates depend on weather conditions, work conditions, and other activities in the communities, but residents and visitors become accustomed to this irregular scheduling. Accurate dates and approximate dates may be obtained by writing to the chambers of commerce or to the individual organizations sponsoring the events. Visitors to the eventful state can be certain that there are many events, celebrations, and festivals in progress nearly every week of the year at one or more of the cities, towns, and outposts. The local newspaper offices and the Alaska Department of Natural Resources in Juneau provide up-to-the-minute reports to keep everyone informed of "today's" events.

CHAPTER V. HUNTING, FISHING, AND TRAPPING

Hunting

HUNTING OF BIG-GAME ANIMALS

Alaska's wildlife resources are of vital importance to its economy and to the welfare of its residents. All government fish and wildlife agencies and conservation services, such as the Izaak Walton League of America, Kodiak and Alaska Guide Associations, and the state sportsmen's clubs, are actively engaged in protecting and preserving this resource. Hunters can assist by carefully adhering to the regulations and reporting to conservation agencies any potential dangers such as fire, traps, or other natural or man-made hazards.

Bears

Alaska's big and varied bear population includes the Alaska brown bear, largest meat eater on land, whose top weight is as much as 1,600 pounds. This bear and its cousin, the grizzly, still roam vast areas of Alaska, up the mainland coastal mountains to sub-Arctic regions, and among the mountain ranges of the interior. They are numerous on Admiralty, Baranof, and Chichagof islands, the Kodiak-Afognak group, and the Alaska Peninsula.

There is a noticeable resemblance between brown and grizzly bears. Scientifically they have been separated into nine groups, made up of about thirty species and subspecies, with a wide range in color and size.

The Toklat grizzly of the Alaska Range, for instance, is cream-colored, while the Shiras brown bear of Admiralty Island is almost coal-black. The grizzly of Norton Sound is comparatively small, but the Kodiak brown bear is a giant.

The Kodiak bear is distinguished by his enormous size, huge head, and massive shoulders and claws. Probably nowhere else in the world is there such a powerful beast. It is almost unbelievable that these monsters are only six inches or less when born and weigh only a pound. They are born during the latter part of February and early March while the mother is still hibernating. At that time their eyes are closed and they are completely helpless, and they are very similar to a young cat or dog. The mating season is from the middle of May into early June. The period of gestation is about nine months.

Although the Kodiak bear does not mature fully until seven or eight years, a young female will mate when only three to four years old. When mated for the first time she will usually have one cub, but every other year thereafter three cubs are born. Occasionally she will have two, and, in some instances, four. During the mating season the male will try to eat, kill, or drive off any cubs the female may have when he finds her.

The life span of the Kodiak bear is estimated at between 35 and 50 years. A full-grown male will weigh approximately 1,250 to 1,450 pounds and measure as much as 13 feet.

The muscular development of these bears is amazing. They can scale steep cliffs and mountainsides with no apparent effort. Their sense of smell and hearing is exceptionally keen, but their eyesight is somewhat poor. Younger cubs have much better eyesight than older bears, although they are not so alert.

On Kodiak Island, the hills above the salmon streams are like giant checkerboards with the well-trodden trails of these huge animals. Some trails are over three feet wide and a foot deep.

Probably the most dangerous time to encounter a Kodiak bear is during the mating season. A large male will go completely crazy if disturbed and will charge. Any movement will attract their attention and it is dangerous to be near them unless completely armed and prepared for hunting.

Brown and grizzly bears are of prime interest to big-game hunters. When wounded, they will put up a fierce fight. Mothers with cubs have been known to attack people.

Black bears are among the most important of the big-game animals and range over three-fifths of Alaska, but there are none on the islands of either Frederick Sound or the Alaska Peninsula, or on the treeless tundra along the Bering Sea and the Arctic Ocean.

The weight of an adult black bear is from 200 to 300 pounds, though some have reached 500 pounds. In Alaska, this bear is usually black, but cinnamon and blue strains are found. The oddest and rarest is the bluish-colored glacier bear. Its range is limited and lies between Lynn Canal and Cape St. Elias.

The young of black bears are born in January, while the mother is still in hibernation. There are from one to four cubs, which stay with the mother for two years, as the female breeds only every other year.

Black bears eat grass, berries, fish, rodents, insects, moose calves, and occasionally other small animals. They are great scavengers, and along the coast their flesh is seldom palatable because they eat dead fish and carrion. In the interior and when they are not eating flesh, bear meat is good.

As a rule, black bears are not hunted for trophies, though glacier bears are prized by some sportsmen because of their unusual color.

The polar bear is one of Alaska's larger bears. Males weigh from 700 to 1,600 pounds. Strong and graceful swimmers, these huge white animals live mostly along the southern border of the ice pack in Arctic waters. They move south in winter to follow the food supply as the ice shifts, then head back north to the frozen packs in summer. A sudden advance of ice sometimes brings them as far south as Bering Strait.

Females, which weigh around 700 pounds, have young every two years. The hairless cubs are born in late December or early January, and do not open their eyes for six weeks. All polar bears except pregnant females, the only polar bears to hibernate, are constantly on the search for food, for fish, seals, walrus, kelp, sea ducks, eiders and scoters, and other birds.

A polar-bear hunt is a dangerous undertaking. Polar-bear meat is welcome food for hunters or anyone stranded in Arctic regions. To avoid trichinosis, it should be well cooked. The liver should never be eaten, as it contains so much vitamin A that it causes a sickness called hypervitaminosis, similar to the shock caused by an overdose of protein. The fat is used by the Eskimos, who also make garments of the pelt and ornaments of the teeth and claws. The pelt is quite a prize, and about one hundred of them, worth six to eight dollars a foot as measured from nose to tip of tail, are exported yearly.

Seasons, Limits, and Regulations—Hunters are allowed to take one brown or one grizzly bear of either sex each year in most areas that are not designated as reserves. The season ranges from about September 1 through December 31 in most areas. In some places, as around Ketchikan, Juneau, Kodiak, and certain parts of the Alaska Peninsula, the season is open until May or June. In all areas cubs and females accompanied by cubs may not be taken.

Black bear of either sex including its brown, blue, or glacier bear color variations are limited to two a year in southeastern Alaska. In other areas the limit is three a year. The season is open from about mid-August through June in the southeastern, southwestern, and south central sections. In all other places, with the exception of the Fairbanks area and game reserves, there is no closed season.

With the exception of cubs and females accompanied by cubs, the polar-bear season is year-round and hunters are allowed one a year.

Mountain Sheep

The Dall mountain sheep is the only wild white sheep in existence. The white coat and the long curled horns of the ram make it one of the handsomest specimens of Alaskan wildlife, and one of the most prized trophies on the North American continent.

The gun or camera hunter must work hard to get within range of these sheep. They are found only in rugged terrain, high in the mountain ranges from Kenai Peninsula to within a few miles of the Arctic coast. A little less than half of the estimated population is found in the remote Brooks Range north of the Arctic Circle. This species declined greatly in numbers between 1940 and 1945 but, with the help of complete protection in some areas, it is increasing.

Young Dall sheep are born in May or June. A single lamb is the rule, twins are rare. Lambs develop strength rapidly, and in less than a month are able to follow their parents high up in the Alaskan mountain crags.

These sheep feed almost entirely on alpine grasses, supplementing their diet with minerals from licks. Their enemies are few. Aside from man, the wolf and the coyote are probably the most important predators. Even these are not as harmful as the severe winters. Eagles may kill newly born lambs on rare occasions, but their importance as predators has been exaggerated.

Rams that reach maturity weigh from 175 to 200 pounds, and ewes weigh less than 150. Both sexes have comparatively short life spans—females seldom live beyond twelve years, while males are "ancient" at fourteen. It is these ancient rams that furnish the prize trophy heads.

Seasons, Limits, and Regulations—One ram is allowed each licensed hunter in most areas except specified game reserves from mid-August to mid-September. However, it is required that the horn growth be a three-quarter-growth-curl horn.

Mountain Goat

The mountain goat lives among the cliffs and crags of the mighty coast range between Portland Canal and the Kenai Peninsula, inland along the Chugach and Talkeetna mountains, and into the Copper River Valley. They are not found on the islands of southeastern Alaska, except on the Baranof Island where they have been successfully stocked.

Both sexes of these hardy, long-haired, and sure-footed white animals have short black horns. A grown billy weighs from 200 to 300 pounds, a nanny somewhat less. Grasses, ferns, and lichens make up the summer diet. In winter, when the deep snows of the coastal mountains cover most of their food, the goats are forced down to lower elevations or onto wind-swept slopes where they browse on alder twigs or whatever vegetation they can find. They will travel to the salt-water beaches for salt when licks are not available.

Many goats get killed by snowslides or by falling from rocky trails. There is little evidence of predation by wolves, bears, wolverines, or other natural enemies. Goats are usually hunted in a few accessible areas. The heads and hides make interesting trophies, and the meat of the kids is good. Several refuges and closed areas have been established where terrain or inaccessibility are not sufficient protection against overhunting.

Seasons, Limits, and Regulations—Kids may not be taken at any time, but two adults of either sex are allowed each year in southeastern areas and in the sections around Cordova and Valdez. None may be taken on Chichagof or Prince of Wales islands. In all other areas the limit is one a year except in the game reserves. The season in all areas runs from about mid-August through October, although an extra month is allowed in the southeast and in the Cordova and Valdez areas.

Moose

The Kenai moose is the largest of its kind on earth. Bulls reach a weight of 1,400 pounds or better and the cows somewhat smaller. With an antler spread of six feet or more, bulls are a fine hunt trophy. Moose furnish the winter's meat supply for hundreds of Alaskans.

In late summer, bulls congregate in the higher country and polish their antlers in preparation for the mating season. From mid-September to late October, they vie for supremacy in struggles that sometimes end in death for the weak; then the victor claims from one to several cows.

May or June of the following year sees the birth of one or two long-legged, reddish-brown calves. As a rule only 50 to 60 per cent of the cows produce calves.

Antlers of the older bulls are usually shed in December, while the younger bulls retain theirs a little longer. Antler growth starts again in April and is completed in late August. Between the sixth and tenth year, antlers attain maximum spread, then diminish in size as old age approaches.

Scrub growth of willow, birch, and aspen provides the winter range essential to large moose herds. In a day one moose will eat 40 to 50 pounds of this browse. Unchecked, a moose herd can increase beyond the capacity of the winter forage plants to support it. This results in deterioration of the range and subsequent starvation in the herd during severe winters. Moose populations fluctuate over long periods because of changes in habitat.

Natural enemies of the moose are wolf and bear which prey especially on the calves. Accidental death is caused by breaking through thin ice, falls on glare ice, being caught in snares or other entanglements, drowning of calves in river crossings, and battles during breeding seasons.

Management of the moose by the Fish and Wildlife Service includes yearly inventories, studies of range capacities, and regulation of hunting seasons to maintain the herds. Refuges are established to meet the moose's need for large areas as free as possible from human interference. Some of these are inviolate sanctuaries; others have limited hunting.

Seasons, Limits, and Regulations—One bull a year with forked antlers or larger is allowed in all areas except portions around Cordova and Valdez which temporarily have a closed season. The open seasons vary greatly from area to area. Each area allows a month or less at any one time in which moose hunting is permitted, but from approximately mid-August through December one or more is always open.

Caribou

Despite a great decrease in the past few years, the wandering caribou is still the most abundant big-game animal in Alaska, where it ranges widely over the high plateaus and mountain slopes. All of Alaska's caribou are barren-ground caribou. Woodland caribou are not found here but are farther south in the forested portions of Canada. The two species of barren-ground caribou are the great caribou of the Alaska Peninsula and the stone caribou of the eastern half of the interior and the Arctic shelf.

In days gone by, when there were millions of caribou, their migrations would hold up paddle-wheel steamers for hours while they crossed the Yukon River. Even today some herds travel hundreds of miles to new ranges and all herds are constantly on the move in search of the slow-growing lichens or reindeer moss, their principal winter food supply. One large herd moved from the Fortymile region of eastern Alaska to the vicinity of Kotzebue on the Arctic coast, a trek of about six hundred miles.

They weigh from 100 to 500 pounds and have antlers. The large males shed their massive branched horns in November and December, and the females and some of the younger bulls shed theirs in May or June.

In October the bulls collect harems of two to fifteen cows. In May or June, each cow has a single russet calf. They cross-breed readily with reindeer, and some caribou herds are well mixed with reindeer.

Throughout their range, these antlered nomads are hunted for trophies and meat, but extensive hunting, forest and tundra fires, and predation by wolves have reduced their numbers so sharply that the phrase "millions of caribou" no longer applies. Greater protection is the only means of preventing even small migrations from becoming spectacles of the past.

Seasons, Limits, and Regulations—Caribou of either sex may be taken where hunting is allowed. The entire Alaska Peninsula is open from about mid-August through December, and the limit is one a year. Nearly all of the inland area between the Gulf of Alaska and the Arctic Circle, including all of Seward Peninsula, is open from mid-March through December, and the limit is three a year. All land north of the Arctic Circle, as well as Atka and Umnak islands in the Aleutians, is open the year round and there is no limit.

Deer

So far as is known, Alaska has only one true deer, the Sitka black-tailed deer. Its natural range is on the islands of south-eastern Alaska, with a few on the narrow mainland strip. Its range has been extended by transplants north to the islands of Prince William Sound, and to Yakutat and west to Kodiak. There are reports that another species of deer, the mule deer, may be spreading into eastern Alaska from Yukon Territory.

In May or June the spotted fawns of the Sitka black-tailed deer are born, sometimes three, but generally one or two. The young are hidden by the mother, perhaps in a thicket of big-leafed devil's clubs. If found, the fawns must not be picked up as "orphans."

Characteristic of these deer is their vertical migration. As the snow melts from higher elevations, many of the deer, particularly bucks and yearlings, climb as high as 2,500 feet, where they stay until late fall when the deep snows force them to lower feeding grounds. By midwinter, if the snow is very deep, all deer may be driven to the beaches where they eat kelp and other marine vegetation. Ordinarily their food consists of huckleberry bushes, ground dogwood, fine meadow grass, skunk cabbage, and cedar.

In late summer or early fall, hunting the black-tail means a climb of two thousand feet or more. Later in the fall many bucks are taken within a few hundred feet of tidewater. Hunter reports indicate that more deer are taken each year than any other big game in Alaska.

Seasons, Limits, and Regulations—The open season for deer hunting is from mid-August through November. Only one deer a year is allowed in the Kodiak area; however, the limit is four deer in the Cordova-Valdez, Yakutat, and entire southeastern sections of the state. During most of the season there are restrictions against taking does, and fawns may not be taken at any time.

Wapiti, or American Elk

In 1928, a group of eight wapiti, or American elk, were captured in the Olympia Mountains in Washington State and eventually liberated on Afognak Island. These large, deerlike animals have increased slowly, but the winter range is somewhat restricted, which limits the potential size of the herd. However, it is a source of stock for other areas which will one day supply trophies for big-game hunters.

Seasons, Limits, and Regulations—In the Kodiak area and the coastal strip of the Alaska Peninsula directly across the Shelikof Straits from Kodiak Island, one bull a year may be taken. The season is broken into two parts, usually ten days around September and then two or three weeks in October or November.

Bison

It has been estimated that at their peak there were about sixty million bison, popularly called buffalo, on the North American continent. By the turn of the last century there was one small wild band in Yellowstone Park and a few animals in Canada. When it looked as if this humpbacked animal would soon be extinct, conservationists took action. In 1902 a buffalo-restoration project was started in Yellowstone Park under the auspices of the federal government. Fifty years later, the animal that gave William F. Cody the nickname of "Buffalo Bill" is thriving on a limited range.

In 1928, six male and seventeen female buffaloes were transplanted from the National Bison Range in Montana to Big Delta, some ninety miles southeast of Fairbanks. These representatives of an animal unknown in Alaska for centuries have increased to a herd of 350.

Although this is a satisfactory increase, these buffaloes have not extended their range, and have reached the limit of their present range support. In 1950 a new herd was started in the upper Copper River Valley by transplanting seventeen bison from Big Delta.

These animals are big game in every sense of the word. Bulls weigh from 1,600 pounds to a ton. Cows are considerably smaller. Neither has good eyesight, and they depend on hearing to detect danger.

Calves are born in April or May, and are cared for by both parents. Twins and albinos are rare, though three albinos were born on the Big Delta Range. None of these white buffaloes is alive today.

Seasons, Limits, and Regulations—There are no open seasons and bison may not be hunted.

Musk Ox

Whalers and traders exterminated the musk ox in Alaska nearly a century ago. But today a small herd maintains itself on Nunivak Island, a national wildlife refuge in the Bering Sea.

This herd, numbering ninety in 1959, was established when thirty-four were brought from Greenland in 1930.

One-time associate of the woolly mammoth, the musk ox is built and upholstered for a glacial climate. Its deep, dense wool undercoat is overlaid by very long, coarse, flowing hairs that almost touch the ground.

The sexes look alike, with broad flat hollow horns that are permanent. The musk ox uses horns, hoofs, and nose to get at its food beneath the crusted snow. It browses on dwarf willows, mosses, lichens, and other alpine plants. When fighting, the animal gives off a very noticeable odor from a small musk-filled gland below each eye, hence its name.

To defend themselves, musk oxen form a circle. Effective against wild predators, this ancient battle formation made the animals easy targets for rifle hunters, who could pick them off from a safe distance. Still adhering to this form of defense, musk oxen need complete protection in the land where their ancestors roamed.

Seasons, Limits, and Regulations—There are no open seasons and musk ox may not be hunted.

Reindeer

Although tremendously important as a food source for the Eskimos, reindeer are not classed as wildlife because they are semidomesticated. These relatives of the caribou are not native to Alaska, but were brought in from Siberia between 1891 and 1902, when 1,280 were imported. For some years food and other conditions were favorable, and by 1936 the reindeer had increased to 600,000, but there are only about 20,000 now. This drastic decline is attributed to depletion of winter ranges, increase of destruction by wolves, poor management practices, excessive butchering, and loss from mixing with migratory caribou herds.

Reindeer in Alaska are under the jurisdiction of the Alaska Native Service, and purchase of live reindeer for export must be approved in writing by that agency. By law, only natives may own them. This animal might again become important in the economy of northwestern Alaska if its numbers could be increased.

Herds are distributed over the tundra from St. Michael on the south shore of Norton Sound to Barrow on the Arctic Ocean. There are herds on the Pribilofs, and on Nunivak, St. Lawrence, Kodiak, Atka, and Umnak.

Seasons, Limits, and Regulations—There are no open seasons and reindeer may not be hunted.

HUNTING AND TRAPPING OF FUR ANIMALS

Since the dawn of history Alaskans have lived by trapping. Twenty-odd varieties of land fur animals are the source of most of the income of hundreds of Indians, Eskimos, Aleuts, and other trappers.

The bulk of furs brought into various trading posts each year is purchased by professional fur buyers who travel regular routes over Alaska for the big Eastern fur houses. Neither the tourist nor any other newcomer to Alaska should expect to buy pelts at bargain prices. Usually pelts left after the buyers have made their choice are irregulars.

Alaska fur revenues make it the third most important of the natural resource industries. During the eighty-three years of Russian occupancy, from 1784 to 1867, $45,000,000 worth of furs were shipped to the mother country. Since its purchase by the United States, Alaska has exported furs valued at more than $145,000,000, exclusive of the Pribilof fur-seal pelts with a raw value of about $90,000,000.

About fifteen thousand natives depend on the fur industry and share in the average annual return of around $2,500,000 from the sale of pelts.

Mink

The value of the annual harvest of mink pelts exceeds that of any other fur animal. Mink is widely distributed south of the Brooks Range, in areas having plenty of fish and shellfish. It is found both in wooded and tundra areas, and is semiaquatic, living along the margins of streams and lakes. It is especially numerous in southeastern Alaska, but thins out inland where the weather is colder and the food scarcer.

Wild mink vary in color from light brown to deep blackish

brown. The best prices are paid for the larger and darker pelts. Away from the coast the fur is of high quality, color, and durability, but on the coastal islands it is more variable. Mink trapping is a vital part of the economy of inland Alaska, and whole communities are dependent for their livelihood on the sale of mink pelts. Fur farming has been successful in areas where fish are abundant. Alaska consistently exports about forty thousand mink pelts annually.

Marten

The marten is found in forested areas from southeastern Alaska north to the limit of coniferous trees. One of the most beautiful and graceful of the forest animals, it weighs from five to six pounds, and measures nearly two feet in body length. The outer fur ranges from rich brown to light red or gray, depending on environment.

Martens make their homes in hollow logs, in holes, and among rocks. One to eight young are born in March or April in an annual litter. After a period of nurturing and schooling, they are forced out on their own at the approach of winter. From then on, they are among the most solitary of animals, except for a brief mating season in July and August. These strictly nocturnal and elusive animals are great travelers, and have been known to cover twenty-five miles in a single night. Their food consists of squirrels, mice, hares, small birds, birds' eggs, and berries in season. Having no fear of traps and being very inquisitive, they are easily trapped. They can be attracted readily by a few feathers, a bright object, or an enticing scent. Fur farming has not been commercially successful, although martens have been reared in pens at the Department of Agriculture Experimental Fur Farm at Petersburg.

Land Otter

Semiaquatic and rather solitary, the land otter is plentiful in southeastern Alaska and on the Alaska Peninsula, but less common northward to the Brooks Range.

Its coat is a rich dark brown, and makes one of the most durable and valuable furs. Southeastern pelts are noted for their size, color, and quality, with first-class skins bringing from ten to fifteen dollars. In addition to their economically valuable coat, the otter is an entertaining animal. Its favorite sport is sliding down a stream bank into the water like a small boy on a toboggan. If caught when young, otters make affectionate and gentle pets.

Weasels

Weasels range over all of Alaska except on the islands west of Umnak in the Aleutian chain. During the summer the fur of this slender animal is light brown, but in winter it becomes white, except for the tip of the tail, which stays black as jet. Although essentially a ground-dwelling animal, the weasel is a fair climber, and is often seen in the lower branches of trees. Small birds and mammals are the normal foods of this inquisitive, bold, and bloodthirsty little animal, which in its smaller Alaskan form is the world's littlest carnivore.

Wolverine

A gluttonous killer and the largest member of the weasel family, the wolverine is said to attack anything but bears and men. This solitary animal looks like a small bear and measures from three to four feet in length.

Wolverines are cabin-invaders and despoilers, and notorious trap-line robbers. The fur, of little commercial value, is generally used by Eskimos to trim the hoods of their parkas because it is frostproof. The wolverine inhabits mountainous timbered areas, including the Alaska Peninsula. Its population remains constant because trapping is difficult.

Muskrat

The muskrat is found from southeastern Alaska north to Kotzebue Sound. Its foods are sedges, horsetails, pondweeds, mussels, and even small fish. Its predators are legion, coming from land, air, and water, with the mink as its arch enemy. Biggest cause of muskrat loss in Alaska is deep icing of shallow ponds, which kills tens of thousands in a single hard winter. Fall and early winter trapping is used to gather pelts that would otherwise be wasted by winter freeze-outs. The take of muskrat pelts has been quite uniform, about 144,000 skins every year, representing an income of about $216,000.

Beaver

The beaver is found over most of the interior from Brooks Range south to the base of the Alaska Peninsula. There are a few in the southeastern mainland and on some of the larger islands, especially Prince of Wales.

Monogamy is the rule for beavers. Litters of from two to five are produced in June, and the young animals are cared for by the parents until the second year. The beaver is a vegetarian, and eats bark, aquatic plants, berry canes, buds, and leaves. A beaver colony must have an ample supply of aspens, cottonwoods, or willows for food, and a site where water does not freeze to the bottom.

Alaska's beaver pelts come principally from the Anchorage-Susitna-Matanuska region, the Fairbanks trade area, and also the Minto Lakes section. The annual take of beaver has increased generally over the last few years and now averages about 20,000 skins valued at $300,000.

Foxes

There are two distinct species and five color variations of Alaska foxes. Beautiful red foxes inhabit the entire mainland, and Unimak, Umnak, and several other islands in the Aleutian chain. Foxes are darker in the more heavily timbered areas, and lighter in open, coastal localities. Arctic foxes range from the Aleutian Islands north along the coast line to the Arctic. The white phase occupies a narrow coastal strip from the Kuskokwim River north to Point Barrow, and eastward along the Arctic shoreline. In winter they are silky and snowy white with a black-tipped tail. In summer they become slate-colored. The blue-coated fox is found mostly in the Aleutians and the Pribilofs. Lemmings, mice, hares, grouse, ptarmigan, and waterfowl are favorite foods but beach fleas are eaten when other food is scare.

Wolves

Wolves are everywhere from the islands of southeastern Alaska to the Arctic coast, and as far west on the Alaska Peninsula as Unimak Island. They prey on valuable big-game animals, except bears, and have contributed to the great decline of reindeer and caribou herds, as they follow the migrating herds throughout the year.

They usually run in family groups of from three to eight, though larger groups are sometimes reported. In color they are all shades and combinations from black to white. The darkest wolves are more common in southeastern Alaska, and lighter ones in the Arctic.

Though they are seldom seen, their presence can be detected by their large doglike tracks along beaches and river bars. Because wolves are predators, there is a $50 bounty on them, and the Fish and Wildlife Service through its Branch of Predator and Rodent Control carries out control measures.

Coyote

The coyote, named from an Aztec word, *coyotl*, or brush wolf, was not present in Alaska until about the turn of the century. It entered through the Yukon Territory of Canada. There are a few on the mainland of southeastern Alaska and all through the interior, but they are most abundant in the Matanuska and Copper River valleys and on Kenai Peninsula. They destroy mountain sheep, ground-nesting game birds, and occasionally domestic fowl and farm animals. There is a $50 bounty on this predator, and the Fish and Wildlife Service has a coyote control program.

Lynx

The shy lynx is the only wild member of the cat family in Alaska. It looks like a giant tabby cat, and its exceptionally soft fur is a light gray streaked with brown. The lynx is found throughout the timbered valleys of interior Alaska, and is fairly numerous along the Copper River and on Kenai Peninsula. Although its major food is snowshoe hare, the lynx preys heavily on grouse and ptarmigan, songbirds, and rodents.

Other Fur Animals

Marmots, ground squirrels, tree squirrels, and Arctic and snowshoe hares are relatively unimportant so far as the dollar value of their pelts is concerned. About $500 worth are sold on the markets each year. But these small species are an important source of food for other animals and are used locally for human food and clothing.

The catch of predaceous fur animals rises and falls with the numbers of small rodents on which they prey. Signs of field mice and lemmings, tree squirrels, and snowshoe hares in spring and summer have proven to be a reliable basis for forecasting the catch of lynx, marten, and fox.

Like grouse and ptarmigan, many of the rodent species go through more or less regular population cycles which at times bring them near the vanishing point. Low periods are often preceded by migrations, such as the famous lemming marches off the cliffs to the floes below.

These unaccountable marches follow periods in which lemming populations reach a peak. The little animals start westward, followed by predators of all sorts, and those that survive predation continue their march to the ice floes and swim out from one floe to another until at last they drown.

Seasons, Limits, and Regulations—There is no annual limit on the number of mink, marten, lynx, weasel, wolverine, land otter, muskrat, fox, marmot, squirrel, wolf, and coyote. However, in the southeastern part of Alaska the regulations vary greatly as to seasons and kinds of animals that may be taken. In other areas the open season is usually sometime between November and March. The limits on beaver vary from ten to forty a year depending on the area being trapped. There is no open season for raccoon, and the regulations do not apply to specified game reserves which are closed to trappers.

Fur animals cannot be taken with a machine gun, shotgun, artificial light of any kind, a steel beartrap, or any other trap with jaws having a spread larger than nine inches. Poison may not be used, dogs are not allowed, and traps and snares cannot be placed within twenty-five feet of beaver houses, or within one hundred feet of fox dens. Chemicals and smoke are prohibited.

Traps may be set during closed season on mink, land otter, weasel, fox, wolverine, lynx, and marten if the trapper secures a special permit from the game commissioner and specifies the need and purpose of the permit, clearly indicating the exact areas to be trapped and the extent of the proposed operation.

HUNTING OF SEA MAMMALS

In the waters around Alaska there are a surprising number and variety of sea mammals. Some, like the fur seal, are of great economic value; others, like the playful porpoise, are merely interesting. And there are many of the most massive mammals of all time, the great whales of the north.

Sea Otter

Most often talked about is the sea otter, whose fur is unmatched in fineness, durability, and beauty. The sea otter's coat was responsible for its near extermination. Its gentle and trusting nature made it easy prey for Russian fur hunters who slaughtered sea otters by the thousands.

Slaughter of the sea otter did not stop even after Alaska was sold to the United States. Adventurers of various nationalities continued taking them. Finally, in 1911, all killing was prohibited. This gave the remnant of the once-abundant sea otter herd a chance to re-establish itself in the Aleutian Islands area.

Sea otters lead a community existence. They live in a unit known as a pod, and stay very much in one locality. Most of their life is spent on the ocean's surface where they feed, rest, play, and rear young. The young are born ashore, and births occur at any time throughout the year. Sea otter pups are cared for solely by their mothers. Males take no interest in the young, but frolic together in the kelp beds, which all sea otters frequent because the thickly growing fronds afford protection from killer whales, their only enemy at sea.

Sea otters weigh from seventy to ninety pounds, are about four feet long, and have a thick tail a foot long. Their fur is a rich dark brown or black, lustered with gold or silver. Their white-whiskered faces appear toothless and make them look like quizzical old men, but they do have teeth, and toothaches. Cavities are frequent. Part of this trouble may be the result of breaking open hard shells with their teeth. The sea urchin is their principal item of diet, with mussels next. Rock oysters, scallops, sculpins, chitons, snails, limpets, flounder, and crabs are eaten, shells and all. After eating, sea otters delicately lick their paws, either to savor the last morsel of food or because of their habitual cleanliness.

Sea otters may not be taken under any circumstances.

Alaska Fur Seal

From its oceanic wintering grounds, the world's largest and most valuable fur-seal herd returns to the Pribilof Islands every summer. Once nearly exterminated by fur hunters, this herd is now approaching its peak under the management of the Fish and Wildlife Service, whose success with the seals is an outstanding example of conservation in action. (See Pribilof Islands, Chapter VII.)

Aleuts, Eskimos, and Indians are permitted to take fur seals by killing them at sea. No one else may hunt them.

Other Seals

Other species of seals in Alaska's waters are the Pacific harbor seal, the ringed seal, the ribbon, and the Pacific bearded seal. The first of these, the Pacific harbor seal, is the most abundant, and the only hair seal found in southern Alaskan waters. They are sometimes called the leopard seal because of spots on the yellowish gray coat. The ringed seal has small yellowish rings or patches on its coat, and is like the harbor seal in build and size. It is the common seal of the Arctic. The dark brown ribbon seal has yellowish streaks around its neck, forelegs, and rump. It lives along the shores of the Bering Sea, and little is known of its habits. The bearded seal gets its name from a tuft of white bristles down each side of its muzzle. Not very numerous, it lives in Arctic waters.

Seals have long been the staff of life for the Eskimos of the far north and may be taken only by the natives.

Sea Lions

Sea lions are common along the Aleutian chain, on the Barren Islands, in Prince William Sound, and on some of the south-eastern islands. Sea lions prefer quiet inlets and bays, particularly during the winter season, where they are sheltered from the rough seas. Males are usually twice as large as females, and often measure more than ten feet and weigh as much as a ton. Their hides have no commercial use, and even the natives no longer hunt them.

Walrus

Called *valross*, or whale horse, by old Norse sailors, this ungainly mammal summers in the Arctic Ocean and winters in the Bering Sea. The law now prohibits the killing of walruses in Alaska, except by natives for food and clothing, or by others for emergency food. Killing for ivory alone, even by natives, is not allowed, and ivory can be exported only as finished articles of handicraft. With these restrictions, the Pacific walrus, whose tusks sometimes measure thirty-nine inches, should be plentiful for years to come.

Seasons, Limits, and Regulations—On occasion, the laws prohibiting the hunting of walrus are relaxed for a brief period of time and nonnatives are allowed to hunt. At that time, a special license is required by all nonnative residents at a fee of $25. The nonnative, nonresident fee is $50. The walrus may not be hunted without a native guide accompanying the hunter and the limit is one bull walrus. The nonnative hunter may keep none of the meat, which must be given to the natives. The Department of Interior Fish and Wildlife Service in Juneau should be contacted to determine the most current regulations in effect.

Whales

Many of the world's whales, which once roamed all oceans by the millions, are still fairly common in Alaska's waters. There are two kinds of whales, the toothed and the "whalebone" or baleen whales, which are toothless.

The Blue whale, a toothless species, is the largest mammal that has ever lived. It frequents the polar ice pack of both hemispheres in summertime. These marine giants grow to almost unbelievable sizes, the females reaching greater lengths than the males. Three females taken in the Antarctic measured 100 feet. Another Blue whale measured 89 feet, and weighed nearly 120 tons. How much such a behemoth can eat is a matter of speculation, though it is known than an ordinary-sized whale can eat a ton of sardines for its morning meal.

Another toothless species, the bowhead or Arctic whale, is a stable item for sea Eskimos from St. Lawrence to Point Barrow. Every part of the whale is used by the Eskimos, even the jawbone, which is used as a grave marker. The bowhead is recovering from decimation by whalers, and there are appreciable numbers in the North Bering Sea and the adjacent Arctic Ocean.

Largest of the toothed whales is the sperm whale. Uniformly gray, or dark bluish gray, it is one of the most widely distributed of all. Old males summer in the Bering Sea, while females and their young stay in tropical waters.

Killer whales, a toothed species, travel in packs and prey on all warm-blooded sea animals, which are terrorized by them. Hair seals, for instance, will leave open water and swim frantically toward the beach at the approach of a pack of killers.

These four species are only a few of the whales that visit Alaskan waters. They are usually more than thirty feet long, with the exception of the pygmy sperm whale, the beluga, dolphins, and porpoises.

The kind of whale can be identified by the spout; a slanting forward spout means that a sperm has surfaced, a short, broad, straight spout denotes a humpback, and a high, slender one is the sign of a finback.

A whale doesn't spout water. On surfacing from a deep dive, it exhales violently, and the warm moisture-laden breath condenses. This condensation can be seen for several miles, and can be heard a mile away on calm days. Spouts in Alaska waters will hold together as a cloud for several minutes in cold air.

Seasons, Limits, and Regulations—Everyone may hunt whales but those taken must be surrendered to the natives.

HUNTING MIGRATORY WATERFOWL

Alaska plays an important part in maintaining the continental supply of migratory waterfowl. Vast expanses of tundra, muskeg, and river bottom are dotted with countless potholes, lakelets, and sloughs, providing nesting sites for a great variety of birds. Ducks, geese, swans, and other shore and water birds are all familiar summer residents. From the Arctic coast to the tip of the Aleutian chain and extreme southeastern Alaska, each species is able to find a nesting habitat to its liking. Although many of these nesting areas do not individually support large concentrations of waterfowl, they combine to produce a huge annual crop of birds.

The most outstanding single nesting area is the coastal tundra between the Yukon and Kuskokwim rivers. Here, in addition to other species of ducks and geese, is found an unusually large number of nesting black brant and cackling geese. Further inland along the great river bottoms, pintails, baldpates, mallards, green-winged teal, white-fronted and lesser Canada geese, and many others nest and raise their broods on the brush- and grass-covered banks of each body of water. The tree-nesting American goldeneye is also abundant, and nests in the large dead cottonwoods lining the rivers. Farther north, along the Seward Peninsula and Arctic slope, the coastal tundra and pothole areas provide nesting habitat for lesser snow geese and for four species of eider ducks, as well as for other widely distributed species of waterfowl.

In central and northern Alaska, the first waterfowl arrive in April or May and often start nesting before the ice has left the rivers. The next three months are a busy and clamorous period as the young birds mature. Some fall victim to marauding seagulls, jaegers, and various other predators, including gigantic pike. By August and September the birds are again on their way south, their numbers multiplied by the new generation.

Birdbanding records have shown that Alaska-raised birds find their way to most of the other forty-eight states and into Mexico. One great flight path from the north leads through the Cold Bay area at the tip of the Alaska Peninsula, where hundreds of thousands of pintails, black brant, cackling geese, and others concentrate before making the long hop to the Pacific Coast states. These birds, together with lesser Canada geese and other species from elsewhere in Alaska, are the waterfowl that provide most of the sport for Pacific Coast hunters. At the same time, many of the ducks and geese from the northern part of Alaska migrate east to Maryland and as far south as Louisiana.

Alaska is not entirely deserted by its birds during the winter. Thousands of scoters, eiders, scaup, and other sea ducks winter in sheltered bays from the Aleutians through Prince William Sound to the Panhandle. Many mallards and a few other pond ducks and geese remain in southeastern Alaska during winter. Alaska's "own" goose, the emperor, rarely strays beyond the country's borders. This medium-sized, bluish, seagoing goose winters up and down the Aleutian chain and Alaska Peninsula and nests in the Yukon-Kuskokwim region and along the north coast of the Seward Peninsula.

The largest species of waterfowl in North America, the trumpeter swan, once on the verge of extinction and still alarmingly rare, has been found wintering in southeastern Alaska, and recently two were reported on Cook Inlet. The smaller whistling swan has always been found thinly scattered over the northern nesting regions.

Seasons, Limits, and Regulations—Migratory game birds' seasons and limits are subject to the Migratory Bird Treaty Act Regulations which require the use of unexpired federal migratory hunting stamps, and current regulations should be obtained from the Department of the Interior Fish and Wildlife Service, Juneau, Alaska.

Hunting game birds

Alaska's native game birds offer excellent shooting. So far, bird shooting has been incidental to other types of hunting, but, to the explorer, prospector, or trapper, grouse and ptarmigan are important food. They are fine-flavored, especially in early fall when berries and various seeds are the main diet. Ptarmigan may be seen in flocks of several hundreds. Grouse are seen in family-sized groups. Ptarmigan hunting with a small-bore shotgun is much like quail hunting, and calls for fast and accurate shooting.

Ptarmigan

Largest of the ptarmigan and most widely distributed of Alaska's game birds is the willow ptarmigan, found from the Arctic tundra to southeastern Alaska. In winter, these birds are almost pure white, with the exception of the black tail feathers. Rock ptarmigan, usually smaller than the willow, are found at higher elevations. They may be distinguished from the willow by a black line from the bill to the eye. White-tailed ptarmigan, smallest of the group, are found around Mount McKinley, Cook Inlet, and Glacier Bay. They inhabit the high peaks and are rarely seen at low elevations.

Grouse

The blue grouse, sometimes called sooty, dusky, or hooter grouse, is Alaska's largest game bird, weighing as much as three and one half pounds. It is distributed throughout southeastern Alaska from Glacier Bay to British Columbia, and may be identified by its large size and dark grayish color. Franklin's grouse, smaller and darker than the blue grouse, is in southeastern Alaska from Prince of Wales Island southward. The spruce grouse ranges widely from Kenai Peninsula north to the Yukon River drainages and east to the border. The ruffed grouse is in the Yukon and Kuskokwim drainages in the interior, and in the Taku and Stikine drainages in southeastern Alaska. The sharp-tailed grouse is found throughout central Alaska from the north fork of the Kuskokwim to the eastern border.

Seasons, Limits, and Regulations—The limit is ten grouse a day in all areas except on the Kodiak-Afognak Island group. The limit on ptarmigan is twenty a day anywhere in Alaska. The season on grouse and ptarmigan ranges from mid-August through mid-April although in some southern sections of the state the season closes at the end of December. The hunter may use a shotgun no larger than No. 10 gauge, which holds no more than three shells, or a rifle, pistol, bow and arrow, spear, or dog for hunting grouse and ptarmigan.

Fishing

SPORT FISHING

Alaska's fresh- and salt-water fisheries give the angler a choice of many excellent fishing grounds.

The fresh-water fisherman can try his luck in two kinds of streams. Coastal streams are short and fairly swift, flowing through deep, narrow, densely wooded valleys, with banks often covered by heavy brush. The many clear pools and riffles and the numerous waterfalls make Alaska a beautiful and exciting state for a fishing trip.

Inland clear-water streams are usually longer. Rising from snow-fed mountain lakes, their upper reaches flow on high plateaus sparsely covered with dwarf willows and alders. The lower reaches are reasonably free of dense undergrowth. The large rivers have their sources in glaciers and are silt-laden, but most of their tributaries are clear and carry masses of game fish, except in waters near cities.

Salmon

From the sportsman's point of view, the best marine fish to go for in Alaska are the king or Chinook and the silver or coho salmon. These may be caught by trolling, spinning, or casting, and both species are widely distributed, but they appear in greatest numbers in waters adjacent to the Pacific Ocean.

King salmon run larger and can be distinguished from silver salmon by the action when hooked. A king generally takes the hook below the surface and sounds at once, taking out as much as two hundred feet of line, doing most of the fighting below the surface. They have become an exceptionally popular sport fish, particularly in southeastern Alaska where the species is the basis for annual salmon derbies.

The silver will strike even when the bait or lure is in sight of the boat. When hooked, it makes a fast run of thirty feet or more, breaks water, and leaps several feet into the air. It continues on the surface until played out, and for that reason is regarded by sportsmen as a superior game fish.

One of the best areas for silver salmon is southeastern Alaska. There, behind island barriers, long stretches of protected water allow fishing without hazard. Chatham Strait, the channel dividing the Chichagof and Baranof islands from Admiralty Island, is the finest. Stephens Passage, Lynn and Behm Canals, Frederick Sound, Clarence, Sumner, and Icy Straits, and waters off the west coasts of Prince of Wales and Baranof islands also have big runs of these fish.

In contemplating fishing in southeastern Alaska, fishermen must remember that there are few roads in the area and transportation is mostly by boat or plane. Shelters are few and rainy weather can be expected. However, there is wonderful fishing and many good lakes and streams for those willing to rough it. It is possible to camp out comfortably with outfit containing cooking gear, food, and sleeping bags.

Salmon fishing is available close to towns such as Juneau, Ketchikan, Sitka, Petersburg, and Skagway, and is usually done from outboard-powered skiffs. Skiffs, as well as tackle, can usually be rented. Charter trips aboard cabin cruisers can be arranged through guides and outfitters. King salmon are large, and good catches are made during May, June, and July. The silver salmon enter the fishery later in the season, usually August and September, and they are also taken in the lower reaches of the streams where they are a very sporty fish on proper tackle.

Tackle needs depend upon the likes or dislikes of the sportsman. The usual salmon reel is a star-drag affair with three to four hundred yards of line. Baits are plugs, spoons, or herring. The rod is generally seven to nine feet long, and fairly limber. Heavy spinning equipment is also becoming popular in salt-water salmon fishing.

Trout

A long-time study has shown that steelhead and rainbow trout are salt- and fresh-water forms of a single species resembling the Atlantic salmon in habits and appearance.

Rainbows are brilliantly colored along the side and are heavily spotted. They are found in coastal rivers from Dixon Entrance northward, and in waters of the interior south of the

Yukon drainage. They are stocked in some landlocked lakes, particularly in southeastern Alaska. Their average size is smaller than that of the steelhead, but individuals of twenty-seven to thirty inches are common in a few areas.

Steelhead trout are silvery gray, and lack the brilliant colors of the rainbow. In fresh water, coloration may become more pronounced. This sparsely spotted fish, which recently came into its own in the sporting world, may be found in most of the large coastal streams and in many of the smaller ones. Average weight of the steelhead in Alaska is eight to ten pounds, but larger ones are often taken.

These two trout offer the best of sport fishing. Both will go for all types of lures, including flies, spinners, or bait. Where fish are rising, they will take flies very well but all too frequently the fish are larger than a flyrod can handle and either the rod is ruined or the fisherman discreetly breaks the fish off.

The Dolly Varden is the most abundant trout in Alaska. It is a native of all the coastal streams and lakes from Alexander Archipelago, bordering British Columbia, to the islands of the Aleutian chain and Bering Strait. Golden fin, bull trout, and Mountain Dolly are local names for this fish, which varies widely in appearance.

This species is distinguished by its light or pink spots—other trout have dark spots—and by its larger mouth. It ranges in length up to thirty inches, although there are fish stories of its measuring four feet or more. The Dolly is usually anadromous, spawning in fresh water and spending most of its life in the ocean. The Arctic variety, the so-called Arctic char, stays in fresh-water lakes, except when ascending tributary streams in the fall for spawning.

The Dolly has suffered considerable abuse through the years. Many sport fishermen won't try for it because of its supposed lack of fight. Commercial fishermen and salmon packers have long demanded its destruction, insisting that it is harmful to salmon runs because it feeds on salmon eggs and young. Substantial sums in wages and bounties have been spent by salmon packers and the government for eradication in westward areas, particularly in Bristol Bay.

Actually the Dolly has every bit as much fight as the Eastern brook trout or the lake trout, and few people would be able to distinguish the cooked flesh from that of any of the preferred game species. Although it is condemned for destroying salmon eggs, studies indicate that it usually eats drifting eggs that would be lost anyway. This trout will strike almost any lure, and is at its best for food when taken at sea or on its way upstream.

One of the finest game and food fishes in Alaskan waters is the coastal cutthroat trout. This trout is a salmonoid shape, with silver sides, white belly, blue, green or brownish spots, and a profuse covering of black spots, even over the tail region. The cutthroat is one of the two black-spotted trouts in Alaska. Two red lines on the jaw give the cutthroat its name, although on fish just in from the sea these marks are often greenish or yellow, or occasionally missing. Cutthroat will run as much as twenty-five inches in length. They are found in many of the coastal streams from the southern end of southeastern Alaska to the western end of Prince William Sound.

The cutthroat generally spawns from February to May, though it may be as early as December. After a summer at sea, adults re-enter the streams in the fall, and it is tnen that the greatest numbers are taken by sport fishermen.

Though not as large as other trout, the coastal cutthroat puts up a spectacular fight when taken on light tackle. A variety of lures. Spoons are probably most productive when fished at the cutthroat may be taken at sea where it travels in schools. And when a school has been located, the angler can catch them as fast as he can put out a lure and pull in the fish. The favorite salt-water lure for this purpose is the "pop gear" type of combination flashers and spinners, trolled behind a boat.

Lake or Mackinaw trout is one of the lesser-known game fishes in Alaska. It belongs to the group known as char, which includes the Dolly Varden and brook trout. Lake trout is the largest of the chars, and is distinguished by teeth on the tongue. Its body tapers to slenderness toward the forked tail, and it has brown sides, a brownish back, and white ventral fins edged with orange. White spots are profuse on sides, back, and tail. Because few Alaskan specimens have been recorded, the size they reach is unknown, but thirty-pounders are not unusual.

This trout, found in the Brooks Range, is most abundant in western Alaska. Although the favored habitat is in the deeper lakes, it also likes lake outlets where it feeds on migrating salmon fry or fingerlings. It feeds on mice and lemmings, too, if they accidentally fall into the water. Because Mackinaws are principally carnivorous, fresh bait or simulated fish are the best lures, such as flies, spinners, and salmon eggs, are effective. The outlets of lakes, although plugs are used with good results. "Pop gear" flashers and spoons are effective in deep trolling. The size of the Mackinaw, a fall spawner, makes it a rather formidable fish to have on the end of a light line, although it does not compare with any of the other trout in fighting qualities.

Fishermen in Alaska like to broil trout or salmon by lashing the fish to a split log and standing the log before a fire until the fish is done.

Availability of Trout and Salmon

Anchorage-Kenai Area—Because of the increase in both military and civilian populations in the Anchorage-Kenai area, most waters with easy access along the less than one thousand miles of highway linking Seward, Homer, Anchorage, and Glennallen are already heavily fished. Only a few major waters continue to have satisfactory yields. Most fishermen in search of a full creel travel to remote fishing locations by light aircraft.

Dolly Varden, salmon, lake trout, and steelhead fishing is available on the Kenai Peninsula. Spring fishing, beginning in late May, is eagerly awaited by roadside anglers. This is the period of king salmon and steelhead runs in the streams of the Lower Kinai Peninsula. By the time the season is open king salmon are moving in numbers into fresh-water streams of Lower Kenai Peninsula. Kings run until late June followed by Dolly Varden which are available in early or mid-July. In August and through September, silver salmon and steelhead enter the streams offering the sportiest of fishing. The interior lakes and streams offer the best catches of rainbow and Dolly Varden trout during

June, but during the summer catches drop off, except in remote waters, then increase again in the fall.

In the Palmer lakes area, rainbow and Dolly Varden trout are subjected to extremely heavy fishing pressures.

Adjacent to the Glen and Richardson highways, and particularly between Sheep Mountain and Paxson, good fishing for grayling and lake trout is available. Lake trout fishing is best in the spring and fall when these fish are in shoal water. Grayling fishing, although best in the spring, can be found in accessible waters throughout the summer.

Kodiak-Afognak Area—Streams on the Kodiak-Afognak group of islands provide some excellent fishing. The best spots are remote from the town of Kodiak, which is the hub of travel connections for the region. Small amphibian airplane service provides transportation to the many fishing areas, and all streams are within sixty minutes by air from the town. Small boats can also be chartered for trips as the majority of fishing sites are within walking distance of salt water.

The fishing pressure on game fish is concurrent with the movements of fish into the bays and within the watersheds. The Dolly Varden trout, which receives the greatest pressure, begin to show in the bays during the middle of May. At this time, sport fishing is almost limited to surf casting. These early sea run Dolly's enter mostly the streams that originate from lakes, such as Buskin River where there is extensive fishing during this upstream migration of trout. This early run of trout tapers off rapidly and sport fishing lulls until the second run of mid-July, when salmon and trout move into the streams together. Fishing for Dolly's, then, remains consistently excellent until late fall.

There is an exception to this early fishing of Dolly Varden trout in the Karluk, Red, Uganik, and Afognak rivers which provide good Dolly fishing from early spring until late fall. The fish in these streams do not leave the river proper but remain throughout the period. Some of the largest Dolly Varden caught in this area measure twenty-four inches, but the average fish measures from twelve to eighteen inches.

Steelhead trout fishing on Kodiak-Afognak islands is excelled in few places in North America. The steelhead begin to move into the watersheds of this region in late September and by November are amassed in the streams. This is the period when trout are fresh and prime, and fishing is at its greatest. These fish remain in the upper parts of the streams throughout winter, and in May they move downstream to spawn. Good fishing is again enjoyed in May and June after the spring breakup. A comparatively small number of rainbows remain over the summer and are available to the sportcaster. Winter weather conditions limit fishing during the remainder of the year.

In September silvers move into the streams in large numbers and provide excellent sport fishing.

King salmon fishing is confined entirely to the Karluk and Red rivers and is a sport almost untouched by local fishermen. The best fishing for kings occurs near the mouth of the streams in June and July; however, only a few sportsmen can take advantage of this activity as both areas are remote from the normal places of fishing on these rivers.

Alaska Peninsula Area—The Alaska Peninsula streams and lakes offer excellent fishing in remote locations and reasonably good fishing in the few accessible locations. Fishing camps have been developed in and near Katmai National Monument, and air service is available to the fishing grounds.

In the large lakes and streams, tributary to Bristol Bay, there are good populations of large fish—rainbow, Dolly Varden, and lake trout, grayling, and northern pike. Flies and spoons have proved to be very satisfactory lures in these waters and live bait is not needed.

Farther out along the peninsula, Becharof Lake and River system produces Dolly Varden trout and salmon. Oil Lake is well populated with rainbow and Dolly Varden, and the Cold Bay area provides Dolly Varden trout and silver salmon.

Grayling

Found in every major river drainage north of the Gulf of Alaska and throughout the Alaska Peninsula, this beautiful troutlike fish has an insatiable appetite for flies. Predominantly a surface feeder, it takes anything, even gaudy red-white-and-blue creations, and comes clear out of the water to try for flies on a graceful downward plunge. When hooked, it starts its fight with a quick run downstream, follows with a cross-current rush, and winds up with a short series of acrobatics, then tries again to take the fly to the bottom.

This game sport fish has an apt scientific name—*Thymallus signifer*. *Thymallus* refers to the sweet odor of thyme that is noticeable in freshly caught grayling, and *signifer*, or standard bearer, describes the enormous dorsal fin which readily distinguishes it from trout.

Grayling measure up to twenty-three inches and weigh as much as four and one-half pounds. Their color is unsurpassed, seeming at first to be purple, then changing to bluish-gray and silver, all beautifully iridescent. Markings are pure white underparts, V-shaped black spots between head and middle dorsal fin, and reddish stripes with several rows of rosy circles along the sides.

Northern Pike

This fish, one of the largest and most plentiful of Alaska's fresh-water fish, is also one of the least popular. It is not even rated as a game fish under Alaska law. But with proper tackle, anglers will find that pike fishing is good in most of the backwaters, sloughs, and bottomland lakes of the Yukon and Kuskokwim valleys, and north to the Arctic coast. During July these fish spawn in weedy shallows, and a plug or streamer fly will produce instant action. Though bony, the flesh is firm and edible.

Sheefish

One of the least known of Alaska's sport fish is the unique sheefish, or *inconnu*. *Inconnu*, meaning *unknown*, is quite appropriate, for this fish is found nowhere else under the American flag, and in Alaska it is largely confined to northern rivers.

The sheefish has been described as a cross between a whitefish and a salmon, though in action and appearance it might be called an Arctic tarpon. The average weight of shees is about twenty pounds, but occasionally one will tip the scale at eighty-five. This great fish is a clear silvery white on the sides and underparts and a dusky olive on the back. Fins are pale and colorless and scales are dime-size.

Sheefish make such excellent eating that there is a market for them in Nome and other northern communities. It is during the spawning season, in summer, when they migrate from brackish or salt water into certain fresh-water streams, when sport fishermen can best try the tackle on these big, still-unexploited fish. A minnow-type fly or large bright spoon cast into a deep pool on one of the northern streams is usually productive, though it often takes skill and persistence to get a sheefish to strike.

Other Fish in Alaskan Waters

The Arctic char, which is more highly colored and larger than the Dolly Varden, is caught in the rivers flowing into the Arctic Ocean. This fish weighs up to and sometimes more than twenty pounds. Brightly colored streamer flies behind a spinner or a red-and-white wobbling spoon are often used in fishing for the char. White sturgeon have seldom been caught in Alaska but are considered the largest of the fresh-water fish found there. They are monsters up to thirteen feet long and weigh up to half a ton each. Halibut, gray cod, Alaska pollock, Atka fish, Alaska greenfish, and red or scarlet rockfish are other varieties found in Alaskan waters.

Seasons and Limits for Sports Fishing

Regulations vary in different areas of the state as to exact bag limits, but in most areas they range from ten to fifteen fish daily. Possession limit is two daily bags. This applies to rainbow, steelhead, cutthroat, Eastern brook, Dolly Varden, and Mackinaw or lake trout, grayling, and northern pike. However, the limit is three fish over twenty inches in length per bag, and in the Chatanika River near Fairbanks, no fish under twelve inches may be taken. Most areas are open the year round with the exception of the areas around Seward, Anchorage, and the Kenai and Alaska peninsulas.

Fish Derbies

Sportsmen from all over the world vie for many valuable prizes in Alaska fishing derbies. Among derbies held annually are Ketchikan Salmon Derby, mid-March through mid-July; Craig and Klawock Salmon Derby, May; Wrangell Salmon Derby, April to July; Valdez "Fish for Fun" Derby, May to August; Petersburg Summer-long Trout Derby; Juneau, Golden North Salmon Derby, late July; Seward Silver Derby, August; Cordova Silver Salmon Derby, Labor Day weekend. Other derbies are in Kodiak, Petersburg, and Sitka.

Fees and Regulations

FEDERAL AND STATE LICENSE FEES

A person must have both federal and Alaska state licenses to hunt or fish in Alaska. Licenses are obtained from licensing officers located in all principal villages, towns, and cities in Alaska. In addition to the following fees, the issuing agent charges $1.00 for each license issued.

Federal

Resident—Trapping, $3, which includes the privilege of hunting and fishing. Hunting, $2, which includes the privilege of fishing. Fishing only, $1. Licenses are not required of native-born Indians or Eskimos, or residents under sixteen years of age.

To establish residence in Alaska it is necessary to live in the state continuously for a one-year period. Three years' residence is required to be eligible for a resident trapping license.

Nonresident—General hunting, trapping, and game fishing, $50 for a license. Hunting and game fishing, but not including big game, $10, and game fishing, $2.50.

Alien—Special hunting, trapping, and fishing, $100, but game fishing is only $2.50.

State

Resident—Fishing and hunting, $4; fishing only, $2; hunting only, $2.

Nonresident and Alien—Fishing and hunting, $20; fishing only, $10; hunting only, $10; or a special ten-day fishing license, $5. In addition to these licenses, hunters must obtain special tags prior to hunting big game. Fees for the various tags are: Polar bear, $150; walrus, $100 plus a special $50 federal license in addition to other federal license requirements; brown or grizzly bear, $75; bison, moose, sheep (each), $50; elk, goat, caribou (each), $25; black bear, deer (each), $10.

Penalties for Illegal Hunting and Fishing

A fine of not less than $25 or more than $500, or imprisonment for not longer than six months, or a combination of fine and imprisonment may be imposed on anyone convicted of disobeying the hunting and fishing regulations.

Emergency Hunting and Fishing

When in need of food and none is available, an explorer, prospector, traveler, Aleut, Indian, or Eskimo may take animals, any birds except migratory birds, or game fish at any time for emergency food.

SPECIAL REGULATIONS

It is illegal to take wild game while on any railroad or highway, or within one hundred feet of the center line of any highway.

Game animals may be taken only with a shotgun not larger than No. 10 gauge and not capable of holding more than three shells. Rifle, pistol, except those using rim-fire cartridges, and bow and arrow may also be used. It is illegal to use dogs, machine guns, spears, pits, deadfalls, fires, jacklights, searchlights or any artificial lights or two-way radio communications, or artificial salt licks.

It is illegal to hunt game animals by means of aircraft, motor vehicle, motorboat, or any other boat except one propelled by paddle, oars, or pole. An animal may not be taken when it is swimming. Rabbits may be taken by snares and dogs.

No hunting is allowed in wild-game reserves or in areas declared emergency closures.

Game fish cannot be taken by the use of snag or gang hooks. Fishing is not allowed within three hundred feet of any fish weir or fish ladder in operation, nor is it allowed in posted waters where game fish planting or restocking is being conducted.

Hunting Dogs

Hunting dogs may be used for hunting grouse and ptarmigan and nongame birds, but cannot be used for any other hunting purposes. It is illegal to feed dogs any meat from game animals, fish, or birds.

Hunting Records

Hunters must keep records to show the kind and number of each species taken and must submit a written report to the game commissioner on or before the thirteenth day after the expiration of the hunting, fishing, and trapping license.

Evidence of Sex and Identity

The horns of dead mountain goat and mountain sheep must accompany the animal while it is in possession of the hunter or is being transported until it is inspected and approved by the game commissioner or his representatives. Whenever the taking of any big-game animal is restricted to the male sex during all or any portion of the open season, positive proof of sex must remain on the carcass until it is inspected and approved by the game commissioner or his representatives.

Shipping Regulations

No part of any game animal, bird, or fish may be shipped unless the package is accompanied by a special permit obtained from the game commission. The outside of the package must carry the permit number and markings describing the contents.

Available Copies of Regulations

The regulations relating to game and fur animals, birds, and game fish in Alaska are revised every year and are issued on June 15. New regulations remain in effect from July 1 through June 30 of the following year. Anyone planning a hunting or fishing trip should apply in person or write to the Commissioner, Alaska Department of Fish and Game, Alaska Office Building, Juneau, Alaska, to obtain a complete and current copy of the regulations for the year.

Hunting and Fishing Guides

Until recently nonresident hunters seeking big game were required to hire a guide to accompany them; however, in recent years the law was changed and it is no longer a requirement. Nevertheless, it is very dangerous and risky for any individual to set out in Alaska on a big-game hunt without the services of a guide because of the dangers not only to hunters but also to the proper conservation of Alaska's wildlife. In all likelihood the law will be revised again so that guides will be required. Fishermen and hunters planning trips to interior lakes and the isolated regions of the state should always have registered guides because of their knowledge of the trails and terrain, weather conditions, and the best locations for fish and game. The various guides charge from $85 to $150 per day per person, all expenses included except equipment. Most have spring and fall hunting parties that vary from ten to twenty days, with two or more scheduled each season.

Alf Madsen, Kodiak, Alaska

Alf Madsen, head of a pioneer hunting organization on Kodiak Island, has a vast knowledge of the habits and haunts of the Kodiak bears. He has been in the guide and outfitting business since 1928. Madsen hires other guides in his organization and guarantees that each guide has at least twenty-five years of hunting and guiding experience on the island. One of his hunting camps is located on Uganik Bay on the west side of Kodiak Island and it is complete with modern cabins and conveniences, such as oil heat, spring beds, radio-telephone, and others, in spite of the isolated location of the camp. Other interior camps are at Karluk Lake, Hidden Canyon Lake, Little River Lake, and Spiridon Lake, all on Kodiak Island. Hunters are taken to the hunting grounds either by de luxe cabin cruiser or private plane. Trophies are packed and shipped to the taxidermist at the completion of the hunt. Reservations and inquiries should be directed to Alf Madsen, P. O. Box 925, Kodiak, Alaska.

Hal Waugh, Juneau, Alaska

Hal Waugh is a big-game hunter with world-wide experience, operating a guide and outfitting service from Juneau, Alaska. He arranges guided big-game and fishing trips to the Alaska Peninsula, south central Alaska, Kodiak Island, and the Endicott Mountains. Waugh's services include camp, food, air mattresses, heating stoves, gas lanterns, cots or bunks, and trophy preparation. He specializes in all Alaskan big game. Reservations and inquiries should be directed to Hal Waugh, Box 1982, Juneau, Alaska.

Kristjan Helgason, Kodiak, Alaska

Helgason's camp is located at Terror Bay on Kodiak Island and is complete with cabins, electric lights, oil heaters, three-quarter beds, warm bedding, and radio-telephone. Meals are prepared and served by Mrs. Helgason. Hunting expeditions travel on a thirty-two-foot power boat which cruises the shores, bays, and inlets during the day and returns to the base camp at night. Reservations and inquiries should be directed to Kristjan Helgason, Kodiak, Alaska.

Other Guides and Outfitters

The Kodiak Island Guides Association is a group of fourteen registered guides that operate on Kodiak Island. The association should be contacted through Park Munsey, Box 83, Kodiak, Alaska.

There is also the Alaska Guides Association which is contacted through Tom A. Moore, at Box 1457, Anchorage, Alaska.

The Civil Aeronautics Administration issues a list of pilots available for hunting and fishing trips in Alaska which is available from Box 440, Anchorage, Alaska.

Polar-bear hunts may be arranged through Nelson Walker, Kotzebue, Alaska, or Bob Curtis, Box 4055, Spenard, Alaska.

Hunting Equipment

The .30-'06 with 180 or 220 grain loads, the .300 Magnum with the 180 load, or the .375 with a 270 load are all recommended rifles. Receiver sights have proven better than scopes for spring bear hunts. Binoculars are necessary and should be either 7x35 or 9x35 power. The hunter must have a skinning knife, and clothing should include two pairs of medium-heavy woolen pants, one down-filled or woolen jacket, a cap with ear flaps, two pairs of warm gloves, one pair of sunglasses, one pair of Shupacks with felt lining, or leather shoes, and at least three pairs of woolen socks. Rain clothing for a bear hunt should consist of jacket, pants, a hat, and hip boots with felt lining, if they are not included in the equipment supplied by the guide-outfitter.

Every hunter and fisherman should carry a camera and fishing tackle.

Shopping for Equipment

Nearly every village, town, and city in Alaska has one or more stores carrying excellent supplies of clothing and equipment for the outdoorsman. Prices are usually higher than in other states, but the local stores offer the advantage of having equipment and accessories especially adapted for local conditions.

CHAPTER VI. SOUTHEASTERN ALASKA

Ketchikan — Wrangell — Petersburg — Sitka — Sitka National Monument — Juneau — Glacier Bay National Monument — Haines and Port Chilkoot — Skagway — Whitehorse, Y.T., Canada — Yakutat

The southeastern coastal region consists of many islands and a strip of narrow mainland called the Panhandle. The wooded islands, ranging from an "Alaskan dot on the water" to areas greater than one hundred miles in length, are exposed to the open seas on one side and on the other form a completely sheltered waterway that stretches one thousand miles from the Strait of Juan de Fuca at the northeastern tip of the State of Washington, to Skagway, Alaska. It is known as the Inside Passage, the homeland of the Indians of the Pacific Northwest who named this waterway "The Road That Walked."

Southeastern Alaska is separated from Canada by mountains that rise sharply from the water's edge to heights of nine thousand feet or more, shaped by many glaciers and waterfalls, and forested with spruce, hemlock, and cedar growths that form the sixteen-million-acre Tongass National Forest.

An abundance of wild flowers blanket the mountain ridges and steep slopes, providing memorable scenery that is equaled only in the lands of the Vikings.

To the north of this area is the Malaspina Glacier near Yakutat which is larger than the state of Rhode Island, and the ice fields at Juneau are larger than all of Switzerland. They are only two of the five thousand gigantic Alaskan glaciers.

Ketchikan

The Indian name for Ketchikan was Kach Khanna, meaning "spread wings of prostrate eagle." Today it is known as Alaska's

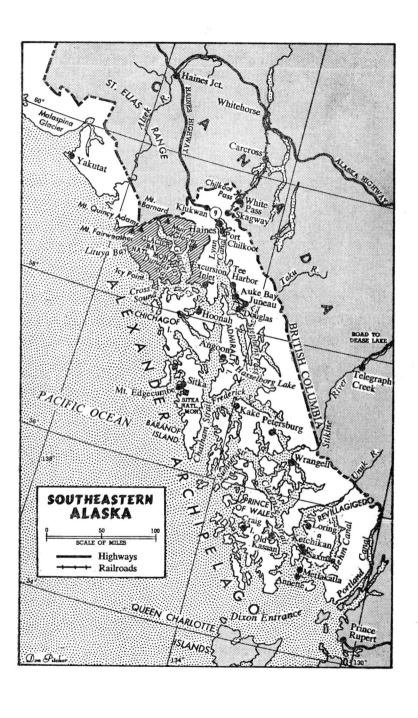

SOUTHEASTERN
ALASKA

SCALE OF MILES
0   50   100

Highways
Railroads

"First City," the "Salmon Capital of the World," and "The Totem City."

Ketchikan is located about seven hundred miles north of Seattle, less than three hours' flying time. It is the first port of call in Alaska for northbound steamships and is the leading port in southeastern Alaska.

It is built on the side of three-thousand-foot Deer Mountain on the southwest shore of Revillagigedo Island, across the Inside Passage from Prince of Wales Island. The climate is temporate but rainfall is heavy.

The setting is picturesque. The downtown section is modern and most of the homes hug the mountainsides and are reached by long wooden stairways. They stand out against a background of evergreen trees that cover the high craggy mountains immediately behind the town. A waterfall cuts down the mountainside and flows through the center of the town where, from the latter part of July to October, salmon can be seen climbing the fish ladder.

In the downtown area most of the streets are paved, but there are a few made of wooden planking and built on stilts over the water to protect them from the high tides. Except for Front Street, which runs along the water front of the Tongass Narrows, the streets are narrow and wind up the hill and around the town. There are roadways leading out of town, extending from nine to fifteen miles each way, following the coast where many homes are built along the fringe of the road, giving Ketchikan the appearance of being a long and narrow city when viewed from the air.

Most houses are of wood construction, largely of spruce or cedar. The homes are well tended and citizens are proud of their rock gardens and the landscaping in their yards where flowers blossom abundantly in giant sizes. In the parks, gardens, the fronts of public buildings and in show windows of stores and shops, many totem poles add to the color and background of the town.

The population of the area includes whites, Negroes, Filipinos, and Indians from the Tsimpshean, Haida, and Tlingit tribes. Living costs are approximately 20 per cent higher than in cities in other states, but they are the lowest in Alaska. Everything that comes to Ketchikan, both people and freight, must come in by either ship or plane—which accounts for the higher cost of living. There are no trains or highways connecting Ketchikan with the rest of the mainland.

Ketchikan's principal industries are based on its fishing, timber, and mining resources but it is striving for an outdoor sports, recreational, and tourist industry. The Ketchikan commercial fishing fleet numbers over two thousand vessels of all types engaged principally in halibut, salmon, black cod, and herring fishing. There are five salmon canneries within the corporate limits and many more in the surrounding area. In addition to the canneries, three large cold-storage plants, a salmon and trout hatchery, and a fishery products research laboratory are in town. The new $2,400,000 small-boat harbor is nearing completion and will give protected moorage to an additional six hundred vessels, more than the existing Thomas Basin and City Flat mooring areas which can handle five hundred vessels. Servicing the marine fleet is an important industry in Ketchikan and includes the operation of marine railways, shipyards, machine and welding shops, marine supply shops, and allied services.

In the early days, industry centered around the gold and copper mining that characterized much of the early development of Alaska, and around the huge salmon and halibut resources. Over the years gold mining has fluctuated so that it is no longer of consistent importance in the area. Ketchikan is still considered an important mining area, however, with the only uranium-producing mine in the state. But the cost of shipping minerals has been much too prohibitive for industry to take even the slightest advantage of the large storehouse of gold, copper, uranium, marble, and others that exist in the area.

Lumbering is of major importance because the town is situated in the Tongass National Forest. The thick forest is so vast that the potential of this resource is not known. But it is being developed and processed through the facilities of one of the most modern sawmills on the Pacific Coast, owned jointly by American Viscose and the Puget Sound Pulp and Timber Company. It includes approximately forty-five logging camps, a cedar processing mill, and a $64,000,000 rayon pulp mill, the Ketchikan Pulp Company. This pulp mill covers fifty-three acres of land six miles north of the town and is one of the most modern in the world and Alaska's first.

TRANSPORTATION TO KETCHIKAN

There are daily flights from Seattle via Pacific Northern Airlines or Pan-American World Airways. From Prince Rupert, B.C., Ellis Air Lines planes fly to Ketchikan in approximately forty minutes and the round-trip fare is about $31. There are daily flights to and from Ketchikan to most communities in Alaska.

The airport and main passenger terminal is located on Annette Island, a fifteen-minute flight by seaplane from downtown Ketchikan, operated by Ellis Air Lines. This flight is included in all fares ticketed direct to Ketchikan, but passengers en route to other points and requesting a lay over at Ketchikan must pay additional fare from Annette to Ketchikan unless tickets indicate the Ketchikan stopover.

To reach the town by automobile, it is necessary to drive to Prince Rupert, B.C., which is ninety miles south of Ketchikan via the Cariboo Highway #97 and Skeena Highway system from Vancouver, B.C., a distance of 1,025 miles, or 1,200 miles from Seattle. Travel from Prince Rupert to Ketchikan may be made by ships that have facilities for transporting automobiles. The passenger fare one way is $16.31, the automobile rate is $49.50.

Principal steamship carriers are Canadian Pacific Steamships and Alaska Cruise Lines, Ltd. Service is limited during the winter months but is excellent in summer from May through September.

All freight must be sent by regular scheduled or chartered steamship, or by plane. Railway Express maintains an office in Ketchikan, as does the North American Van Lines, Inc.

LOCAL TRANSPORTATION

Automobiles may be rented by the day or longer from Lah-meyer's Avenue Service. The local city bus service, and a scheduled bus service to the outlying Clover Pass and Mountain Point areas, is available and convenient. There are several twenty-four-hour taxi services. Charter boats are located at Heckman and Ketchikan wharves for short cruises and fishing excursions in and around Ketchikan or for longer trips. Cabin cruisers and yachts are available for charter from individual owners. Rates range from $40 to $100 per day and include gas and oil and a skipper to run the boat. Average boats will accommodate from four to eight persons. Inquire at the Ketchikan Yacht Club at Thomas Basin or write P. O. Box 1694. Outboard boat and motor rentals range in price from $8 to $15 per day, depending on the boat and motor size.

Seaplanes are chartered from a number of local services operating direct from the city airplane float and seaplane base during daytime hours. They include: Alaska Coastal Airlines, Ellis Air Lines, Webber Air Service, Pacific Northern Airlines, and R. W. Simpson.

Charter planes and boats are always available, but there are frequently boat shortages during the three-day Ketchikan King Salmon Derby Days event.

HOTELS

The Ingersoll Hotel is the best in Ketchikan. It is the only one offering most of the conveniences of a metropolitan hotel. Located in the heart of the city, it is a reinforced concrete building, fireproof, with 60 rooms, 55 with bath, offering studio-type accommodations, as well as twin-bed or single rooms. Singles are $7, and doubles from $9 to $11. Pan American World Airways and Pacific Northern Airlines have offices in the lobby.

The Stedman Hotel, one of the old city landmarks, is comfortable and conveniently located. The Stedman has 45 rooms, 12 baths, and singles range from $4 to $6, doubles $5.50 to $10.50. In addition there is the Gilmore and seven smaller and lower-priced hotels in the downtown area.

RESTAURANTS

Most food in Alaska is American-style, plain and good. The restaurants and coffee shops in Ketchikan offer a modest variety of foods at reasonable prices. Breakfast costs from $.40 to $1.35;

lunch $1 to $1.50; dinner $1.50 to $2.50. The food is mostly well prepared, and seafood is featured along with steaks, chicken, and a selection of everyday cookery. The Narrows, one and one-half miles out on South Tongass, features dining and dancing nightly.

CHURCHES

Denominations of many faiths have churches which are open to visitors and residents for services as well as community social activities throughout the year. The churches include: Assembly of God, Catholic, Christian Science, Church of God, Church of Christ, Church of the Nazarene, Baptist, Methodist, Gospel Tabernacle, Latter-day Saints, Lutheran, Pentacostal, Presbyterian, and Seventh-day Adventist.

SCHOOLS

There is a completely modern school system in Ketchikan which includes a new $3,000,000 high school with an auditorium seating 1,200 and a gym seating 2,500. In addition there are two large grade-school buildings and a community college operated as a branch of the University of Alaska. Enrollment in the Ketchikan school system numbers about 2,000. There is one private school operated by the Seventh-day Adventists.

SHOPPING

Gifts and curios are sold at The Trading Post, Tom Sawyer's, Schallerer's Photo Shop, and Alaska Specialties Company. For those interested only in authentic native crafts such as totem poles, masks, carvings, moccasins, and so on, ask specifically for items bearing the Alaska Native Arts and Crafts label (ANAC), the guarantee of authenticity and value.

Sears Roebuck, Ben Franklin, Heckman's, and the Bon Marché are general department stores with sizable selections of clothing, household wares, accessories, and sundries. Twelve specialty shops carry men's, women's and children's clothing and accessories, and furs and fur products are purchased at the Ketchikan Fur and Tailoring Shop. The Stan Lee Drug Store has a large selection of photo supplies, equipment, and processes film.

Ketchikan has several sporting-goods stores with stocks of sport supplies, clothing, and equipment. Salmon and trout tackle may be rented at reasonable rates. Any of the Ketchikan dealers will personally help in outfitting and planning a fishing or hunting trip, including Paul M. Hansen, Nordby Supply Company, and the Tongass Trading Company.

SERVICES

In the downtown area there are two banks, First National and the Miners and Merchants Bank; two barbershops and four beauty salons; four cleaners, one laundry doing finish work, and one laundromat with quick service. There are four drugstores and two florists. A public stenographer is available at the Credit Bureau of Ketchikan. There is one investment broker, one shoe repair shop, one typewriter repair service, and three jewelers. The local travel bureau is Alaska World Travel Service.

In spite of the fact that there are no roads leading into Ketchikan from the outside, there are six automobile dealers handling the major American and imported cars, four garages, six gasoline stations, and two used-car lots.

Health—The seventy-five-bed Ketchikan General Hospital services the city and surrounding area. There are four dentists, seven physicians and surgeons, and four optometrists. A twenty-four-hour telephone answering service for doctors is maintained by the Ketchikan Medical Association.

Telephone and Telegraph—The local telephone system is a part of the community-owned public utility agency, the Ketchikan Public Utilities. Long-distance calls and telegrams are handled by the Alaska Communications Systems of the United States Army Signal Corps.

Publications—The Ketchikan *Daily News* and the *Chronicle* are the two newspapers published in the city.

Radio and Television—The leading radio station is KTKN and KATV is the local television station.

CIVIC AND SOCIAL ORGANIZATIONS

There are more than twelve state, national, and international organizations represented in Ketchikan, including the American

Legion, American Red Cross, Elks, Eagles, Masons, Salvation Army, and Sons of Norway.

ACTIVITIES

Swimming is popular in summertime when the water is warm. Summer is also the occasion for boat races and regattas on the inlet waters and there is a huge Fourth of July celebration.

In addition to salmon fishing, trout streams offer excellent opportunities for fishing and they may be reached by plane or boat, taking from ten- to twenty-minutes' flying time by plane to reach the better lakes and streams. The principal species of trout are plentiful. The United States Forest Service maintains shelter cabins and boats on many of the trout lakes in the area at no rental charge. Most of the lakes are accessible only by air, although some may be reached by trails from tidewater.

Hiking, mountain climbing, photography, and sight-seeing offer unlimited opportunities. The major trails are marked and well maintained.

Tours of the salmon canneries are conducted in late August and September. The fish hatchery and pulp mill may be visited the year around. There are daily water-front tours during the fishing season for close inspection of the commercial fishing fleet and fish-processing plants with their interesting exhibits of octopus, wolf eel, sea cucumbers, lobsters, and king crabs, as well as other specimens of the Alaskan waters. A variety of sight-seeing tours are operated by the local plane, bus, taxi, and boat services.

Annual Events—King Salmon Derby events begin about March 15 and end July 15 each year. Weekly prizes are awarded for the largest salmon and grand prizes are awarded to top entries caught during the season. A special three-day derby is held in late May or early June of each year, known as Ketchikan King Salmon Derby Days, and the prizes exceed $10,000 in value. The entry fee is $10 and covers both events.

Ketchikan also has an International Basketball Tournament sponsored by the Ketchikan Junior Chamber of Commerce between Canadian and Alaskan teams, during the close of the basketball season.

Night Life—Ketchikan has eighteen cocktail bars and two movie houses. Some of the cocktail bars have dancing and occasional floor shows with live entertainment, but generally they do not offer special attractions. The movies are current and change frequently. There is a local roller-skating rink open nightly from seven to ten.

SIDE TRIPS

Ward's Cove recreation area, a few miles northwest of Ketchikan, is easily accessible by auto, bus, or taxi and is excellent for swimming, picnicking, boating, hiking, and camping. There wildlife, including Chinese pheasants, deer, bear, and beavers, make their public appearance during spring, summer, and autumn. There is a large campground with bathhouses, water, and sanitary facilities. Excellent trails lead to four lakes in the area where there is fine fishing. There is skiing in winter but the conditions are only fair. Ward's Cove is also the location of Ketchikan's ultramodern pulp mill.

Totem Pole Park in Saxman, a tiny Indian village standing two miles south of Ketchikan available by motorcar, includes the largest Indian totem pole collection in the world.

The art of carving these "history sticks," as they are called, reached its peak in the middle of the last century, but thousands were chopped down and burned when Christianity came to Alaska, and the rest were left to rot in the backwoods.

Realizing the value of the poles as primitive artifacts, the Civilian Conservation Corps in 1938 combed deserted Indian villages attempting to collect the remaining poles. Indians were paid to stay home and carve copies of totems that could not be restored. Copying a totem conforms to Indian custom, but repainting an old pole is often taboo.

Carved from giant cedars, they were trimmed, peeled, and hollowed into a half shell. The skilled carver was paid the equivalent of $50 in blankets for six feet of work. As an artist, he had little freedom, since the family in charge of the monument supervised his efforts every inch of the way.

The totem collection near Ketchikan contains several types of poles. Prominent is the genealogy pole which stood at the gate like a mailbox to identify the family in the house. A native, so the Indians say, could tell at a glance whether the ruling clan would welcome him or slam the door in his face. Numerous, too, are the house pillars, used to support beams, and the mortuary poles with a single box at the top for the ashes of the dead.

One pole tells how a white trader had been adopted into a tribe with great fanfare and showered with gifts at a potlatch. When the trader failed to stage a return potlatch to repay his benefactors, a ridicule pole was set up to embarrass him. The ridicule pole shows the white man in the form of a raven at the top with a woodpecker below protesting that the trader was a cheat.

As white men penetrated the northwest coast, the totems became more realistic. Typical of the European influence is the Chief Skowl totem, done in the 1880's; with angels and eagles, Russian bishops and saints, the pole records how the chief and his family were baptized into the Russian Orthodox Church.

The totem stories are all read from top to bottom of the poles. Excellent examples of totems may also be seen at Mud Bay and in Ketchikan City Park.

The villages of *Metlakatla, Wacker,* and *Loring* are reached by boat and all are within twenty miles of Ketchikan. They are primarily small Indian villages of interest, not only because of the local fishing and lumbering activities, but because they were once centers of Indian culture where there are still fascinating native artifacts, totems, buildings, and native burial grounds. Metlakatla is a model Indian community, established in 1887 by missionary William Duncan of the Church of England, who helped the Indians build homes, establish trade, and create a successful co-operative venture which continues to this day. Ellis Air Lines has charter plane service to Metlakatla and round-trip fare from Ketchikan is $10.80.

The deserted village of *Old Kasaan* is a part of what was formerly a national monument covering twenty-eight acres on the east side of Prince of Wales Island. The village was built by Indians belonging to the Haida tribe and is worth seeing for the ruins of totem poles, graves, and framework of buildings representing aboriginal American civilization. Old Kasaan is thirty miles from Ketchikan and can be visited by charter boat or via Ellis Air Lines for $27 round trip.

RESORTS

Bell Island Hot Springs, forty-five miles north of Ketchikan, is open the year around and is reached by boat or plane. The boat fare is $7.50 and the plane is $11 each way.

The hot springs consist of several sizable basins ranging from 125 to 162 degrees and flowing approximately 8 to 10 gallons a minute. The mineral content of the water is high and is predominantly sodium chloride with some sulphate. The water from these springs is used for heating buildings as well as for health baths.

Heated cabins complete with bedding and dishes rent from $5 to $7 a day and from $25 to $35 a week. Family-style meals are also available and there is a grocery store and cocktail lounge. The mineral baths are free, outboard and motorboats can be rented, fishing tackle is for sale or rent, and fishing is excellent.

Clover Pass Resort is fifteen miles north of Ketchikan by road. Cabins for 4 people are $10 a day, $58 a week, smaller cabins for 2 people are $8 a day or $48 a week. They are completely furnished with oil heat, electricity, bedding, and cooking facilities. Outboard and motorboat rentals are $12.50 a day; boats only are $8.50. Complete salmon fishing tackle may be rented for $3 a day. Guide service is available at reasonable rates, and the resort has a complete tackle store, grocery, and coffee shop.

PROSPECTIVE SETTLERS

Job opportunities are limited in all industries with a local labor pool sufficient to fill the normal needs. There are occasional openings for trained clerical personnel, especially stenographers and bookkeepers. Salaries are high and usually balance out the added cost of living at 20 per cent above the wages in other states. Inquiries about job opportunities should be directed to the Alaska Employment Service, Box 159, or to the various unions with offices in Ketchikan which include: the Alaska Fisherman's Union, Alaska Logger's Association, Bartender and Culinary Workers, Cannery Workers Division ILWU, Carpenter's Local #1501, Construction and General Laborers ILWU or Local 62, International Woodworkers of America, Operating Engineers Union, and the Teamster Union #959.

There is need for professional people, doctors, dentists, lawyers, chemical engineers, chemists, and educators, for example, but this need is not as great in Ketchikan as it is in other cities in Alaska.

The business opportunities exist primarily in the field of servicing the increasing tourist trade. There are industrial opportunities requiring considerable capital investment in the fields of timber processing, such as plywood mills, specialty cedar products, and pressed wood products. Special tax incentives are available for new industries locating in the Ketchikan area, where a trained work force is available. The Ketchikan Chamber of Commerce maintains current and comprehensive information for persons interested in investing or opening a business in the area.

Housing—A plentiful supply of housing is available at Ketchikan, mostly in the apartment rental field. Housing can be obtained without advance arrangements, mainly because the town overbuilt during the pulp mill construction boom. A few home rentals are available from time to time. There are two 130-unit apartment buildings, built under the Federal Housing Authority at a cost of $2,000,000 each. Apartments rent for $75 to $140 per month. Electricity is used almost exclusively in all homes for cooking purposes.

Wrangell

Wrangell, the third oldest city in Alaska, is in the heart of the Alaskan Panhandle on the Inside Passage in an area of great scenic beauty.

Named in honor of Baron Ferdinand Petrovich von Wrangell, the Russian explorer and scientist, this city of 1,500 people is 89 miles northwest of Ketchikan, 125 miles south of Juneau, and 820 miles from Seattle, Washington. It was established in 1834 by a Captain Zarembo, and used as a Russian fortress for the Russian-American Company to keep the rival Hudson's Bay Company from the fur-rich Stikine River.

The town boomed and faded under many economies. It thrived first as a fur center when pelts were a major item in Alaskan economy, then as a transportation center when gold was discovered in 1870 in the Cassiar district on the Stikine River. It boomed as a tent city of 15,000 in 1897, when the hazardous Stikine River was thought to be a short cut to the gold-mad Klondike, but quickly faded when the Dyea Trail opened from Skagway. It prospered in the early 1900's under a fish economy, then boasting of the largest cannery in Alaska. Since that time the town's economy has depended largely on catching and processing the wealth of the sea, but the current focal point is on the great timber resources consisting of hemlock, spruce, and cedar. The immediate area is known to be rich in minerals including marble, gold, silver, and lead.

Wrangell has a large fishing fleet which supplies the raw materials for the three shrimp canneries and the large salmon cannery which is a seasonal industry. The community also has two boat shops and cold-storage facilities as allied industries. The sheltered harbor is open all year around and has light, water, and fuel services at the floats.

Alaska Wrangell Mills, operated as the Wrangell Lumber Company and affiliated with the Alaska Lumber and Pulp Company of Tokyo, Japan, processes and ships over twenty-five million board feet of lumber a year. Much of this has been carried direct to the Orient in large Japanese freighters and negotiations are under way with another company to operate a large lumber and pulp mill on a fifty-year lease from the Forest Service on 399,000 acres of timber in the Wrangell-Petersburg area, with an announced initial expenditure of $4,500,000.

In addition there are four local sawmills supplying salmon boxes for canneries in the state and a shingle mill producing Alaska red cedar shingles. The lumber industry is nonseasonal.

Wrangell suffered a disastrous $1,500,000 fire in 1952 which wiped out over half of the business district, causing a severe business slump. However, in anticipation of an increased population, it has expended $750,000 in public facilities, including the dredging of its harbor and a new sea wall. Additional funds have been spent on a $350,000 school improvement, a water system costing $300,000, a sewer system costing $296,000, and improvements on six miles of roads amounting to $200,000. The light, power, and water systems are municipally owned.

Wrangell has a moderate climate characteristic of the southeastern part of the state. In the immediate vicinity are hundreds of miles of sheltered waterways with countless bays and inlets offering excellent salmon fishing for the angler. The many streams and lakes have abundant rainbow, cutthroat, and Dolly Varden trout, and the near-by islands, as well as the mainland and Stikine River area, are full of a variety of big game. Because there is good hunting and fishing, Wrangell is an important outfitting point for big-game hunters, sport fishermen, and guides are available for hire in the community.

TRANSPORTATION TO WRANGELL

There is daily seaplane service to Wrangell from Ketchikan or Juneau via Alaska Coastal Airlines or Ellis Air Lines. Steamship passenger service in summer is available from Canadian Pacific Steamships and Alaska Cruise Lines, Ltd.

The Ritchie Transportation Company ships autos by barge in summer on the Stikine River, a distance of 163 miles, between Telegraph Creek, B.C., and Wrangell, then continues by water via Dease Lake to the Alaska Highway. United States and Canadian immigration and customs offices are in Wrangell.

HOTELS AND FOOD

The New Thunderbird Hotel has modern accommodations and all rooms are with private bath. Rooms without bath are available at Gartley House. Rates are from $4 to $8 single. There are several restaurants serving good American food and one, the Cassiar Café, serves Chinese dinners. From time to time specialty food dinners are served by local organizations which are open to the public and the menus vary from potluck suppers to sukiyaki.

CHURCHES AND SCHOOLS

The Presbyterian Church in Wrangell, called the "Oldest Protestant Church in Alaska," has a neon cross on top of its church spire which serves as a "lighthouse beacon," making it one of the two churches in the world so designated on nautical charts. There are also Assembly of God, Catholic, and Episcopal churches in the city.

Wrangell's school system is modern and well housed, with fully accredited grades through high school. The grade school is brand new and the recently completed high school has a gymnasium, tennis court, and large playfield. School enrollment is approximately three hundred.

SHOPPING AND SERVICES

Wrangell has a bank, curio shops, a drugstore, the Igloo Potters, and general stores with a good but modest selection of merchandise, and complete stock of fishing and hunting equipment and clothing. There is auto service and maintenance facilities. The Wrangell *Sentinel* is the local weekly newspaper giving excellent news coverage on all local activities. The offices of the *Sentinel* welcome visitors and provide information about the community and surrounding area. Long-distance communications are handled by the Alaska Communications System to any point in the world via radio, radio-telephone, and telegraph. There is twenty-four-hour taxi service and boats or planes may be chartered at the seaplane and boat floats at the wharf. There is a twelve-bed hospital which is modern, well equipped and well staffed.

CIVIC AND SOCIAL ORGANIZATIONS

The community has several fraternal orders and civic organizations, a Salvation Army post, Elks Club, Masonic Lodge, American Legion, Boy Scouts, and Business and Professional Women's Club.

ACTIVITIES

Wrangell has two movie theaters and an occasional Saturday night dance at The Brig. During the winter season, residents participate in the Alaska Music Trail concert series. Basketball tournaments between the Wrangell Thunderbirds and teams from other Alaskan communities are a high light of winter. In summer the emphasis is on outdoor sports and activities.

Shakes Island Community House and the many totem poles in the city are authentic restorations of a fascinating era in the life of the Tlingit Indians. The Bear Totem Store has one of the finest privately owned collections of native art and curios in the world. Shakes Island is located in Wrangell Harbor and is accessible by foot bridge from the main thoroughfare.

Wrangell Institute, an Alaska Native Service boarding school, with an enrollment of several hundred children from communities all over Alaska, is maintained at Shoemaker Bay, six miles from the downtown area and reached by automobile. Native crafts and artifacts are on exhibit at the school.

Visitors are always welcome to visit the canneries and lumber mills of this hospitable water-front city.

SIDE TRIPS

The Stikine River provides one of the world's most thrilling boat trips. The journey goes between Wrangell and Telegraph Creek, a mining camp in British Columbia and one of the few remaining typically frontier towns. Through canyons, gorges, and rapids, and 163 miles inside the Canadian Cassiar district, this scenic side trip is made on a steamer of the Ritchie Transportation Company. Along the way, passengers thrill to the sight of almost a hundred glaciers, formed like jagged mountains of ice.

At Telegraph Creek, the passengers live on board the steamer and have the opportunity of taking several short trips farther into the interior by automobile. One of these trips goes to the Cassiar mining district, another to the Tahltan Lava Beds, and still another to Dease Lake on the Arctic watershed.

The round trip requires four days from Wrangell, including

a stopover at Telegraph Creek. Because of the strong current, the upstream trip requires thirty-two hours, while the return downstream takes about twelve hours. The boats operated by the Ritchie Company are modern, with staterooms, dining rooms, electric lights, and all conveniences throughout. Sailings are once a week and the round-trip fare is $75, which includes berth and meals.

RESORT

The Diamond B Guest Ranch is located on the Stikine River, twelve miles below Telegraph Creek, and may be reached from Wrangell on boats of the Ritchie Transportation Company.

The main lodge at the ranch, cabins, corrals, and other ranch buildings are set in a beautiful surrounding of high evergreens, poplars, cottonwoods, and wide green meadows. Fresh water is piped to the lodge and cabins from Fizz Creek which runs through the ranch. The meals are served in the main lodge and are wholesome and well prepared, usually featuring a variety of fresh game. The cabins are comfortable and attractively furnished.

Hunting parties may be outfitted at the ranch with pack train, guides, cooks, wranglers, and complete camping equipment. The Diamond B furnishes saddle horses, and activities include riding the saddle trails which wind through the hills to near-by fishing streams. In the evening old-time music is played for dances in the main lodge.

The weekly rate is $80 per person and includes all ranch facilities and a saddle horse for each guest.

PROSPECTIVE SETTLERS

Existing opportunities of Wrangell are primarily in the fields of lumber, fishing, and recreational industries but the supply of labor is enough to fill employment needs. Investments which would establish supplemental businesses to the major industries provide the most likely opportunities. Processing or manufacturing mills and plants, the building of sports and recreation areas, lodges, camps, and so on, are types of businesses which suit the current economy.

Housing—Rentals are few. There are often houses for sale and usually the furnishings must be purchased with the house.

Petersburg

Petersburg, in the heart of the Tongass National Forest, is said to be the richest town per capita in the world. It is known as "Little Norway" because of the Norwegian fishermen who migrated to America and eventually settled in the community.

Actually this town of two thousand people was named for Peter Buschmann who arrived in 1897 and built a salmon cannery and sawmill on the picturesque site, situated on Mitkof Island midway between Ketchikan and Juneau, and approximately forty miles northwest of Wrangell at the mouth of the Stikine River.

Petersburg is surrounded by snow-capped mountains and a setting of glaciers, high mountains, and fiords. Fishing and logging are the main industries in the area. Two large cold-storage plants freeze halibut, cod, and king salmon, while three canneries process shrimp, crab, and several varieties of salmon. About seventeen million pounds of fish are processed and shipped annually. There are nine individually owned logging camps in the area and one sawmill which operates most of the year.

Petersburg is headquarters for an eight-thousand-square-mile United States Forest Service Ranger District in the center of Tongass National Forest, which includes the towns of Wrangell and Kake.

School, church, and civic groups are strongly united in a community spirit and interest. The public school system extends from kindergarten through high school. A staff of 23 teachers serves an enrollment of 450. The new high school building has a 500 seat auditorium for public use.

Seven church groups of Protestant and Catholic faiths are represented. Most fraternal organizations have local chapters and an excellent city library is sponsored by the American Legion Auxiliary and financed by the city.

The Presbyterian mission ship, M.V. *Anna Jackman,* is based in Petersburg and, along with the floating church, M.S. *Princeton-*

Hall from Juneau, churns through the waters of southeastern Alaska, serving logging camps, weather stations, and far-from-church villages.

Petersburg's climate is mild and wet with an average annual rainfall of 108 inches. Summer temperatures vary from 50 to 70 degrees, turning the numerous fresh- and salt-water beaches into havens for swimmers. There is less than a month of below-freezing weather, with waterways ice-free at all times. Skiing and skating are frequently enjoyed.

In 1957 and 1958 a million-dollar hydroelectric plant was completed. Extensive street and sewer improvements were made, including the concrete paving of Main Street.

TRANSPORTATION TO PETERSBURG

Daily plane service is maintained to Seattle via Juneau and Ketchikan, with connections to other points in Alaska and to Canada via Ellis Air Lines. There is a nonpassenger weekly freighter service on boats of the Alaska Steamship Company.

HOTEL, FOOD, AND SERVICES

The local hotel is the Mitkof, a modern hostelry that is comfortable and can accommodate thirty-five people. Rates are $3.50 single, $5.00 double. There are several good cafés serving American and Scandinavian specialties and featuring seafood. Telephone and telegraph communications are available, and there are general stores with basic shopping services.

A locally owned twenty-one-bed hospital was completed in 1954. Volunteer labor had a large part in the construction of this and several other public buildings.

ACTIVITIES

Big-game hunters and sports fishermen start from Petersburg to go on charter trips by boat and plane to near-by hunting and fishing grounds. On display in downtown Petersburg at the municipal office is the World's Record King Salmon, 126½ pounds, and the 36-pound World's Record Chum Salmon.

The Norwegian holidays are celebrated in the colorful Spring

Festival on the seventeenth of May each year. St. Hans Day
in June and the Fourth of July celebrations are wonderful occasions, with special religious services, street dancing, *smörgås-
bords,* salmon barbecues, boat races, logrolling contests, and a
variety of outdoor entertainment. The annual Yulefest in December is a high light of the winter season.

SIDE TRIPS

There are flights over LeConte Glacier, southernmost active
glacier in North America, only five minutes by air from Petersburg. Auto trips may be taken along the Mitkof Highway. Approximately twelve miles from town is the recently completed
$200,000 Fall Creek Fish Ladder, where the salmon climb to
reach their spawning waters.

Also on the Mitkof Highway is the Experimental Fur Farm,
operated by the University of Alaska, where interesting experiments are conducted in conjunction with the fur farming in this
and other parts of Alaska.

About one and a half miles from town is the Sandy Beach
Recreation Area which can be reached over a boardwalk across
the muskeg.

PROSPECTIVE SETTLERS

Because of fishing regulations and weather factors, local industries are seasonal. The lowest period of employment occurs
between mid-February and mid-April while the high runs from
May through September.

A considerable number of workers migrate southward during
the winter months and return in early spring. Canneries bring
their regular crews from outside the state each year but they
hire only local people to fill their personnel needs for the actual
canning season during July and August.

The local labor force expands each year in proportion to the
growth of the logging, lumbering, and construction industries.
The growth of available local labor has been large enough to meet
most normal employer demands, making opportunities for newcomers extremely limited.

Sitka

Sitka, the old Russian capital of Alaska, is a historic community originally populated by Tlingit Indians, then by the Russians, and finally by Americans. Representatives from many lands established their homes in this city.

In the last quarter of the eighteenth century, ships from Spain, Britain, Russia, and the United States visited southeastern Alaska in ever-increasing numbers. Most of them were merchantmen trading with the natives for sea otter skins. They found the Sitka area rich in furs. They also found that the people were shrewd bargainers and dangerous enemies. Shore parties were in constant danger of ambush and robbery and ship captains remained alert against seizure of their vessels by the natives.

Finally the Russians founded trading settlements in the Aleutians and along the Alaska coast north of the Panhandle, but by 1799 sea otters were growing scarce near these Russian posts, and Alexander Baranof, general manager of the Russian-American Company, decided to expand his settlements to the southward.

In that year he established the fortified post of St. Michael, about six miles north of the present Sitka. In 1802 the Sitkas surprised the settlement and wiped out most of the Russian and Aleut inhabitants. The fort was completely destroyed but the site is still known as Old Sitka.

Baranof was determined to re-establish his colony, but it took two years to marshal sufficient resources at the company's headquarters on Kodiak Island. In 1804 he appeared near the site of the present Sitka with a force of about 150 Russian hunters and 800 Aleuts, who had made the long journey in their tiny skin bidarkas. Here Baranof received an unexpected reinforcement from the *Neva*, a Russian warship.

The Sitkas awaited the attack in a position atop Baranof Hill. But when they saw the force against them, they retreated to a stronger fort near the south boundary of the present Sitka National Monument. Here, behind thick log walls, they defied the Russian cannon, which did little damage. An assault, led by Baranof himself, was repulsed by murderous fire, killing ten Russians and wounding twenty-six, including Baranof.

The Russians then brought their guns closer and settled down for a siege. After several days the Sitka Indians ran out of ammunition and, believing their cause to be hopeless, fled in the night and made their way to the northeast side of the island. As a result of their retreat, the way was left open for the Russians to develop the area of Sitka in this New World.

Baranof at once re-established his settlement on the site of the present town. A residence for the general manager and his officers was built on Baranof Hill, and by the following spring eight substantial buildings and several gardens were evidences of progress and prosperity. The post was officially named New Archangel, but it was generally known as Sitka, a Tlingit word meaning, "the village on the outside."

During the Russian administration, Sitka became a thriving industrial city. In its iron and brass foundries cannons were cast and many of the famous mission bells of California were molded. Among other industries were lumbering, shipbuilding, and tanning. Ice harvested on Swan Lake was shipped to San Francisco, and the first railroad in Alaska ran from where the ice was cut to the shipping docks. For many years an extensive trade was carried on with the Spaniards in California and the Hawaiian Islands. Baranof soon transferred the company's American headquarters to Sitka, which remained the capital of Russian America until Alaska was purchased by the United States in 1867.

The official transfer of the territory took place on October 18, 1867, in the presence of two American generals, three Navy captains, 250 enlisted men, and the residents, who stood in a rain storm while the Russian flag was lowered and the American was raised in its place. Ships in the bay fired salutes announcing that the vast country was changing authority in Sitka.

Surrounded by heavily timbered mountain peaks, Sitka is located on the west side of Baranof Island facing Sitka Sound and the broad sweep of the North Pacific Ocean, approximately 980 miles north of Seattle. Its harbor is dominated by the snow-capped peak of Mount Edgecumbe, an extinct volcano which is a twin to Japan's Fujiyama. The climate is mild and moist. The population in the immediate area, including the community of Mount Edgecumbe, is approximately six thousand.

Fishing, lumbering, and a sizable government pay roll make up the town's economy. Most recently, the extensive activities of the Alaska Lumber and Pulp Mill, with a new $50,000,000 pulp plant, and the Columbia Lumber Company have made large contributions to the economic stability of the town. The harbor houses more than a thousand small fishing boats and there is a large salmon cold-storage plant. The cost of living in Sitka is approximately 28 per cent higher than in Seattle, Washington.

The major downtown streets are paved and the roadways, extending a short distance from the town to the new pulp plant, the residential, and the commercial areas, are well maintained.

TRANSPORTATION TO SITKA

Alaska Coastal Airlines operates two flights daily between Juneau and Sitka, while Ellis Air Lines offers service twice weekly between Sitka and Ketchikan. Both air lines connect with Pan-American and Pacific Northern air lines to points in Alaska and other states. Freight is handled by the Alaska Steamship Company and by the air services.

LOCAL TRANSPORTATION

There are three taxi services, and charter boat and plane service is available, as well as local city bus service. A ferry operates between Sitka and Mount Edgecumbe, a five-minute boat trip with departures and arrivals approximately every half hour from 6:00 A.M. to midnight.

HOTEL AND FOOD

The Sitka is the leading hotel, with clean sleeping accommodations, a friendly comfortable lobby, and a small café. There are four restaurants in the community serving plain American food, also one drive-in restaurant and Beacom's 57 Steps, a tearoom with a private museum and a fine view.

CHURCHES

There are many churches in Sitka, including Lutheran, Episcopal, Roman Catholic, Presbyterian, Russian Orthodox, Pentecostal, Assembly of God, Church of Christ, Seventh-day Adventist, Church of the Nazarene, Southern Baptist, Christian Science, Baha'i, and Unitarian Fellowship.

SCHOOLS

There are close to one thousand students in the public school, which includes kindergarten through high school. Sheldon Jackson Junior College, established in 1878 and operated by the Board of National Missions of the Presbyterian Church, offers education to both high school and junior college students. It is the oldest school in Alaska and the Sitka campus is made up of 352 acres and 27 buildings to house the student body. The school is accredited by the Northwest Association and is a member of the American Association of Junior Colleges.

SHOPPING AND SERVICES

The community has a selection of stores, shops, and services, including two banks, clothing and specialty shops, gift stores, craft shops, two radio stations, KIFW and KSEW, garages, drugstores, a flower shop, a weekly newspaper, the *Baranof Banner,* and the *Daily Sitka Sentinel,* photo studios, a bicycle and hobby shop, service stations, beauty parlors, and cleaning and laundry services. Sitka has one movie theater, one pool hall, one bowling alley, and five cocktail bars.

Health—Sitka has a modern, fully equipped twenty-five-bed hospital, six physicians, two dentists, and one optometrist. A large government hospital is maintained at Mount Edgecumbe for native beneficiaries. The Pioneers' Home operates its own hospital.

CIVIC AND SOCIAL ORGANIZATIONS

Sitka has many organizations represented including a Teenage Club, Women's Club, the Business and Professional Women, Alaska Nurses Association, Lions, Rotary, Elks, Moose, Masons,

Baranof Arts and Crafts Association, 4-H, and Boy and Girl Scouts.

ACTIVITIES

Alaska Day Festival on October 18 of each year is celebrated with a colorful historical pageant re-enacting the transfer of Alaska to the United States. In July, the annual Sitka Salmon Derby is held. Sport fishing and big-game hunting are excellent in the area.

St. Michael's Cathedral—The old-world influence is evidenced in the cathedral of St. Michael's in downtown Sitka. The cathedral, completed in 1848, is of Eastern Orthodox design and is decorated with icons, paintings, jewels, and contains a priceless treasure of religious art from the old world. The structure was built in the design of a cross from logs and timbers salvaged from the wrecked warship, *Neva*.

The Pioneers' Home—The Alaska Pioneers' Home is near the dock on the former parade grounds of the Russian and American troops. The home is for retired men and women who pioneered the settling of Alaska. The buildings are surrounded by landscaped grounds featuring native Alaskan plants. Back of the home is the first Russian cemetery. Crumbling marble slabs mark the graves of many persons prominent in Sitka's history.

Sheldon Jackson School Museum—Many of the books, papers, and maps pertaining to the settling, purchase, and history of Alaska are on display in this fine museum along with Indian and Eskimo arts, crafts, and artifacts, Russian relics, and special exhibitions of local artists and craftsmen.

Baranof Hill—Also called Baranof's Castle, where Baranof and succeeding directors of the Russian-American Company resided, was the scene of important events so far as Russian activities in America were concerned. There have been three or four buildings on this site; one of them, the historic building generally known to early Americans as Baranof Castle, was completed in 1837 and burned in 1894, and the present building was built by the United States Department of Agriculture. Baranof Hill was where the transfer ceremonies took place.

Mount Edgecumbe—This Federal medical-educational insti-

tution is located on four of the sheltering islands, five minutes
by ferry from downtown Sitka. The installation, named after the
3,467-foot Mount Edgecumbe, has a residence school for Eskimo
and Indian children, as well as complete hospital services. It is an
interesting installation to visit for its scenery and school activities, and to see the superior handicrafts being made by the
students.

Sitka Magnetic Observatory—The Russians maintained a first-
class meteorological and magnetic observatory in Sitka from 1842
until 1867. Later the United States Coast and Geodetic Survey
built a magnetic observatory on the small knoll behind the Cathedral Apartments and in 1942 the observatory was moved to its
present location at the northeast corner of town.

In addition to the varied landmarks already described, Sitka
has a display of anchors from the old sailing ships in Totem
Square, the Russian cemetery notable for its headstones dat-
ing to 1799, and petroglyphs. Old Sitka, which is the site of the
Indian rebellions of 1802, the Blarney Stone where Baranof is
said to have spent many hours sitting and meditating the events
of his day, the cold-storage plant, where fish are stacked like
cordwood; and along the road to the pulp mill is Jamestown Bay
and a panorama of the area.

Sitka National Monument—Sitka National Monument is open
all year around and is within three-quarters of a mile of downtown Sitka, easily available by foot or motor transportation.

The monument was established to protect an outstanding collection of Alaskan Indian totem poles and to preserve the historical value of the vicinity.

Within the monument are eighteen of the finest totem poles in
the world, and the largest and most famous of them stands on
the site of the old Sitka fort. This totem, called Fog Women,
belonged to Son-I-Hat, a Haida chief who lived at Old Kasaan.
It is fifty-nine feet high, one of the tallest in the world, and has
more carved figures than any other Alaskan totem pole. Around
it are four smaller "house" totems.

The poles were not objects of religious worship. They record
family and tribal history, describe significant events, and stand
as monuments to the fame or ill-repute of outstanding persons.

Their carvings and paint tell of the earth's origin and the creation of certain fish, birds, and animals. The bright, contrasting colors were made from crushed rock, minerals, and clamshells, mixed with fish eggs as the binding agent.

PROSPECTIVE SETTLERS

The opportunities that exist in Sitka are in the nature of investment. There is need for greater tourist facilities and businesses that are allied to tourist trade, as well as lumber and, to a lesser degree, fishing. Jobs are not plentiful because the local labor market can meet most needs but, as the pulp plant and lumbering industries expand, there will of course be more employment. Work in the government installations is obtained through the United States Civil Service and inquiries about openings in other established industries should be directed to the union offices or Alaska Employment Service in Ketchikan or Juneau. There is homesteading land available in the area.

Housing—Few rentals are available and rents run high. New subdivisions and homes are in the planning stages, though some are under construction to handle the increase in population that is expected as a result of the new pulp industry.

Juneau

Juneau, the capital city of Alaska, is situated at the foot of Mount Juneau and Mount Roberts, which tower over the city and crowd it to a narrow strip of land along the water's edge. A highway and bridge over the Gastineau Channel connects Juneau with the community of Douglas. These two cities, with a combined population of eleven thousand, are known as the Gastineau Channel Community.

Juneau is approximately one thousand miles northwest of Seattle in a beautiful mountain setting, where elevations range from two to four thousand feet along the coastal areas and over eight thousand feet inland. Snow remains on the peaks as part of the Juneau landscape until midsummer. Heavy forests blanket the lower elevations of the mountains and the vast network of islands that lie in the channels, bays, and fiords for many miles around Juneau. Extensive ice fields cover much of the mainland east of Juneau to the Canadian border, less than one hundred miles away.

The harbor at Juneau is open all year around. It has seaplane floats and service facilities, a protected moorage for small boats, and a large steamer wharf. The water level changes rapidly each day and, in July, the tides go from minus one foot to over thirteen feet in less than six hours.

Juneau has a moderate, damp climate, with cool summers and mild winters. It is the most cosmopolitan community in southeastern Alaska, and is the transportation crossroads of the entire area.

Narrow, crooked, concrete streets and sidewalks climb the steep hills to the old and the new homes in the residential areas. The downtown area is crowded with commercial activity, office buildings, stores, hotels, restaurants, bars, and a jumble of street traffic. There is a fine public library, the Governor's Mansion, and many historical landmarks.

Juneau began as a boom town after the discovery of gold by Joe Juneau and Dick Harris in 1880. It became the capital in 1900 and has remained the center of federal and state government activity.

The leading industries are fishing, mining, lumbering, transportation, tourists, trade, and government. There are over five hundred businesses in the city, including a large lumbermill, a plywood plant, and headquarters for the Columbia Lumber Company which has state-wide interests in sawmills, logging camps, and lumberyards. The secondary industries include dairying, agriculture, and poultry raising which supply part of the local needs for these food products.

TRANSPORTATION TO JUNEAU

Pan-American Airways and Pacific Northern Airlines offer daily service to and from Seattle as well as other points in Alaska. Alaska Coastal Airlines has regular scheduled flights to and from the cities of the southeastern section of the state. The airport, located nine miles north of Juneau, has an attractive passenger terminal, and taxi or Grayline bus service is available to and from downtown Juneau at $1.75 per person.

From May to November the auto ferry between Haines and Juneau is available and links the city with the Alaska Highway. Summer passenger service from Vancouver, B.C., is available via Canadian Pacific Steamships and Alaska Cruise Lines, Ltd. The Alaska Steamship Company serves Juneau with year-round service weekly for freight only.

LOCAL TRANSPORTATION

A city bus system goes to Douglas and points along the twenty-eight-mile Glacier Highway and Douglas Highway. There is twenty-four-hour taxi service. Grayline Tours, with offices in the Baranof Hotel, operates buses to the local scenic points of interest with a good selection of tours by bus, car, plane, or boat. Grayline also has a U-Drive car rental service, with rates at $12 per day plus 10 cents a mile, and a limousine service to the docks. Autos may also be rented from W. D. Field Motor Company. There are many charter planes including Alaska Coastal Airlines, Dean Goodwin Air Service, and Ken Lokken's Juneau Air Taxi Service; rates are $20-$30 an hour. Charter boats are operated by Northwind Cruises, Chuck Porter, Roy Conner, Trever Davis, and several others.

The excursion boat, M.V. *Sea Otter*, offers trips through Lynn Canal, Glacier Bay, and the numerous waterways to Sitka and return. It is a modern steel cruiser with informal but comfortable stateroom accommodations. It has a package vacation plan which includes round-trip air transportation between Juneau and Seattle and a six-day cruise with a price range of $475 to $500 per person, all expenses included.

HOTELS

The Baranof Hotel is the finest in southeastern Alaska. It is modern and contains a fine coffee shop, banquet rooms, handsome lobby with huge Alaskan murals, cocktail lounge, grill, drive-in garage, and is the meeting place for civic, social, and business organizations of the community. Rates are $12 single and $16 to $22 double. Other hotels include the Hotel Juneau and the Gastineau, which is a small, clean, and comfortable commercial hotel with 98 rooms and 38 baths; singles are $4.50 to $7, doubles from $7 to $12.

RESTAURANTS

There are nineteen restaurants in town and on the outskirts. They serve mainly plain American cooking and there is an emphasis on seafood and steaks. The prices range from $.75 to $1.75 for breakfast; $1.25 to $2 for lunch; and dinner from $1.50 to $4.50.

CHURCHES

Juneau has many churches including Assembly of God, Catholic, Church of God, Methodist, Presbyterian, Pentecostal, Latter-day Saints, Nazarene, and Baha'i Faith.

SCHOOLS

The Juneau-Douglas school district has ninety-two classrooms in six schools, including a new high school and grade school. The total professional staff numbers eighty-seven. Juneau also has a parochial grade school. There are three day nurseries, one art school, and one dance studio.

SHOPPING

The business section offers the most complete shopping facilities in southeastern Alaska. In addition to the gift and curio shops, camera stores, and a selection of hunting and fishing outfitters, the community has three well-stocked department stores, including Sears and Montgomery Ward, specialty shops for music, hobby supplies, jewelry, clothing, and books. The grocery stores range from small neighborhood operations to large supermarkets with a good variety of foods to choose from.

SERVICES

Juneau has two banks, B. M. Behrends and the First National; architects, lawyers, accountants, and other professional services are available. There are four beauty parlors, several barbershops, cleaning, pressing, and laundry services, and three drugstores.

Garages and service stations are numerous and auto dealers carry most makes of imported and domestic cars.

Health—There are two hospitals, one private and one government, with 138 beds, two private clinics, and a United States Public Health Center, in addition to the seven dentists, eight physicians, three optometrists, and one chiropractic clinic.

Telephone and Telegraph—Juneau has a modern dial telephone system. All outside communications are handled by the Alaska Communications System including messages to ships at sea. Long-distance rates to all other states range from $5.25 to $8.25 for three-minute daytime calls.

Publications—Two newspapers are published in Juneau, the *Daily Alaska Empire* and the *Juneau Independent*. *The Alaska Sportsman*, Alaska's nationally circulated magazine, has main offices here.

Radio and Television—There are two radio stations, KJNO and KINY. The television station is operated by KINY, which is a CBS affiliate, showing first-rate filmed and taped programs. It is estimated that over three thousand homes and business firms have television sets in the Juneau-Douglas area.

CIVIC AND SOCIAL ORGANIZATIONS

Juneau has groups representing all civic, business, and social organizations located in Alaska.

ACTIVITIES

In addition to the usual summer and winter sports activities, the salt-water and fresh-water fishing, as well as all types of hunting, are superior. Planes, boats, and experienced guides are available for hire to hunting parties.

The Juneau ski area is located across Gastineau Channel near Douglas, a ten-minute drive to the base of the ski trail. The bowl is located some three miles from the highway, with the Sno-Cat or helicopter providing the most popular means of transportation up the hill. A rope tow is in operation and there are overnight facilities available for members and guests of the Juneau Ski Club. Two warming huts are on the trail, which is a three-mile downhill run from the bowl to the highway, one of the features of the area.

Museums—The Alaska Historical Library and Museum is located on the second floor of the Federal Building. It contains the largest Eskimo art and craft collection in the world, including the famous Neuman Eskimo Exhibit and the Wickersham collection of Alaskan memorabilia. The library contains more than fifteen thousand volumes, with a large collection of Alaska newspapers on microfilm. On display are examples of Attu basketry, jade artifacts, Chilkat blankets, minerals, fine art, and historical relics of the Russian occupation. The museum is open the year around from 8:30 A.M. to noon and from 1:00 to 5:00 P.M., Mondays through Fridays. From the middle of May to late September the doors are open in the evenings from seven to ten. The library has research rooms available for students and researchers with microfilm services available.

Another museum in Juneau is located at The Nugget Shop where the art gallery is devoted to paintings by many leading Alaskan artists, as well as to many native Indian and Eskimo artifacts. This is primarily a retail gift shop but it is one of the landmarks of Juneau and the collection of arts and crafts is unusual and worth while.

Annual Events—In July, the biggest event of the year is the Golden North Salmon Derby with prizes totaling over $15,000. During the three days of the Salmon Derby no one works in Juneau. The entry fee for the derby is $5 per day or $10 for three days and anyone in Juneau on those days is eligible to participate, including children under sixteen when they are accompanied by an adult. The salmon caught and entered in the contest must have been taken with salmon sport fishing rod and reel. Each contestant is allowed to fish with one pole only. The Salmon Derby is sponsored by the Territorial Sportsmen, Inc., of Juneau and entry blanks may be obtained in person or by writing to the sponsors.

Other annual events are the Trout Derby, 4-H Club Fair, and Flower Show in August, a Creative Arts & Crafts Exhibition in March or April, the Gold Medal Basketball Tournaments at the close of the state-wide basketball season, a traditional Fourth of July celebration, the southeastern Alaska Ski Championships in March, and the Boat Show in April.

Night Life—Two movie theaters, the Capitol and the Twentieth Century, show the most current features. There are seventeen bars, the Red Dog Saloon being the most famous with frontier atmosphere and occasional entertainment.

The Baranof Hotel has dancing nightly in the Bubble Room. Other dances and parties held under the auspices of civic, fraternal, or business organizations are numerous and invitations are frequently extended to visitors. Most of these events are informal, and notices of dates and times appear in the local newspapers.

SIDE TRIPS

Glacier Highway goes north out of Juneau approximately twenty-eight miles and is of particular interest. The highway is lined with country homes, summer cottages, fur farms, and dairy land, and goes through forests of hemlock, cedar, and blue-tipped spruce. Alpine bluebells grow on the mountainsides and wild flowers are abundant along the way, growing in mixed clusters of purple lupine, wild hyacinth, yellow cowslip, dwarfed dogwood, fireweed, bog laurel, yellow water lily, and violets. Thirteen miles from Juneau is Mendenhall Glacier, jumbled masses of rocky moraine, and remnants of a buried forest sheared off by the advancing ice and later exposed when the ice retreated. This is one of the few glaciers in the world that can be reached by auto. The strange blue of the seventeen-mile-long ice mass, crevices, caverns, and swift streams of water that flow at its edges can be viewed from trails on either side of the glacier. It is easily accessible from the recreation area on the Mendenhall Loop road where there is a small campground, drinking water, sanitary facilities and, on the same road, two other comparable recreation areas are located at Skaters Cabin and at Dredge Lake.

Along Glacier Highway is Auke Bay, a sport-fishing center. Auke Village, fifteen miles north of Juneau and two miles west of Auke Bay, has a large campground with bathhouses. There is good boating, salmon fishing, totems, a beach, drinking water, picnic tables, fireplaces, and sanitary facilities. A similar recreation area is two and one-half miles further along the highway at Lena Cove. At Auke Bay community there are two grocery stores and a hardware store.

Tee Harbor, the loading point for passengers and autos traveling the seventy miles to Haines by ferry, is located nineteen miles out the Glacier Highway and is one of the starting points for contestants in the Salmon Derby. The Shrine of St. Therese, just off the highway, is a Catholic retreat located on a small island connected by bridge to the mainland. The chapel is built of stone in a beautiful miniature setting of trees and foliage, and visitors are welcome.

Hiking trails lead from the city of Juneau to the top of Mount Roberts and Mount Juneau. The four-and-a-half-mile trail to the 3,600-foot summit of Mount Roberts goes through a dense forest of evergreens and wild flowers, and the view from the top of the inland waters, mountains, and glaciers is spectacular. Other trails are at Basin Road and Salmon Creek, maintained and marked for hikers.

The Treadway mine in Douglas and the Alaska-Juneau mines in Juneau can be visited, but neither is in operation and there are no conducted tours of the properties.

Hoonah—The native village of Hoonah, a typical Alaskan fishing village, is about seventy-five miles southwest of Juneau and can be reached by boat and plane from Juneau. There are three stores, one crab cannery, and a salmon cannery one and one-half miles from the village. Hoonah has one of the best harbors in Alaska, a new school, and a health clinic. There are no overnight accommodations and no restaurants.

Angoon—This is a colorful Indian village situated on a narrow neck of land between Chatham Straits and Kootznahoo Inlet on Admiralty Island about sixty miles south of Juneau. There is one school, five teachers, and a general store with everything from candy bars to purse seine boats costing as high as $70,000. The population of Angoon is about 375, with four churches— Presbyterian, Salvation Army, Pentecostal, and Russian Ortho- dox—but no hotels or restaurants. The only possible place for a transient to stay overnight is the home of the Alaska Coastal Airlines agent.

Alaska Coastal Airlines from Juneau goes to Angoon three

times a week for mail delivery but it has charter service for passengers at any time. The Island Transportation Company of Juneau handles freight for the community.

The village is almost deserted in summertime when the men go fishing and the women go to work in the canneries at other towns. A health nurse is stationed in the village all year around. Some of the natives are engaged in handcrafts, making moccasins from hair-fur seals and weaving baskets. The town site is considered very old and anthropologists have found evidences of arrowheads and native artifacts within three or four feet of the ground surface predating the white occupation of Alaska.

There are two local basketball teams that play in the Recreation Hall where Saturday night dances and occasional church socials are also held. Hunting and fishing are good and the beach has a good supply of clams and cockles. There is some agriculture and plenty of wild berries. Prices for staple products are from 50 to 80 per cent higher than Seattle, and as a result, most of the residents shop from mail-order catalogues.

Glacier Bay National Monument—Glacier Bay National Monument can be reached by chartered plane or boat from Juneau and is one hundred miles northwest of Juneau by boat. It contains nearly 3,600 square miles and the bay itself is about 50 miles long. It is fed by glaciers that descend from towering mountains clothed in perpetual snow. There are over twenty tremendous glaciers and many others almost equally impressive, illustrating all stages, from actively moving ice masses to those that are nearly stagnant and slowly dying.

These glaciers are rivers of ice, hundreds, sometimes thousands of feet deep, which flow slowly down the mountain valleys because of the great weight of the snow and ice constantly accumulating at their sources, high in the mountains. Along the southeast coast of Alaska, drenched by a continuous succession of westward-moving storms born in the Aleutian region, such glaciers are fed so constantly that many of them flow all the way to the ocean where they end in towering cliffs.

The famous Muir Glacier, one of the most active on the Alaska coast, has a sheer face rising from 265 feet above the water, and is nearly two miles wide.

The southeast end of the monument, toward the mouth of Glacier Bay, is thick with spruce and hemlock. A visitor by boat or plane, with an opportunity to go ashore, can push through the low, dense alder thickets beyond the beach and step into a luxuriant primeval forest where perhaps no man has walked before.

Alaska brown bears, grizzlies, black bears, and the rare bluish color phase called the glacier bear, inhabit these forests, as do marten, mink, red fox, beaver, wolverine, and Sitka black-tailed deer.

Visitors are likely to see mountain goats among the lofty crags on Mount Wright, and glimpse porpoises and spouting whales in the broad, sheltered stretches of the bay, or hair seals asleep on the floating ice cakes. Large numbers of waterfowl dot the coves and inlets. Spawning salmon crowd the rushing streams in the spring, attracting many bears, particularly in Bear Track Cove where the animals have worn broad, winding trails along the stream banks.

Flying time from Juneau to the monument is about thirty minutes one way via Alaska Coastal Airlines or chartered plane. A small boat requires about three and one-half days for the same trip. The best overnight anchorages are located at Bartlett Cove, North and South Sandy coves, Hugh Miller Inlet, and Berg Bay.

Floating ice sometimes occurs in enormous quantities at the foot of the glaciers in the upper end of the bay. Ice blocks, some of which are over 250 feet high, continually crack off the faces of the glaciers, crashing into the sea and creating waves as much as 30 feet high. Therefore, small boats are warned not to approach closer than half a mile to active glaciers. Icebergs should not be approached closely because, if disturbed by swells from a small boat in passing, they may roll over.

Shoals and kelp beds are present. Daily tides average between eighteen and twenty feet, and surveys of the area are incomplete. For these reasons, and because of the frequency of Alaska coastal storms, navigation of the bay by small boats is not considered safe unless an expert guide is along.

Admiralty Island Recreation Area—Admiralty Island covers an area of over one million acres of excellent fishing, and some restricted hunting, boating, hiking, photography, and mountain climbing. While this is a wilderness area, it has been made accessible by a system of trails, boats, and shelter cabins constructed and maintained by the Forest Service.

The recreation area is most easily reached by seaplane, available in Juneau, Petersburg, and Ketchikan. About thirty minutes is required to reach Camp Sha-heen by plane from Juneau. Another way of reaching Admiralty Island is by charter boat available at any of the coast towns. The travel time by boat from Juneau to the east-side harbors where the trails begin is from nine to ten hours.

Three main trails on the island lead from marked points on the coast to the lakes, and the entire lake system of the recreation area is made accessible by boats and trails between lakes.

Eleven shelter cabins are available to visitors on Admiralty Island. They are of log and shake construction with one side open, adaptable for campfire heating and cooking, located at the beginning of all trails leading to the lakes, as well as on the lakes themselves. There are no cooking utensils or facilities for sleeping at these cabins.

On the south bank of Pack Creek, about a quarter of a mile from tidewater, a secure platform with roof, guardrail, and seats, reached by an iron ladder some twenty-five feet in height, has been built by the Forest Service around a large spruce tree, affording a safe place of concealment for observing and photographing the numerous bears while they are fishing in the creek.

Camp Sha-heen lodge was built by the Forest Service on the east side of Hasselborg Lake at an attractive point where the lake narrows. It is a log structure 14 by 20 feet with three rooms, consisting of a combined kitchen, living room, and two bedrooms each containing a double-deck, double-width bunk. The kitchen is equipped with cookstove and a few cooking utensils. This lodge is open for public use without permit. The only requirements state that the premises be kept clean and the stovewood replaced. The regional forester at Juneau should be consulted about the availability of the lodge.

Flat-bottom skiffs for public use are well distributed at Admiralty Island's various shelter cabins. The majority are twelve feet in length and should not carry more than three persons and a small amount of luggage. A few sixteen-foot skiffs will safely carry five persons and their gear. All boats are designed for outboard motor use but are also equipped with oars. The maximum-sized motor suggested for the smaller skiffs is three horsepower, and five horsepower for the larger. It is imperative that each skiff be returned to the place from which it is taken.

RESORTS

Taku Lodge is located thirty miles southeast of Juneau on the bank of the Taku River, four miles above Taku Glacier. It is reached by the M.S. *Redwing,* a river boat, or by plane with Alaska Coastal Airways from Juneau.

There are accommodations for forty-eight people in charming rustic log cabins with stone fireplaces and all modern conveniences, including hot showers and electricity. The cabins house from two to six people. The rates are $20 a day per person, American plan, and fine food is served family style in the main lodge.

The lodge carries a supply of hunting and fishing equipment and clothing which may be purchased or rented; experienced guides are on hand for hunting and fishing excursions.

There is good swimming in a warm-water lake, plenty of opportunities to fish, take pictures, hike, or go out in the river boats. Hole-in-Wall Glacier is immediately out the front door of the lodge.

Tongass Lodge, at Excursion Inlet, fifteen minutes from Juneau by plane on Alaska Coastal Airlines, offers hiking, swimming, boating, tennis, archery, hunting, and fishing. For strictly Alaskan sights, the canneries, the gold and silver mines, the sawmill, the historical Indian cemetery, and Tlingit Indians fashioning handcrafts should be seen. There are eighty-five miles of roads weaving in and out of the dense forests. Tongass Lodge is open from May 30 until Labor Day, and the rates are $18 per day per person. The hearty meals feature seafoods, and the sleeping accommodations are comfortable and attractive.

Professional and office workers are usually in demand but otherwise there are not many job opportunities in Juneau or Douglas. The federal and state government agencies have openings occasionally. Tourist travel to Juneau is expected to increase considerably and there are business opportunities for building recreation sites, lodgings, and facilities to handle the influx.

Housing—It takes several weeks to locate housing facilities. There are some rentals, mostly apartments and a few houses for lease. Apartment rentals range from $75 to $150 a month and there are approximately twenty-nine apartment houses. The leading one is Mendenhall Apartments which has one- and two-bedroom efficiency apartments that may be rented furnished or unfurnished. Houses rent between $125 and $185. Heating is primarily oil and cooking is by electricity or bottled gas.

Haines and Port Chilkoot

Haines and Port Chilkoot, adjoining communities, are the only cities in southeastern Alaska with direct motor service to the other states and Canada, being the starting point of the Haines Highway which extends 159 miles to the Alaska Highway.

The twin cities, surrounded by Rainbow Glacier and towering mountain ranges, stand on the Lynn Canal which marks the northernmost tip of the Inside Passage.

Though Haines is noted for its giant strawberries and other fine garden produce, fishing is the primary industry. Two canneries and two lumbermills are in operation. The Port Chilkoot Cannery and Smoker prepares delicious smoked salmon and other delicacies for market.

The Colby Lumber Company has a mill capable of fifteen thousand board-feet daily output and is located one mile from the downtown areas. The Moose Valley Lumber Company, twenty-eight miles away, is capable of fifteen thousand board-feet per day. Both mills supply local sales and ship lumber to interior Alaska by truck via the Alaska Highway.

Port Chilkoot has the Alaska-Yukon Refiners and Distributors, Ltd., tidewater pumping and storage terminus of their 3,000-

barrel-per-day oil pipe line to the Yukon and interior Alaska, as well as a 6,500-barrel-per-day oil refinery. The United States Army operates a $30,000,000 8-inch pipe line between Haines and Fairbanks.

The area is strategically located for industrial expansion. The Klukwan Iron Mine, one of the richest magnetite deposits in the world, is only twenty-two miles away and a mountain of limestone touches the highway thirty-eight miles from tidewater. In near-by British Columbia and Yukon Territory, there are rich copper, nickel, cobalt, lead, asbestos, silver, and gold ores.

TRANSPORTATION TO HAINES AND PORT CHILKOOT

Alaska Coastal Airlines flies to Haines from Juneau and is the connecting air line for Pan-American World Airways or Pacific Northern Airlines. Canadian Pacific Steamships and Alaska Cruise Lines transport passengers to Juneau and the M.V. *Chilkat* Car and Passenger Ferry operates regularly during May through September, carrying passengers and cars between Juneau, Skagway, and Haines.

By automobile, Haines Junction, which is Mile 1016 on the Alaska Highway, is the turnoff point for the Haines Highway. Driving south from Haines Junction the road is well-graded gravel to the Canadian border and is smooth macadam from the border to Haines. Canadian customs are located at the border, United States customs are in Haines.

LOCAL TRANSPORTATION

Takhin Air Service and Haines Air Service have charter planes, rates are about $30 per hour, and there are boats for hire, but there is no auto rental service or city bus service. Taxi service is very limited.

HOTELS, FOOD, AND SERVICES

The Halsingland at Port Chilkoot is the leading hotel and thirteen of its thirty-eight rooms have baths. There is a family-style dining room serving Swedish-American cooking. Rooms are $5 for a single, $6 to $10 for a double. This hotel also has dormitory accommodations, family rates, and the American plan available on request. The hotel is open from March 15 to December 15. The Chilkoot Inn offers single rooms at $4 to $7, double $5 to $12. Haines has three hotels, the Gateway, rates $7 for a single and $10 for a double; the Schnabel, $5 single and $7 double; and the Grand View, $3.50 single and $5 double, and all are neat and clean.

Except for the dining room at the Halsingland Hotel, other dining facilities are limited to a few cafés in Haines where the food is plain.

The communities have a few stores for shopping; there are good schools, churches, a Lions' Club, Elks' Club, American Legion Post, Women's Club, and Business and Professional Club.

ACTIVITIES

The Haines Strawberry Festival is the big annual event, held in July of each year. Several beaches for swimming are popular during the summer season. Port Chilkoot Beach has an abundance of driftwood and colored pebbles, and the swimming is best at high tide. Chilkat Inlet or Pyramid Island Beach on Mud Bay Road is the site of an ancient Indian village with good views of the islands and glaciers. There is good hunting and fishing.

Sheldon's Museum in Haines is in the original Jack Dalton house, built in 1898. There is a private collection of Indian and gold-rush curios.

Old Porcupine Mine and Ghost Town, across the Klihini River, thirty-five miles away, is an abandoned gold-rush town on the old Dalton Trail. Some placer mining is still being done on Porcupine Creek.

At Klukwan, twenty-one miles out, is an early village of the Tlingit Indian tribe with a population of sixty-six. This is the home of the Chilkat blankets where ceremonial costumes, blankets, hats, carvings, and other relics are on display. There is a graveyard with totem grave markers. A few canoe makers are still living in the village and during summer their canoes are in use on the river for salmon fishing. It was recently discovered that the village is sitting on a very rich deposit of iron ore and the land has been leased for mining.

Other sights in the Haines-Port Chilkoot area that may be

visited are the Haines Packing Company, the pipe-line operations, and the Craft Shop Factory, which produces Alaskan birch and yellow cedar bowls and other wood products.

Camping facilities are located at Haines City Park and Picnic Ground, one mile north of Haines. The Fort William H. Seward Park and Recreation Area is one-quarter mile out on Mud Bay Road. Madsen's Birchdale Park and Homestead, six and one-half miles out on Mud Bay Road, is the best spot to view Rainbow Glacier; it has a small boat float and launching area. Chilkoot Lake, nine and one-half miles on the Lutak Road, is at the edge of the Chilkoot River, and Mosquito Lake is two and one-half miles on a turnoff at Mile 28 on the Haines Highway. The camping areas are not developed and it is necessary to carry all equipment, including drinking water.

Alaska Holiday Adventures, Inc., in Haines offers two to five hours of "Sourdough Guided" sight-seeing trips in the area, priced from $4 to $8, with half rates for children.

PROSPECTIVE SETTLERS

The strategic location of these communities indicates the possibilities for business and industrial expansion requiring considerable capital investments. There is no employment for outsiders and housing facilities are almost nonexistent. Developing and building a home and business requires personal investigation, especially in this area which looks hopeful but has an unknown potential.

Skagway

Skagway, which means "home of the north winds," has retained much of the atmosphere of the gold-rush days. Tread-board sidewalks, false-front buildings, and many of the original landmarks of the days of '98 stand as reminders of Skagway's rough history when it was the gateway to Dawson City and the Klondike, a boom town swarming with prospectors and miners. It is a triangle-shaped town wedged against the mountains of the White Pass and dwarfed by the steep seven-thousand-foot mountains around it. As the southern terminal for the 110-mile White Pass and Yukon Route railway to Whitehorse, Y.T., Canada, Skagway was an important distribution point during World War II for the supplies used in the building of the Alaska Highway.

Skagway's main industry is transportation. It is the entrance for the shortest and the only all-weather surface route into the Yukon Territory, and quantities of freight are handled on its docks and by the railroad which has given Skagway's seven hundred residents steady year-round employment and a stable economy for many years.

TRANSPORTATION TO SKAGWAY

The White Pass and Yukon Route from Whitehorse, Y.T., has a daily schedule, and transports autos and freight as well as passengers. Canadian Pacific and Alaska Cruise Lines have excellent summer service. Alaska Coastal Airlines operates daily between Skagway and Juneau. The Chilkat Ferry provides service during the summer months between Skagway, Juneau, and Haines.

HOTELS, FOOD, AND SERVICES

The Pullen House is a colorful old hotel with singles from $4 to $7 and doubles $7 to $12. There is also the new Sourdough Inn, the Golden North Hotel, which is newly decorated in Gay 90's style, with a coffee shop, dining room, and cocktail lounge, Skagway Inn, and Pack Train Inn. The local cafés have plain American food.

There are three general merchandise stores, a bakery, drugstore, photo shop, movie theater, beauty parlor, barbershop, two cafés, a soda fountain, one bank, a laundry and dry-cleaning service, jewelry and gift shops, taxi services, and approximately thirty other business establishments in the community. The schools are housed in modern buildings; there is a parochial school for native children and a public library. The community has a small hospital, a landing field, and beautiful flower, vegetable, and berry gardens.

ACTIVITIES

In summer the residents dress up in gala frontier costumes to stage a production of "The Shooting of Dan McGrew" and re-enact "The Days of '98" every time steamers arrive with visitors.

Boats can be chartered for fishing. Both the city and Pullen House have pioneer museums with relics and artifacts of the area, and most of the historic landmarks in town are marked, including "Soapy Smith's" grave at the Gold Rush Cemetery, the old Pack Train Saloon, and many other pioneer sights.

At the ghost town, Dyea, fifteen miles by gravel road west of Skagway, there is a trail leading to the foot of Chilkoot Pass over which the miners and prospectors struggled to reach the Klondike.

Whitehorse, Y. T., Canada

Everyone traveling to Alaska via the White Pass and Yukon Route and on the Alaska Highway will go through the town of Whitehorse and many will stop over in this major city of the Yukon.

By ruling of the Canadian government in 1953, Whitehorse was made the capital of the Yukon Territory. Nearly half of the twelve thousand people of the Yukon live in Whitehorse, where some of the firm log buildings from the gold-rush days are still standing, and where summer visitors to this busy, modern community can attend evening lectures in the Old Log Church in which Robert W. Service wrote his famous "Songs of the Sourdough." There are many north country sights to see and things to do in the area. Hunting and fishing are excellent but non-resident hunters are required to hire a guide if they intend to hunt.

One of the points of interest is Miles Canyon south of the city, where the rapids claimed the lives of many early settlers. Another worth-while side trip covers the original Trail of '98 on the White Pass and Yukon Route's railroad from Whitehorse to Skagway.

Museum—In the downtown business section of Whitehorse, one of the historical landmarks, the two-story log building, erected in 1900 to house the government telegraph and personnel, is now the W. D. MacBride Museum, and displays a large and captivating collection of artifacts and historical documents of the Yukon Territory. It is open to the public from May 15 to September 15, from

7:30 to 9:00 P.M. every evening except Sundays; at other times, visits can be arranged by appointment.

TRANSPORTATION TO WHITEHORSE

The city is reached by car on the Alaska Highway or by scheduled bus service operated by Canadian Coachways, and White Pass and Yukon Route. Canadian Pacific Airlines has daily flights from Edmonton and Vancouver. A boat-train summer service operates from Vancouver and Seattle via Skagway. Connelly Airlines in Dawson City, Pacific Western Airlines in Whitehorse, and Dalzeil's Flying Service in Watson Lake will arrange chartered flights.

HOTELS, FOOD, AND SERVICES

All modern services are available in the thriving community including first-class medical and hospital facilities. The list of accommodations is headed by the Taku Hotel with a coffee shop and cocktail lounge. Rates for the twenty-eight rooms with baths are $8 for singles, $13 for doubles, with special rates during the winter months. In addition to a bowling alley and ballroom for dancing, the White Horse Inn has a café and cocktail lounge, and ninety-four rooms with or without bath at $6 to $7 for singles and $8 to $12 for doubles.

Yakutat

Yakutat is a small Alaskan fishing village of about 290 people located on Yakutat Bay. Approximately 216 miles northwest of Juneau, it faces the gigantic Malaspina Glacier which is larger than the state of Rhode Island and reaches to a height of 2,500 feet. This glacier, in addition to its great size, is a rare example of a kind that existed during the Ice Age in Great Britain, the Rocky Mountains, and Norway.

The Yakutat area is noted primarily for excellent hunting, fishing, and magnificent scenery, but there are also interesting remains of the old Russian penal colony which once contained a blockhouse and stockade that was razed by the natives in about 1803. A short-line railroad connects the village with the Situk and Los River fishing camps but the railroad cars are trucks fitted with rail wheels used primarily to carry fish to the cannery.

The airfield built during World War II is one of the largest in Alaska. There is a year-round weather bureau and a United States Coast Guard Station. Approximately one hundred Civil Aeronautics Administration employees are stationed in Yakutat to maintain the various government installations.

A few native handcrafts are made for sale in Yakutat including moccasins and there is one totem carver and one basket-maker. Jay B. Mallott's General Store is the major shopping center, complete with lunch counter. One other store is operated by the local cannery.

Yakutat can be reached by plane from either Juneau or Anchorage via Pacific Northern Airlines or bush pilot. The only accommodations are room and board in bunk lodgings at the airport, run by the Colorado Gas and Oil Company. The cost is about $10 per day.

CHAPTER VII. WESTERN ALASKA

Anchorage—Katmai National Monument—Matanuska Valley—Kenai Peninsula—Valdez—Cordova—Kodiak — King Cove — Pribilof Islands — Bethel — Hooper Bay

On the upper curve of the Gulf of Alaska, bordered by the 150-mile-wide Alaska Range, is the south central coast line. Numerous mineral deposits exist in the Alaska Range, the monumental chain of mountains that is peaked by Mount McKinley, the highest in North America, towering 20,320 feet. There are immense glaciers and volcanoes in the areas near the coast and in the nearby mountains. And there, too, is the renowned Matanuska Valley and fertile Kenai Peninsula.

To the west is Bristol Bay, a great salmon fishing area known to be rich in fur and deposits of gold, platinum, antimony, and other minerals. And to the north is a vast inland region that is wild and little explored. Beyond Bristol Bay are the southernmost waters of the great Bering Sea, cut off from the Pacific Ocean by the long narrow Alaska Peninsula and the Aleutians. These islands are like a chain of steppingstones leading westward toward the Komandorski Islands and the Kamchatka Peninsula of Soviet Russian Siberia. Trees are nonexistent in this area, where there are slopes of moss, grass, scrub brush, glaciers, and smoking volcanoes.

Anchorage

Anchorage, the largest city in Alaska and reported to be the fastest-growing city in the nation, is as far west as the Hawaiian Islands and as far north as Helsinki, Finland.

Fourteen hundred and forty-eight air miles northwest of Seattle and 375 miles south of the Arctic Circle, this modern and progressive city is built on a bluff bordered on the east by the

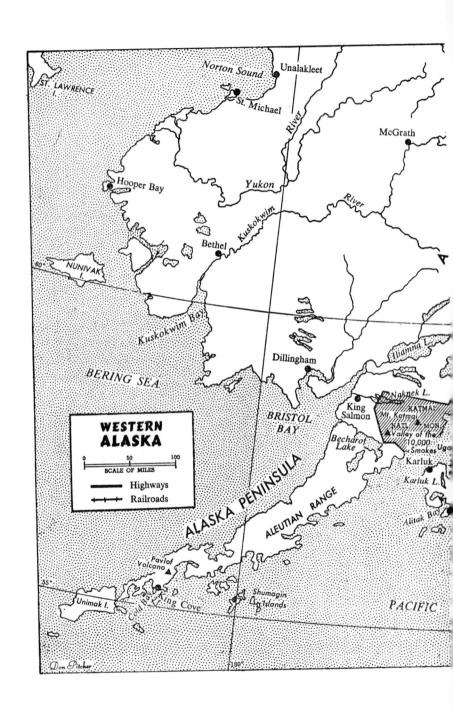

ST. LAWRENCE I.

Norton Sound

Unalakleet

St. Michael

McGrath

Hooper Bay

Yukon

River

Kuskokwim

Bethel

60°

NUNIVAK I.

River

Kuskokwim Bay

BERING SEA

Dillingham

Iliamna L.

Naknek L.

BRISTOL BAY

King Salmon

KATMAI
Mt. Katmai NAT'L MON.
Valley of the 10,000 Smokes

Becharof Lake

Uga

Karluk

WESTERN
ALASKA

0   50   100
SCALE OF MILES

Highways
Railroads

Karluk L.

ALASKA PENINSULA

ALEUTIAN RANGE

Alitak Bay

Pavlof Volcano

55°

Unimak I.

Cold Bay

King Cove

Shumagin Islands

PACIFIC

180°

Don Pitcher

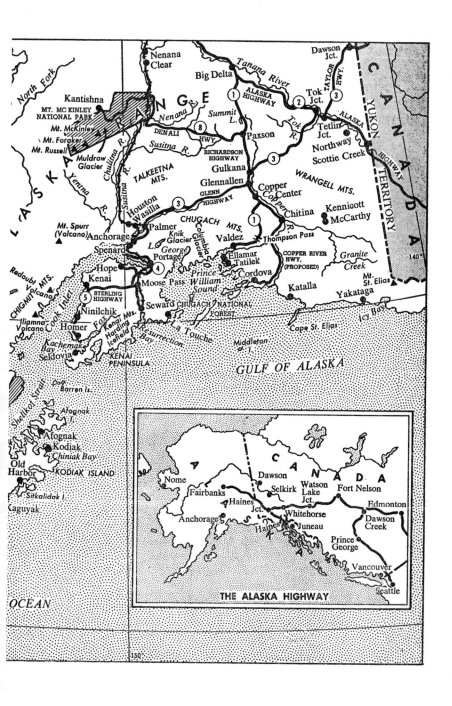

eight-thousand-foot peaks of the rugged Chugach Mountains and on the west and north by Cook Inlet. Across the inlet, in the Susitna Valley, is North America's largest stand of white birch. On the west are the active volcanoes and majestic heights of the Alaska Range.

The climate is similar to that of the northern portions of the Great Lakes states, New England, and the Scandinavian countries, with relatively moderate winters and mild summers. This climatically agreeable area first came into prominence when President Woodrow Wilson signed the Alaska Railroad Bill in 1914, 136 years after Captain James Cook, famed English explorer, had first taken possession of the area for the British Crown.

Anchorage was born when work on the Alaska Railroad started in July of 1914 and the freighter, *LaTouche*, landed a scouting party of four men with twenty-four horses near the mouth of Ship Creek. Two weeks later seventy surveyors, engineers, packers, and laborers arrived. Most of them scattered out along the proposed rail route, but some remained behind to erect buildings and corrals at Ship Creek in what is now the downtown area of the city.

The following spring, ships crowded with settlers arrived. There were no wharves and the passengers were landed upon the sticky mud flats for a trek through mud and grass to the temporary camping site. A tent town sprang up along the banks of Ship Creek, while surveyors laid out the streets of a new town on the bluff overlooking the creek.

Unlike most new towns, Anchorage did not grow up around narrow, unplanned streets created by convenience or necessity. The new city was carefully laid out and was considered a model town by planners. The 347-acre townsite had 60-foot-wide streets and spacious lots measuring 50 by 140 feet.

At two o'clock the afternoon of July 10, 1915, the auctioning of the raw new lots began. In all, 887 lots were sold for a total of $177,105 and, two years later, there was a population of over 3,000.

Railroading was not the only industry. Anchorage began to serve as a supply base and communication center for mining outfits and several salmon canneries were set up. A company was established to raise reindeer on the tundra and moss in the surrounding country. A lumbermill operated near Bird Creek. At the same time Anchorage was regarded as a great potential coal terminal but, after the railroad was completed in 1923, coal possibilities crumbled when the Navy announced conversion to oil.

A second boom came in 1935 when the federal government launched the Matanuska Valley Colonization Project, transplanting two hundred families from the Midwest to the Matanuska farming lands. The third big development came with the defense build-up of World War II and it is continuing because Anchorage plays a key role in the new polar military strategy.

Today the city has fancy shops, neon-lighted thoroughfares, parking meters, wide paved streets, and modern improvements of all kinds. The cost of living is about 35 per cent higher than in Seattle.

It is the retail and wholesale trade, communication, and service center for the state, particularly for all of the communities within a radius of three hundred miles, which contains approximately 70 per cent of Alaska's population. Anchorage is an international transportation center, the hub for North Pole flights between Europe and the Far East. It has the third greatest volume of air traffic of all cities in the United States, operating out of the municipal airport at Merrill Field, Anchorage International Airport, and the seaplane base at Lake Hood.

It is also the focal point for the Alaska Railroad, trucking, and other distribution facilities. The Port of Anchorage is the site of new $8,700,000 docking facilities.

Headquarters for 50 per cent of Alaska's corporations, the annual business of the city exceeds $140,000,000, with retail sales of over $60,000,000 and military purchases amounting to $37,-000,000. The local government pay rolls exceed $119,000,000 annually. The leading nongovernmental industry is construction. The estimated population is 67,300 and a total of over 100,000 people live within a fifty-mile radius which includes Elmendorf Air Force Base and Fort Richardson.

Currently, increased interest in Alaska's natural resources promises a new development in the area. Rich oil resources were discovered in the immediate vicinity and more than $30,000,000 is being spent in the development of oil properties by major oil companies. The city is teeming with activity, as individual investors, speculators, and oil companies arrive to explore the potential. The city is headquarters for geologists, research teams, and oil executives who give it all the appearances of a booming oil town.

In the heart of the community, at Fourth Avenue and F Street, is the Chamber of Commerce tourist information cabin. Nearby is the Z. J. Loussac Public Library with over twenty-five thousand books on its shelves; a block away is the Anchorage Junior High School, directly across the street from the beautiful Anchorage Municipal Auditorium, which seats six hundred and cost $400,000.

Fourth and Fifth avenues are lined with restaurants, hotels, theaters, the Federal Building, City Hall, and the Post Office. On East Fourth is one of Anchorage's two fourteen-story apartment buildings and near by is the $7,500,000 Alaska Native Hospital. Scattered about the downtown area are log cabins from the old days, ultramodern office buildings, homes, a park reserve, and a fine children's playground.

The Alaska Railroad yards, the warehouse and industrial district, the city power plants, the fish canneries and ocean docks, are within walking distance of the downtown area.

North of the railroad yards is Government Hill, a residential area where many of the Alaska Railroad employees live, and the favorite observation points of Mount McKinley, 150 miles away and always visible on clear days. The sunsets are particularly spectacular from the heights of Government Hill.

In the eastern part of the city is Merrill Field, the city-operated airport, as well as the Fairview community, Rogers Park and Mountain View residential areas, Airport Heights, and the new Goose Lake Park recreation area. Fort Richardson and Elmendorf Air Force Base are just beyond the eastern city limits.

To the south of downtown Anchorage is the golf course and country club, the high school, and just beyond is Woodland Park and Spenard, a flourishing unincorporated business and residential area. This is the location of Lake Spenard, popular resort area for summer swimming and winter skating. The lake is linked by canal to Lake Hood, which is the airbase for float planes. Near by is the $12,500,000 Anchorage International Airport, which serves over 200,000 passengers yearly and is a huge air-freight terminal.

TRANSPORTATION TO ANCHORAGE

At Anchorage International Airport, Northwest Orient Airlines operates flights to and from major cities in the Orient, United States, and Canada, including Edmonton, Minneapolis, Washington, D.C., New York, Tokyo, the Philippines, and Hawaii.

Pacific Northern Airlines has flights to and from Seattle, Portland, Ketchikan, Juneau, Yakutat, Cordova, Kenai, Homer, King Salmon, Kodiak, and Dillingham.

Northern Consolidated operates between Anchorage and King Salmon, Dillingham, McGrath, Bethel, and Katmai, with a charter and bush service to many smaller villages throughout the state.

Alaska Airlines has plane service between Fairbanks, Seattle, Portland, McGrath, Unalakleet, Nome, and Kotzebue, and also operates a bush service.

Reeve Aleutian flies the Aleutian Islands and the Pribilofs, offering scheduled flights, charter service, and tours.

Anchorage is a refueling stop on the "short-cut" route between Scandinavia and Tokyo. It is the only stop on the *Scandinavian Airlines* polar route. Flight time from Anchorage to Tokyo is twelve and one-half hours, and to Copenhagen, fourteen and one-half hours. The Scandinavian Airlines nonstop service from Anchorage to Copenhagen, 4,400 statute miles, is one of the longest in commercial aviation. Tourist-class fares, round trip from Anchorage to Europe, begin at $811.

The *Alaska Railroad's* main "Gateway Tour" route runs a distance of 470 miles, beginning 114 miles south of Anchorage at Seward; traveling to Anchorage, it continues on to Mount McKinley National Park and ends at Fairbanks in the heart of the interior. Offering completely modern trains with Pullman berths, drawing rooms, compartments, lounge-car and dining-car accommodations; the rates between Anchorage and Fairbanks are $21.35 one way, $28.50 round trip, and include the privilege of stopovers at McKinley Park. Berths are from $6.55 to $4.70; drawing rooms from $17.75 to $19; and compartments from $11.30 to $14.45. Dining-room prices begin at $1.85 for dinner, $1.25 for breakfast, and there is a la carte service available at all hours of the day and night.

The Alaska Steamship Company handles freight only to Anchorage from Seattle, and Coastwise Lines has a freight-boat service out of San Francisco and Long Beach, California, to Anchorage. The Aero Mayflower Transit Company maintains offices in Anchorage for shipping freight, household equipment and furnishings by truck.

Major highways connect Anchorage to Seward, Kenai Peninsula, Matanuska Valley, Valdez, Fairbanks, and the Alaska Highway to Canada and other cities in the United States.

LOCAL TRANSPORTATION

There are no problems getting around the city with a choice of many twenty-four-hour taxi services, local bus transportation, tours of the city and the outlying districts, and four auto renting agencies, including Avis and Hertz, whose average rates are $10 a day plus 15 cents a mile.

At Merrill Field there are charter planes operated by Spernak Airways, Safeway, Barton Air Service, Gay Airways, and Polar Helicopters, with charter facilities for the entire state.

Lake Hood is a seaplane base where the charter services include Ward Gay's Sea Airmotive and Shellabarger's Flying Service, which also has registered guides for hunting and fishing trips in the area.

Charter boats are located along the water-front areas, including yachts, motorboats, cruisers, and small river craft.

HOTELS

Anchorage has twenty-eight hotels, nine motels, and ten trailer courts. The Traveler's Inn at Seventh and Gambell Streets has excellent accommodations, telephones, thermostatically controlled heat, tiled baths, television in the rooms, and one- or two-room units or housekeeping accommodations. Rates are, single, $9 to $9.50; double, $13 to $17.

The Westward Hotel in the heart of the city has 200 first-rate rooms and 175 baths. There is a coffee shop, cocktail lounge, and dining room. Rates are, single, $5 to $12; double, $8 to $17. Westward Inn, at Fifth and Gambell, has superior accommodations and is a combined hotel-motel with coffee shop and cocktail bar, but no pets are allowed. The rates are, single, $7.50 to $10; double, $12 to $16.

There is a bath with each room at the North Star Hotel at 1430 Gambell Street, where rates are from $8 to $9 per unit. The Anchorage Hotel has good accommodations and pleasant rooms, most with baths; rates are, single, $5 to $11; double, $8 to $16.

Restaurants

Anchorage has the greatest variety of restaurants in the state, serving foreign as well as American-style food. Prices range from $1.00 to $3.50 for breakfast, $1.50 to $4.50 for lunch, and from $3.00 to $6.00 for dinner in most of the better restaurants. The Westward Hotel serves good food in the Chart Room and can handle large banquets and parties. They feature an open-pit broiler for meats and a large menu, including breast of capon and wild rice or porterhouse steak for two at $14.

Don's Café, the Pagoda, the Jade Room, which is air-conditioned, and the Rice-Bowl specialize in Chinese foods. El Sombrero has a good selection of Mexican specialties and boasts of the only tortilla machine in Alaska. For Italian foods there is Joe's Pizza House and the Ritz Venice, which also serves French cuisine. The Garden of Eatin' in Spenard is an intimate restaurant with a good bar and attractive surroundings; the Cloudhoppers Dining Room at the International Airport features homemade rolls and pastries, while the Sabre Jet Room features a sizable menu including steaks, frog's legs, squab, wild rice, lobster, and prime ribs. In all, there are approximately twenty superior restaurants in Anchorage, plus many small coffee shops and cafés.

CHURCHES

Anchorage's churches include the Baha'i, Episcopal, Gospel, Lutheran, Baptist, Catholic, Christian Science, Church of Christ and Church of God, Nazarene, Seventh-day Adventist, Church of the Open Door, Methodist, Presbyterian, Unitarian, Temple Beth Sholom, and the Salvation Army.

SCHOOLS

The Anchorage schools are constantly striving to provide an educational program that will meet the needs and challenges of the community with some of the best schools in the state, including a new $4,000,000 high school. The high school has the finest modern gymnasium and auditorium in Alaska.

All the schools work in double shifts because of the lack of space to handle all students.

Anchorage schools are better than average in the fields of music, art, physical education, and vocational education at the high school level. Instructional materials are of a high standard and include visual aids, maps, globes, recording equipment, texts, references, and good library facilities, all of which contribute to the high academic standards.

The elementary buildings have multipurpose rooms. These schools operate educational clinics to meet rehabilitation needs for those pupils who have missed some of the fundamental stages of education, or have had their education interrupted by frequent moves.

The school system includes the Anchorage Community College, Anchorage High School, Anchorage Junior High School, and eleven elementary schools. Enrollment is nearly nine thousand students.

The Anchorage Community College, sponsored jointly by the school district and the University of Alaska, opened its doors in 1954. It is accredited and credits are accepted in universities and colleges anywhere in the nation. It is possible to earn an Associate of Arts degree or receive on-the-job training in many occupations. College is held in the new high school building in the evening hours, offering over sixty courses of study and excellent library facilities.

Ground has been broken for the $4,000,000 Alaska Methodist University in the Goose Lake area on the east side of Anchorage. The university plans to accommodate one thousand students and will begin classes in the fall of 1960.

SHOPPING AND SERVICES

The city has complete shopping facilities and services. Among the more than 2,500 licensed business firms, there are superdrugstores and supermarkets, and three banks including the City National, First National, and National Bank of Alaska. There are twenty beauty shops, five dance studios, five large department stores, plus two branches of Montgomery Ward's, five florists, two steam baths, three physical therapy services, three pawnshops, and several travel agencies, including Arctic Alaska Travel Service at 616 Fourth Street and Polaris Travel Service at 337 Fifth Street. Many stores remain open until late in the evening for shoppers and visitors.

Health—Medical facilities and services are excellent in the Anchorage area. There are two large and modern hospitals, three medical clinics, over forty-two physicians, and two animal hospitals.

Telephone and Telegraph—Complete communication facilities are available twenty-four hours a day.

Publications—Two daily newspapers, the *Times* and the *News*, are published in Anchorage. "This Month in Anchorage" is distributed free in the hotel lobbies, giftshops, travel agencies, and by business firms in the area, and gives the most current news of activities and events, not only of Anchorage but of the many surrounding communities including Seward and Palmer.

Radio and Television—KENI-TV and KTVA, the C.B.S. affiliate, present all the major television programs and local telecasts. Radio station KENI has the unique program "Mukluk Telegraph," heard six nights a week at nine thirty. This program is used to relay messages to people who live out in the bush, such as the trappers, homesteaders, missionaries, and prospectors; it broadcasts family and personal news, such as the arrival of new babies and word of successful operations, calls for jury duty, the place workers should report for jobs, and the arrival of bush pilots with groceries, packages, and passengers at out-of-the-way landing strips and isolated waterways. Other radio stations are KFQD and KBYR.

CIVIC AND SOCIAL ORGANIZATIONS

Anchorage has many civic, fraternal, social, and business organizations which are active throughout the entire Greater Anchorage area. They include: Odd Fellows, Masons, Eastern Star, Eagles, Elks, Moose, Rebekahs, Pioneers of Alaska, Daughters of the American Revolution, PEO Sisterhood, American Legion, Toastmasters and Toastmistresses, Hadassah, Veterans of Foreign Wars, Lions, American Association of University Women, Inlet Potters, Mental Health Association, Alaska Crippled Children's Association, and approximately 150 more.

The YMCA and two USO clubs are located in Anchorage and there are more than thirty-five homemakers' clubs, garden clubs, and other local organizations.

The city has Boy Scouts, Girl Scouts, the Anchorage Teen Club, Rainbow Girls, DeMolay, Civil Air Patrol cadets, and youth fellowships.

ACTIVITIES

Many concerts are given by the Anchorage Symphony Orchestra throughout the year. This superior music organization also sponsors the Alaska Music Trails concert series, importing fine artists from all over the world to appear during the winter concert season. The Anchorage Community Chorus has weekly meetings to plan and rehearse for their numerous winter and summer concerts.

The Little Theater has a winter theater series in addition to the presentations of the Community College's Theater Workshop. The city's two new auditoriums, the six-hundred-seat Anchorage Municipal Auditorium and the larger four-thousand-seater at Anchorage High School, are active community centers for a wide variety of entertainment, providing facilities for the orchestra, theater, and choral groups, as well as concerts and special foreign and domestic art film programs sponsored by the Anchorage Film

Society. Lectures and meetings are held in the public library building.

For visitors and residents, Anchorage has many folk dance, square dance, and ballet groups. Shops and public buildings feature art and craft exhibits of local artisans and one of the leading art organizations, Studio One, has been established as a conservatory for instruction and exhibition. There are mining and prospecting clubs, historical societies, photography clubs, and just about every kind of hobby club one can think of.

In sport and recreation there are the Izaak Walton League, Alaska Range Association, dog mushers and sled-dog groups, the Ski Club and Skating Club, baseball, basketball, tennis, hockey, curling, and many more athletic organizations. The Trap Shooters Association holds trapshooting meets every Sunday, weather permitting, and organizes hunting parties for members and guests. There is an indoor swimming pool at the Spa.

The high-school games have an enthusiastic following by the entire community. Inter-Alaskan basketball games are scheduled between the various high schools throughout the state. Teams and sizable groups of home-town boosters make the trips from city to city, often covering distances of five hundred miles or more. In the city active leagues in baseball, softball, and basketball are sponsored by the local business firms.

An Inter-Alaskan tennis tournament is held on the city tennis courts annually. On the longest day of each year, local golfers participate in a "short nighters" round at the nine-hole golf course at Forest Park Country Club. The golfers play in the twilight of the Midnight Sun at midnight. Championship matches for men and women are held in September, with a special "Governor's Cup Match" as one of the high-light events.

The Jonas Brothers of Alaska maintain a free museum with the most complete collection of mounted Alaskan animals in the state. Many are the prize record-winners, including one of the largest salmon ever caught, the largest walrus, polar bear, mountain sheep, and Kodiak bear.

At Parliament Stadium, there are stock-car races every Friday night combined with motorcycle races. The stadium is located on the Base Cut-off Road just past Boniface Road. Every Sunday, motor races at the Alaska Speedway are held by the Alaska Race Car Owners and Drivers Association. The Alaska Speedway is a quarter mile of paved track located on the corner of Bragaw and DeBarr roads in Mountain View.

The Anchorage area is one of the best places in the state to enjoy winter activities. The ski runs are at Arctic Valley, just ten miles from the center of the city, and at Mount Alyeska, near Girdwood, some thirty-eight miles south of Anchorage. Arctic Valley has six rope tows, warming huts, and hot meals. The ski season is from December to March, with dry powder snow prevailing throughout the entire winter. Many tournaments are held during the ski season.

Ice skating on the several outdoor rinks is a winter-long sport in Anchorage. The weather is mild enough so that ice hockey is featured at lighted outdoor arenas during the evening hours.

Bowling in the Anchorage area is a very popular sport. There are a total of fifty-two lanes in the city, with sixteen more at Fort Richardson and twenty-six at Elmendorf with plans to open another twenty-four lanes. In the downtown Anchorage area the alleys include the Anchor Bowl and Elks Lanes; the Center Bowl is in Spenard. All have automatic pinspotters and alleys of the most modern design.

Annual events—There are three big annual events in Anchorage beginning with the week-long winter carnival, the Anchorage Fur Rendezvous, which takes place in February. The Anchorage Music Festivals are held in June and the last of August, and the Elmendorf Carnival in July or August includes open house at the Air Force Base.

Night life—Anchorage has three motion picture theaters. The Fourth Avenue Theater is one of the finest in the state showing only first-run pictures. There are also the Denali and Empress theaters. All change programs about twice a week. Cocktail bars and nightclubs are everywhere in the city, especially in the downtown area, and many feature a friendly atmosphere and dancing to two- or three-piece combos but there are seldom floorshows or live entertainment. During the summer, swimming, auto racing, golf, baseball, and other outdoor activities continue into the late evening hours. The Forest Park Country Club features entertainment nightly and many of the affairs are open to the public. The club room serves cocktails; there is dining and dancing, and visitors are welcome. Nearly all entertainment and night life in Anchorage are informal.

Campgrounds—Picnic and camping areas, maintained by the Bureau of Land Management, are conveniently located near Anchorage, but they do not have facilities for trailer houses and stays are limited to one week at each campground. These are: Bird Creek, 25 miles south of Anchorage on the Seward Highway; McHugh Creek, 15 miles south of Anchorage at Mile 12 on the Seward Highway; Eagle River, at Mile 13 on the Glenn Highway; Peters Creek, at Mile 21.7 on the Glenn Highway. Thunderbird Falls, at Mile 26 on the Glenn Highway and one-half mile east by trail has a picnic area, fishing, hunting, boating, and swimming facilities similar to Finger Lake, 10 miles west from Palmer on Finger Lake road; Moose Creek, Mile 54.5 on the Glenn Highway; and Big Lake Number One and Two, 31 miles west of Palmer via Wasilla.

At each campground a pile of fuel wood is normally available and additional wood may be gathered using only dead or fallen timber; the cutting of standing trees is prohibited. All fires should be built in the existing fireplaces and thoroughly extinguished before leaving the area. Sanitary facilities are available at each site.

PROSPECTIVE SETTLERS

Seasonal fluctuations cause sharp changes in employment between summer and winter. The construction industry employs a large number of workers, but it is highly seasonal, with few opportunities for year-round employment. The total number of workers employed in the winter is about a quarter of the number normally employed during the peak summer season. Many persons are attracted to Anchorage by the high wages of the construction industry and by the possibility of enhancing their income, but existing resident and transient labor normally fills the needs. Even when the demand is good, newcomers face a waiting period and must have a financial reserve to avoid hardship. At least $400 per month per person should be allowed while looking for work in the Anchorage area, with extra funds to provide for return transportation if it is needed. The combination of time spent looking for a job and the higher cost of living in the Anchorage area can deplete personal savings.

Because of the surge in transient population as a result of statehood, the surplus labor force has tripled in the Anchorage area and is not expected to decline appreciably in the immediate future.

Since many defense construction jobs are in remote locations, there is no family housing at such places and workers frequently must set up homes for their families in Anchorage and be separated from them for long intervals.

Construction workers planning to seek work in Anchorage should first contact the union to establish some assurance of a job before traveling to Anchorage.

There are recurring demands for certain occupational classifications which are usually in short supply. These include most professional engineering classifications, electronic and radio technicians, medical technicians, stenographers, and secretaries. A number of these jobs are with government agencies and are filled through civil service registers.

The business opportunities that exist are similar to those of any city of comparable size. Most basic services and shops are already established and new business firms must compete by offering better services, and more comprehensive or specialized merchandise. Greater Anchorage is considered a good potential business area and the Anchorage Chamber of Commerce, as well as the Alaska Resource Development Board in Juneau, both offer reports and surveys of substantial interest to the prospective businessman considering a Greater Anchorage business location.

The labor organizations with offices in Anchorage include: American Federation of Technical Engineers, Bartenders, Bricklayers, Building Service Employees International, Carpenters, Hotel and Restaurant Employees, International Ironworkers, International Machinists, Electrical, Longshoreman and Operating Engineers, Laborers and Hod Carriers, Lathers, Laundry and Dry Cleaners, Painters, Pile Drivers, Plasterers, Plumbers, Retail Clerks, Sheet Metal Workers, and Teamsters unions.

Housing—Anchorage has seventeen major apartment buildings, with a total of 2,281 units. There are frequent vacancies. Rents are high, ranging from $119 for an efficiency apartment to $155 for a one-bedroom apartment and about $165 for a two-bedroom unit. Luxury apartments are $300 up, and many of the lower rentals are in substandard housing. House rentals are higher priced than apartments, renting from $145 to $185 a month for a two-bedroom house. New homes are being built throughout the city, the suburbs, and in building developments. Prices range from $25,000 to $45,000 for two- and three-bedroom houses, approximately 50 per cent higher than comparable units in other states. There is considerable competition among the local builders but the prices are reasonably stable. The Anchorage economy has fostered a more permanent population, which gives the city a better grade of housing than other cities in Alaska with more transient populations.

The utilities in Anchorage are municipally owned. Garbage collection is weekly at residences and costs $2 a month. In apartment houses each unit pays $1.75 per month. Monthly water rates in the city are $4.75 for homes, $4.25 for apartments, $3.00 for cabins, and $1.50 in rented rooms. Telephones are from $8 to $13.50 a month on a single party line. Electricity is high, averaging about 4½ cents per KWH. Deposits are required for all utilities, $20 to $35 for electricity, $20 for telephone, $10 for water, $5 for garbage.

Katmai National Monument

Katmai National Monument embraces a vast mountain and lake wilderness with one of the greatest varieties of scenery, wildlife, and scientific interest of any area in the National Park system. Situated near the base of the Alaska Peninsula, less than 75 miles west of Kodiak Island, the monument's 2,697,590 acres make it the largest of all of the national parks.

On June 6, 1912, Novarupta volcano erupted and was recorded as one of the most violent eruptions ever recorded, with an explosion heard for 750 miles and fumes that were seen on Puget Sound, 1,500 miles away. For three days after the explosion, a darkness as black as an Arctic night covered the vast territory around the mountain and volcanic ash more than a foot deep was deposited over many thousands of square miles. Two hundred people lost their lives, animals became bald, and, for over a year, volcanic dust filled the air. But the volcano is now inactive, though others in the monument are not.

Evidence of the great explosion, and one of the outstanding features of the monument, is the Valley of Ten Thousand Smokes; originally there were thousands of steam jets, large and small, but today there are only a few active in the valley.

TRANSPORTATION AND ACCOMMODATIONS

The Northern Consolidated Airlines flight to Katmai from Anchorage soars over the Chigmit Mountains, Illiama and Redoubt volcanoes, and Mount Spurr, which erupted in 1953 sending a layer of volcanic ash on Anchorage, seventy-five miles away. The flight provides a full panoramic view of all the important volcanoes, mountains, and other spectacular scenery in the monument. Bush flights may also be chartered from Kodiak and Homer airports for sight-seeing trips over the monument and surrounding areas.

Northern Consolidated Airlines operates five camps in the Katmai wilderness, and their scheduled service leaves Anchorage International Airport weekly during the summer season. The camp accommodations are far from de luxe but they offer superior comforts by wilderness standards. Separate sleeping tents are equipped with wooden floors and sidewalls, and are heated. The tents have screened windows and doors, and all are equipped with steel cots, mattresses, and sleeping bags with changeable liners.

At each camp there is a central cookhouse and dining room where hearty meals are served. There are shower facilities at three of the camps and two have general stores supplied with liquor, sports equipment, and sundries. Four are equipped with washing machines. All of the camps have boats, motors, and guides for the guests, and there is a twenty-six-foot Chris Craft Cruiser at Brooks Camp. Two of them, Brooks and Grovenor, are located inside the monument and the other three are just outside the boundary line.

The camps are open between July 1 and October 1 and tours are operated in conjunction with Northwest Orient Airlines, with weekly flights from all major cities in the other states.

Rates are from $201.60 to $250.30 per person per week, with housing, meals, transportation between the five campsites, but not the transportation to and from the monument.

Matanuska Valley

More famous now than when it was colonized in 1935, the wide, beautiful, and productive Matanuska Valley grows 55 per cent of all Alaska's salable agricultural products. It consists of 1,200 square miles of rolling hills, with narrow level areas between and about 13,000 acres of cropland worth $6,000,000, producing nearly $3,000,000 worth of foodstuffs annually. The population of the valley is about 4,500 people.

Palmer, the hub and main trading point of the valley, is a modern community with varied industries, social activities, and constant progress, 125 miles north of Seward and 50 miles northeast of Anchorage by paved road, or 43 miles by railroad from Anchorage.

Life for the 1,200 residents of Palmer is little different from life in any small town except that the weather is a little colder and springs and summers are shorter; otherwise it has almost the same advantages and disadvantages found in any small Western town. Food costs are higher and fresh foods are difficult to buy in winter, but that is true of any community located off heavily traveled highways.

There are nearly one hundred businesses in Palmer. Many of them are small one-man or family operations and some are only part-time enterprises, which necessitates other employment for the owner, but there are also major stores and business houses, and a new $6,000,000 grain elevator.

Palmer is headquarters for various government agencies. Among these are the Alaska Agricultural Experiment Station, the Soil Conservation Service, the Geological Survey, and the Alaska Department of Agriculture. Palmer has its own letterpress and weekly newspaper, the *Weekly Frontiersman,* published in the modern printing plant of the Matanuska Press.

In the Matanuska Valley, farming and coal mining are the largest industries. The coal fields are among the largest in the state and one of the three major producing coal mines is located near Palmer. A Welsh miner named Evan Jones was responsible for starting the commercial development of the Matanuska coal fields, which today employ over one hundred miners the year around, furnishing coal to the near-by military bases, as well as the civilian population.

For many years, gold mining was the sustaining industry of the valley people. The near-by Talkeetna Mountains are rich in gold and other valuable minerals, but the high costs of materials and labor, and the costly methods that must be used to extract the minerals, have kept mining operations at a minimum. Recent increases in the price of antimony, nickel, copper, and tungsten have spurred some new developments but none are of great importance to the local economy.

One of the up-and-coming industries in the valley, at least from a conversational standpoint, is oil and Matanuska has felt the effect of the Kenai discoveries. Although oil was produced in limited quantities many years ago, it is only in the last few years that an exploration boom has occurred. All the major oil companies have geophysical parties in the field, and the Anchorage Land Office is actually doing a "land office business" in approving oil leases, not only throughout the state, but in the Matanuska Valley as well.

Agriculture—Over half of the income in the Matanuska Valley comes from farm products worth over $6,000,000, yet little more than a half of the food items consumed in Alaska are produced by Alaskan farmers. Since summer temperatures rarely exceed eighty degrees and average around fifty, some types of food cannot be grown in the valley because of low summer or winter temperatures, and some types cannot be stored for full periods between crops.

The Matanuska Valley has about 13,000 acres of cropland, over 2,000 head of cattle, and 15,000 chickens. It produces about 3,750,000 quarts of milk, 3,800 ton of potatoes, 150 tons of cabbage, 160 tons of lettuce, 250 tons of carrots, and 130,000 dozen eggs. There are about 250 farms producing crops for market and almost 800 others in operation that do not produce a marketable surplus.

In addition to the 13,000 acres of cleared land in the valley, 50,000 more are suitable for crops when cleared. Clearing costs range from about $80 per acre, for small second-growth trees cleared on frozen ground in the early spring, to $240 per acre for native spruce, birch, or cottonwood stands. The farmer is still picking up scattered roots five years after the initial bulldozing. It can take as much as a year for one man to clear a single acre of land by hand.

The soils of the Matanuska Valley, like most of the Alaskan soils, are low in fertility. The land varies from rolling to very rough terrain and the soil texture is mostly fine sandy and silt loam. Heavy applications of fertilizers, especially nitrogen, are necessary to obtain top yields. The famous fifty-pound cabbages, teacup-sized strawberries, seven-foot oats, and the twenty tons per acre of potatoes are a result of plenty of fertilizer and the long summer days.

The average length of the growing season is from 107 to 123 days. Tomatoes, cucumbers, green peppers, and eggplants are usually grown in greenhouses. Large fruits are not grown commercially but many small fruits are profitable. A partial list of common commercial crops includes: oats, barley, wheat, peas, strawberries, raspberries, potatoes, lettuce, broccoli, beets, radishes, turnips, parsnips, carrots, sprouts, cabbage, celery, and green onions. String beans are common in home gardens but are not sufficiently dependable for commercial production. All hay and pasture grasses common to the northern states do well in the valley. Neither corn nor alfalfa are grown commercially but clover does well. Commercial crops are primarily small grains, potatoes, and grasses for forage. These three crops occupy about 90 per cent of the cleared land.

Tractors are used for farm operations because of the need for speed in planting and harvesting as a result of the short growing season, and few horses are used because of the high feed costs.

A crop failure has never occurred in the valley. Some years moisture and temperature conditions are more favorable than others and some years plant and animal diseases are more serious than others, but a harvestable crop is assured for a careful farmer.

New and used farm equipment is available at Seattle prices plus freight. Price levels and living costs are about double the Midwestern states costs. Most residents maintain cold-storage lockers and fill them each fall with wild game and fish for the winter to keep food bills down.

Holstein dairy cows predominate in the valley and only the finest are shipped to Alaska for the herds. Very little beef is produced, practically no lamb or mutton, and very little pork. The margin in raising slaughter animals does not compare favorably enough to vegetables or whole milk to make it an attractive enterprise. Some beef cattle can be grazed on the public lands during the summer, but there is not enough cleared land to raise feed for large beef herds. Cattle must be fed seven months out of the year from October to May or June, and local hay sells for from $40 to $60 per ton, which makes the operation very costly.

Poultry raising is primarily for egg production, although there are a few hardy souls who try the frier or broiler business. To be successful in the egg business, a grower must be able to meet Seattle egg prices plus air freight.

Marketing of crops in the valley is handled either by the individual farmer direct to the merchant or through a packing or processing agent. The Alaska Dairy Products Corporation processes and distributes whole milk from the valley producers, but the largest part of the marketing and processing of farm and dairy products is handled by the Co-op.

The Matanuska Valley Farmers Cooperative Association handles its members' farm production. The Co-op, which was organized in 1938, numbers about 125 producers and 300 to 400 consumers. This association does better than $2,000,000 worth of business a year in dairy, produce, garage, grocery store, feed and seed lines, hardware, and miscellaneous activities. It pasteurizes and packages milk, operates a modern steam-generating plant, a continuous-freeze ice cream plant, and processing plants in Palmer and Fairbanks, with storage and distributing facilities in Anchorage. Its products are sold under the name of "Matanuska Maid" throughout the entire state.

The Experiment Station—The Alaska Agricultural Experiment Station has been a constant source of improved farming methods for the residents of the valley. The Experiment Station, ten miles south of Palmer, was in operation fifteen years before the 1935 settlement project. It is a very interesting place to visit. It has developed new potato, wheat, and barley varieties, adapted to the valley's climatic conditions. During recent years the Experiment Station has made great progress in livestock and forage improvements, and was instrumental in inaugurating an artificial insemination program which not only provided the best in sires but eliminated the necessity of each dairyman's keeping one or more bulls.

TRANSPORTATION TO THE MATANUSKA VALLEY

Highways and roadways link Palmer to Seward, Kenai Peninsula, Fairbanks, Valdez, Haines, and all outside points. There are bus lines providing daily service between Anchorage and Palmer, and one bus line operating to Fairbanks with a connection to Dawson Creek on the Alaska Highway. More inaccessible areas in the state are reached by small aircraft operated by numerous bush operators out of the Palmer as well as the Anchorage airports.

HOTELS

Palmer has four hotels, including the modern Matanuska Hotel with 42 rooms and baths, single rate $6, double $9 to $12; the hotel has a coffee shop and cocktail lounge. The Hyland has rooms for $45 a month. Housekeeping rooms and other sleeping accommodations can be rented in the numerous lodges and inns along the highways.

RESTAURANTS

The food in Palmer's numerous cafés and restaurants is good. The Palmer Café features Saturday specials, such as a *smörgåsbord* at $2.50 for adults and $1.00 for children. There is also a drive-in restaurant and the lodges near by serve meals and cocktails. Other restaurants include the Frontier Café, White Spot Café, and Cobb's Café, which has "Ceramic broiled" steaks.

SCHOOLS

There are six hundred students enrolled in the two grade schools and two hundred in the new million-dollar high school located in Palmer. There is a combination grade and high school at Wasilla, twelve miles west of Palmer, with school bus service at both communities for children living in the surrounding area.

During the fall and winter, short courses in agriculture offer residents of the valley an adult education program at the high school, covering farm management and operations.

SHOPPING AND SERVICES

Palmer has the Matanuska Valley Bank, two bakeries, two drugstores, three department stores, two greenhouses, three cleaning and pressing establishments, one lumbermill, and numerous other business firms, including garages, service stations, gift shops, beauty and barber shops, five grocery stores, and three variety stores. The local travel service is Wright's Travel Agency in the Wright Building.

Health—The twenty-seven-bed hospital in Palmer has three doctors, a staff of nurses and technicians, surgery, and all modern equipment. It costs an average patient approximately $33 per day in the hospital. Palmer also has a full-time dentist in residence in the community.

ORGANIZATIONS AND CHURCHES

In addition to the chamber of commerce, the many civic and fraternal organizations in Palmer include the Kiwanis Club, Masons, Elks, Moose, American Legion, Grange, and the Matanuska Valley Sportsmen, which has its own indoor rifle range and clubroom. There are various women's clubs, auxiliaries, homemakers' clubs formed by the University of Alaska's Extension Service, 4-H Clubs, and church organizations. The community of Wasilla has its Community Club, PTA, and a chapter of the VFW and auxiliary. The churches throughout the valley represent most faiths.

ACTIVITIES

The annual Matanuska Valley Fair is held during the Labor Day week end at Palmer and attracts twenty-five thousand visitors during the three-day fair. It is a colorful event and a high light of the year for the residents. The second largest event is Colony Day, held in the latter part of each May, commemorating the colonization of the Matanuska Valley.

There is a movie theater in Palmer, the Valley Theater, with movies nightly and frequent changes of programs. There is excellent hunting and fishing, swimming, boating, picnicking, and hiking, and a variety of outdoor activities in the summer. Winter activities center around basketball for men, women, and high school students alike, and the skating and skiing are excellent. The school gymnasium is also the Community Hall and the scene of community dances, plays, public meetings, and other civic events. Bowling at the Palmer Bowling Center begins every Wednesday after nine and all day Saturdays and Sundays. The valley's television is beamed from Anchorage's stations, KENI and KTVA.

SIDE TRIPS

A trip south of Palmer on the Palmer-Matanuska Road goes through the area where many of the original colonists' farms are located. The Matanuska Experiment Farm is located on this route and visitors are welcome.

Northwest of Palmer and just off the Glenn Highway is a very scenic drive along the mountain road that follows the Little Susitna River to the summit down to the small community of Willow and returns by way of Houston, the site of oil and gas explorations.

At Sutton, north of Palmer, the drive along the Mine Road affords interesting stops for visits to the Matanuska Coal Fields.

In the early summer, between Palmer and Anchorage, the Eklutna flats blaze with the deep pink of countless shooting stars and wild flowers. A side road leads to the colorful Eklutna Indian graves and an old Russian church.

Lake George is situated less than thirty miles from Palmer at the base of Knik Glacier, accessible only by charter plane from the Palmer or Anchorage airports. It is the scene of a strange phenomenon that takes place every July or August after Knik Glacier has created a dam at one end of Lake George, which extends several miles inland. The water pressure in the lake eventually reaches such intensity that it breaks through the tongue of the glacier, dumping the lake and tearing giant icebergs from the glacier's wall that push downstream in a massive flood. When the lake is drained, the process begins again.

The town of Wasilla, twelve miles west of Palmer, came into being as a result of the construction of the Alaska Railroad. Knik, the seaport town on the Knik River, was moved in 1917 to the place known as Wasilla, named for an Indian chief.

Until approximately 1945, Wasilla was a trading center for the gold-mining activity which existed in the Talkeetna Mountains northeast of Wasilla. Two large oil-storage tanks are still standing near the railroad station as mementos of the mining days.

Today the population, including the outlying areas, is close to 250, and the shopping area consists of a general store, a roadhouse, a service station, the railroad, and a bar.

PROSPECTIVE SETTLERS

A small amount of seasonal work is available but it is usually taken by residents. The work consists of construction and road work with the Alaska Road Commission, railroading with the Alaska Railroad, or jobs in business houses, mines, sawmills, trappings, and harvesting.

There is good opportunity in the valley for many small industries. Water is of good quality and quantity, and the area is well served by rail, highway, and communications; there is a reliable labor force available. Suggested industries are a brewery, foundry, birch mill, birch plywood factory, or food-processing plants.

Housing—There are few houses for rent but two large and two small apartment houses in Palmer offer apartments from $85 to $130 per month. The Matanuska Electric Association has a powerline covering the valley with standard alternating current. Electric power rates for farm and home are about 10 cents per

KWH for the first 50, 6 cents for the next 150, and 3 cents above 200.

Farming—Farm lands in the Matanuska Valley may be acquired in three ways. They may be purchased from private owners, from the Alaska Rural Rehabilitation Corporation, or from the government. Only a very limited number of improved farms are repossessed by the ARRC and offered for sale. Most project farms, as they are called, involve the purchase of an equity with the approval of the ARRC required on land that is changing hands and has an unpaid contract balance.

Farm lands may also be leased from private owners. The ARRC does not lease repossessed farms when a sale can be negotiated. No farms are now available for lease or sale by the ARRC.

The third way to obtain farm lands is by homesteading (see Chapter IX).

When farms are purchased from private owners, from 25 to 30 per cent of the purchase price is required as a down payment, and the balance is paid in amortized payments over a period of from ten to fifteen years. Some owners require full cash payment. Government land purchased must be paid in full at the time of purchase.

To purchase government land an applicant must make application in person and be approved by the Land Office, located at 334-336 East Fifth Avenue in Anchorage. The price of such land is from $5 to $100 per acre. Very little good farm land is available for homesteading or government purchase within the Matanuska Valley.

It takes approximately $7,000 to start a farming operation in the valley, not including an allowance for the purchase of the land or buildings. But it does include the cost of making the move, purchasing equipment, and carrying on farming operations through the first year.

A developed farm will usually cost anywhere from $8,500 upward. Usually such farms are sold completely equipped. A fully equipped, twenty-cow, Grade-A dairy has an average price of around $40,000. A minimum of $25,000 over a period of years is

needed to set up a new dairy farm. Developed farms usually consist of a house, well, barn, and other farm buildings.

The rate of interest on realty contracts varies from 4 to 8
per cent.

Financing is not easy to arrange, but there are several sources
that handle financing: the Farmers Home Administration, which
maintains an area office in Anchorage; the state has a loan
program administered by the Commissioner of Agriculture at
Palmer; there are commercial banks; and the Alaska Rural Rehabilitation Corporation, which charges 6 per cent interest on
farm loans.

Developed farms have anywhere from 40 to 320 acres of cleared
land, but the average is from 15 to 100 acres.

The best time of the year to settle in the valley is about the
first of March, so that there is time to plan farming operations
for the coming year.

To assist residents and newcomers, the University of Alaska
Extension Service supplies information on crops, livestock, and
farms and home practices. There are local 4-H clubs and homemakers' clubs that also assist. The Alaska Experiment Station,
Soil Conservation Service, and State Commissioner of Agriculture have headquarters and operations in Palmer, and all are
available to assist with farming problems.

Kenai Peninsula

The thousand-mile coast line of the Kenai Peninsula juts out
of the southern coast into the Gulf of Alaska, immediately south
of Anchorage. Along the picturesque miles are the principal communities of the peninsula—the town of Hope in the north, Kenai,
Seldovia, and Homer on the west coast, and Seward on the
southeast.

The Alaska highway system connects all of these communities,
except Seldovia, by paved roadways from Seward to Anchorage
and partially paved or gravel along other connecting routes. The
two major peninsula highways are Seward-Anchorage, Route #4,
and the Sterling Highway, Route #5. Along the highways are
automobile service facilities, lodgings, and places to eat and to
buy groceries located about ten miles apart.

The entire western length of the peninsula is well protected from severe weather by the Kenai Mountains to the east and the Alaska Range to the west across Cook Inlet, making it ideal for farming and agriculture. The major industrial activities on the peninsula are fishing, trapping, and agriculture. Some of the best agricultural lands in Alaska are situated in these western areas, especially those extending north from Kachemak Bay and the city of Homer to the town of Kenai.

It is estimated that 204,708 acres are suitable for crop production, of which 41,415 are excellent for general agriculture and 90,760 acres for limited agriculture and livestock farming. The remaining 72,533 are suitable for raising forage crops and grazing lands.

Hope

This small village, eighty-nine miles south of Anchorage, was the scene of the first recorded gold strike in Alaska when, in the summer of 1895, prospectors found gold and the word spread to all the large cities on the Pacific Coast. In the spring of 1896, Hope was a giant-sized tent city with a population of 2,500 and twice as many more crowded into the community to establish claims. But in the following year the population dropped to less than 80 people, when the gold-seekers moved on to bigger and more prosperous diggings. Currently Hope is becoming a summer residence resort for the people of Anchorage. Only a few of the pioneer sights remain but these are interesting places to visit in the abandoned mining area.

Kenai

Up until 1939, Kenai consisted of little more than a post office, a roadhouse, a Greek Orthodox Church, and a Protestant mission with a native population of 286, even though it had been an important Russian fur-trading post, founded in 1791 by Grigor Knonvalof who built the fort there.

Today Kenai is a very active community of seven hundred residents and one of the focal points on the peninsula for the oil explorations which are taking place less than fifty miles north of the town in the Swanson Creek area. Two major oil strikes by

Richfield and Standard, and other drilling and seismic studies by Halbout-Alaska Oil Company, all in 1957 and 1958, have led to great speculation of the actual potentials of this area. Estimates based on current findings and results run into hundreds of millions of barrels of oil, and, if developments continue, Kenai should become an important oil city.

Paved highways lead into Kenai off the Sterling Highway, a distance of about 159 miles south from Anchorage. A modern airport handles flights daily to and from the town, operated by Pacific Northern Airlines and charter plane services. Kenai has a large salmon cannery, ten stores including grocery, building materials, hardware, drugs, clothing, a department store, laundry and dry-cleaning services, cafés, and bars.

The Kenai Hotel offers accommodations from $6 to $8 for singles and from $8 to $12 for doubles without private baths. At the new Spur Motel there are eighteen rooms with bath, and singles are from $7 to $8, doubles are from $9 to $13.

The residents of the area are engaged in farming, homesteading, road building, and dock work; there are many fishing families. Kenai has a modern school with gymnasium and school bus service for children living within twenty miles of the community. The Catholic and Russian Orthodox and six Protestant churches are represented.

Many of the original Russian-built buildings still remain, including the Old Russian Church, and sight-seeing in and around the community is very enjoyable. Hunting and fishing are excellent and charter boats are available.

Traveling down the Sterling Highway, following the western shore of Cook Inlet from Kenai to Homer, is a beautiful trip with majestic views of the snowy peaks and the steaming cone of 10,017-foot Iliamna volcano on the far shore of the inlet.

Homer

Homer, at the end of the Sterling Highway, is the largest community on the west coast of the peninsula, 226 miles south of Anchorage and 176 from Seward. The population of Homer and the immediate area is over one thousand and it is a trading center for the west-coast residents.

The surrounding countryside is particularly noted for beautiful wild flowers that bloom from June to September, coloring the many farms, grazing fields, and gardens. Climatically Homer is ideal without extremes of heat or cold, giving it the name the "Shangri-la of Alaska."

The principal industry is fishing and canning, which are tied in closely with the community of Seldovia, only eighteen miles across Kachemak Bay, where there are also processing plants for shrimp, king crab, and salmon, but there is no road link between the two communities.

A wide variety of minerals are found in the adjacent area, including coal along the west shore of Kachemak Bay, clay deposits usable for ceramics or tile products, large limestone deposits near Seldovia, a chromium mine, which is being extensively worked, on the south side of Kachemak Bay, pumice on St. Augustine Island near by in Cook Inlet, and unlimited gravel deposits.

The raising of sheep, beef, and chickens is done on a small scale by some farmers in the community and in the Fox River Valley area, and there is one dairy.

Transportation to Homer

The community has scheduled flight service operated by Pacific Northern Airlines. The airport has paved runways and a seaplane base near by. Charter planes are available at Lawrence Aircraft and Homer Air Service with rates $15 to $30 an hour depending on the size of plane. Boats may be chartered at the docks for excursions of the area. There is scheduled bus service between Homer and other communities on the peninsula. Shipping and freight services are supplied by Alaska Steamship once a month in summer and a large number of trucking firms.

Hotels and food

Hotel rates range from $5 for singles to $10 for doubles and there are several places to stay, including the Heady Hotel which has twenty-four rooms with eleven baths, as well as dormitory accommodations, café, and a cocktail bar; The Seafair Motel, which has some housekeeping facilities; The Inlet Inn with ten rooms and one bath; Land's End; La Fon's Long-Tel Cabins; Chuck's Cabin Court; and, approaching Homer on the Sterling Highway at Mile 173, the Baycrest Motel, with twelve rooms and baths and some housekeeping units.

Seafood is superior in Homer's restaurants which include the Land's End, where there is especially fine food, the Homer Club, and Martha's Café.

SHOPPING AND SERVICES

Homer has a movie theater, bank, self-service laundry, cleaning services, barber and beauty shop, drugstore, giftshops and general stores, machine shops, service stations and garages, a gunsmith, and dairy and taxi services. There is a hospital-health center with a doctor, nurses, and a pharmacist.

The local newspaper is an interesting weekly of six to eight mimeographed pages presenting full coverage of news of the wildlife, oil, marine, and fishing activities, and social and local government news of the near-by communities.

SCHOOLS, CHURCHES, AND ORGANIZATIONS

There is a combined grade and high school, with a staff of twenty teachers, hot-lunch program, and school bus service. The churches in Homer include Baptist, Methodist, Protestant, Catholic, Christian Community, Assembly of God, and Church of Christ. A number of service and business organizations are represented, including Chamber of Commerce, PTA, 4-H clubs, Civil Air Patrol Cadets, American Legion, Masons, and Elks, as well as homemakers' clubs and other youth organizations.

ACTIVITIES

Toward the end of August each year, Homer has a big agricultural fair and the annual Winter Carnival in March. Ice skating is a popular winter sport and there is excellent skiing at Ohlson Mountain Road which has a ski tow. The Mariners, the high-school basketball team, are enthusiastically supported by the residents and home games are played in the school gym throughout the winter season.

Other activities include swimming, berrypicking, clam digging, crab catching, hiking, camping, boating, hunting and fishing. Sight-seeing in and around Homer and Seldovia visitors can enjoy the canneries, the Russian Church, wild-game reserves, glaciers, exposed coal seams, and mines, or have picnics at the public campgrounds.

Homer-Seldovia Tours operates a three-day tour of the area including a limousine tour of Homer, the Skyline Drive for panoramic views of Kachemak Bay, glaciers and the Harding Icecap, a visit to the wild berry cannery on the Sterling Highway and to the king crab processing plants at the end of the four-and-a-half-mile-long Homer Spit. The following day there is an excursion by cruiser of Halibut Cove, waterfowl rookeries, fiords, islands, and the king crab beds, a tour of Seldovia, Camel Rock, the Russian Church, and the canneries. The third day features a hundred-mile bush flight over the Harding Icecap and the glaciers. The tour rate is $69, and operates from June 1 to September 5.

Seward

Seward, the gateway of the Kenai Peninsula, was founded in 1904 and named after William H. Seward, the secretary of state who negotiated the purchase of Alaska.

Located at the north end of Resurrection Bay, about 1,500 miles northwest of Seattle, this city of 3,200 people is the most southerly terminal of the Alaska Railroad and the year-round harbor terminal for freighters from Pacific Coast cities. The new $10,000,000 docks, with 90,000 feet of heated warehouse space, were recently completed by the Alaska Railroad.

In addition to the new docks, three ocean docks within the city limits are maintained by Standard Oil, the United States Army and the city-owned Fish and Cold Storage Company. A large fish and shrimp packing plant, and the bulk cement storage and shipping plant used by the Lone Star Cement Company, add to the activity of the water-front area.

Seward's fishing industry has benefited by the recent enlargement of the Small Boat Shelter Harbor and the construction of a breakwater. King salmon, halibut, king crab, and giant shrimp in large quantities are products of the local fishing industry.

A new hydroelectric plant is located at Crescent Lake, thirty-two miles north of town, providing the city with a large electrical supply that is more than adequate to support new industrial developments.

Three lumbermills work to near capacity, because Seward is almost entirely surrounded by the great Chugach National Forest.

Because of the nature of the soil, which is glacial terrain, and because the thick forest is so close to the city limits, there are no farms in the area. Gardens are highly productive, especially berries, root crops, and leafy green vegetables, which grow rapidly to large sizes in the short growing season. Chicken farming is one of the increasing local industries.

Oil development on the Kenai Peninsula has affected Seward as it has all communities on the peninsula. Speculation is high, and explorations and developments by major oil companies are within seventy-five miles of the city. Currently it is the location of a Standard Oil installation and an oil-distributing point to interior cities and military installations, and is considered to be the logical location for pipe-line terminals and future cracking plants and other auxiliary oil operations.

Seward looks much like a frontier town with false front stores and buildings, but it is really a very modern and progressive community. One of the town's newest attractions is the new post-office building completed in 1956. The city government is operated by a city manager working with the city council and mayor. All utilities are city-owned with the exception of the telephone system.

The city's Women's Club sponsors a "hospitality group" to aid in the entertaining of tourists, while the chamber of commerce maintains an "information cache" which is very helpful to visitors in the city.

TRANSPORTATION TO SEWARD

The Alaska Railroad operates between Seward and Fairbanks with stops at Anchorage, Mount McKinley, and many other communities along the way from the coast to the interior. Daily passenger bus service connects Seward with other cities on the Kenai Peninsula and runs to Anchorage. Cordova Air Lines has daily service to Anchorage, Cordova, Valdez, and other cities in south central Alaska. Trucking companies do much of the freighting into Seward and the Alaska Steamship Company handles sea freight. The M.V. *Expansion* operates between Seward and the Aleutian Islands. Seward is connected by paved highway to all the major roads in the state.

LOCAL TRANSPORTATION

Taxis provide the local transportation. The McDonald Airways and Cordova Air Lines both have charter plane services at the local airport, and boats may be chartered for hunting and fishing trips at the water front.

HOTELS

Seward has two motels and four hotels including the New Seward Hotel which has forty rooms and twenty-three baths. Singles are from $5 to $8, doubles from $8 to $16. The Hotel Renwald has thirty-four rooms and ten baths, with singles from $4 to $6, doubles from $6.50 to $9.00. Murphy's Motel consists of six rooms with bath; a single costs $5 and double from $8 to $10.

RESTAURANTS

All restaurants in Seward have American food and practically no foreign specialties. There are a number of cafés and restaurants including: Don's Café, Clark's, and Tony's, which is mostly a bar and has free buffets on Saturday nights. The weekly feature at the Harbor Club is prime rib roast and free wine for guests on birthdays and anniversaries. One of the many bars and cocktail lounges is the Nobby Club which has an organist and dancing nightly.

CHURCHES

The many churches include Baptist, Assembly of God, Episcopal, Methodist, Catholic, Lutheran, and Nazarene.

SCHOOLS

Seward has three schools, two elementary and one high school. Adjoining the high school is the Seward National Guard Armory used by the schools as a gym and auditorium, seating six hundred. There is one private school, the Loraine Trowbridge Music School. The Jessie Lee Home, two miles from town, is a large Methodist mission school for native children.

SHOPPING AND SERVICES

The stores are small but there is a good selection of merchandise. Among the several gift and souvenir shops is O'Brien's, which also sells flowers and photo equipment, and the Alaska Shop, a general store selling local arts and crafts. There is one bank, the First National, and a cleaning and laundry service. Durant's is one of the best places for all sporting equipment and hardware. Vina's Beauty Salon is equipped with slenderizing facilities and there are two barbershops.

Health—There are two hospitals in Seward, the thirty-two-bed Seward General and the Wesleyan Hospital for Chronic Diseases, which is the only nonnative tuberculosis hospital in Alaska. Seward has a rehabilitation center for the handicapped, three doctors, one dentist, and a public health nurse. The Seward Volunteer Ambulance Corps has a first-aid unit on call for emergencies.

Publications—Seward's weekly newspaper is one of the most interesting published in the state. It is called the *Petticoat Gazette* and is published by the Seward Business and Professional Women's Club. The majority of the news is local, anecdotal, colorfully written, and the paper is the best source for news of commercial opportunities in the city. The price is 15 cents a copy.

CIVIC AND SOCIAL ORGANIZATIONS

There are many organizations, including the American Legion, Beta Sigma Phi, unions, 4-H, the Harbor and Marathon Home-makers Clubs, Business and Professional Women, Pioneers of Alaska Igloo #9, Odd Fellows, Eastern Star, Masons, Elks, and Chamber of Commerce.

ACTIVITIES

The famous Mount Marathon climbing race on the Fourth of July is the best-known sporting event in Alaska. The Seward

Silver Salmon Derby attracts 2,500 to 3,000 sports fishermen in August every year to compete for the $10,000 in prize awards. The Annual Fireman's Ball on New Year's Eve is another big event in Seward.

Swimming, boating, water skiing, skin diving, photography, hiking, softball, basketball, dancing, hunting, and fishing are among the favorite local recreations. The Liberty Theater has nightly programs and changes films four times a week. There is bowling every night at the Dreamland Bowl.

Seward's clubs, lodges, and organizations have many social affairs, and special concerts are presented by the popular Community Chorus and local choral societies. A little theater group, a mineral society, an artist colony, and the Seahawks basketball team from the high school receive enthusiastic support from the community. The local Yacht Club is a very active group promoting a private marina and recreation area at Thumb's Cove, and the Ski Area, in the Chugach National Forest eleven miles from Seward, is excellent. The largest golf course in western Alaska is under construction in Seward. Meetings, lectures, dances, and parties are held in the Civic Center, the Odd Fellows Hall, the Elks, Armory, and local restaurants, and many of these events are open to all visitors.

The Community Library has a small but good collection of books and a fine children's section.

SIDE TRIPS

The mail boat, which delivers the United States mail and freight once a month to the Aleutian Islands and points along the Alaska Peninsula, has accommodations for twelve passengers aboard a 114-foot ship, the M.V. *Expansion.*

The trip is an unusual one and affords an opportunity to visit the peninsula and islands as far out as Nikolski on the Fox Islands, some nine hundred miles southwest of Seward, with stops at Chernofski where two families, a few sheepherders, and 4,500 sheep live. The boat puts in at Kashega, which has a population of two, at Dutch Harbor, the site of a naval air station, the isolated canneries in the Shumagins, Kodiak Island, and a total of nineteen villages and thirty-five ports of call, stopping at most ports from two to six hours to give passengers time to visit and explore the villages and islands along the way. This is not a luxury cruise but the accommodations are good, the atmosphere is friendly and informal, and there is a great deal of adventure. Warm clothes are a necessity.

The ship is a floating supermarket, branch bank, and traveling library, and carries all necessary food and supplies for the villagers, as well as providing transportation between the communities. The *Mailboat Monitor* is the ship's bimonthly newspaper which is distributed along the way and contains a roundup of local news and a "Friendship Society" matrimonial column.

The ship sails about the first of every month from Seward and is back in port the last ten days of every month. The round-trip fare is $258. Reservations should be made well in advance with Captain N. P. Thomsen, Master, M.V. *Expansion*, P. O. Box 537, Seward, Alaska.

Campgrounds Near Seward—Along the Seward-Anchorage Highway north of Seward there are nine campgrounds that have water and sanitary facilities; these include: Grouse Lake, 6½ miles north, a very small campground with a stream near by where the salmon spawn in later summer; Summit Lake, 47 miles north to Summit Lake Lodge and then 2 miles beyond to the very small campground, where the scenery is outstanding and trout fishing is good; Granite Creek, 63 miles north to Granite Creek, then ¾ mile west to the large campground at Sixmile Creek; Williwaw, 80 miles north to Portage, then 5½ miles east of Portage on the Glacier Road to the large campground, which has a trailer parking area and is near Portage Glacier.

Near most of the campground sites there are commercial lodgings and accommodations, and at Moose Pass in the mountains, 30 miles north of Seward on the Seward-Anchorage Highway where the Alaska Railroad makes a stop, there are several good motels, lodges, and cafés, and a small but interesting museum.

PROSPECTIVE SETTLERS

Employment on the Kenai Peninsula is seasonal and there are few openings with an adequate local labor force to fill the needs. There are no homestead lands available on the roadways but there are homesteads in the wilderness areas. Anyone interested in homesteading in the peninsula area should have sufficient funds for at least two years for, although a portion of the family living can be gained from gardening, berrypicking, hunting, clam digging, and fishing, such activities require considerable time, leaving the homesteader little time for earning money for necessities not provided by the land. This practice cannot be counted on to provide a sufficient portion of a family's living on the Kenai Peninsula. (See Chapter IX.)

There are opportunities for new businesses in or near the population centers. The community of Kenai reports the need for a theater, bowling alley, and good restaurants. The chambers of commerce in each town have helpful information available regarding current needs and conditions which is valuable for evaluating the potential business prospects.

Housing—On the west coast of Kenai Peninsula, housing for families is inadequate, with few modern homes available. No program for new home construction has been started in the area; however, lots, improved and unimproved, are for sale in and adjacent to the communities. There are very few houses for rent or for sale in Seward, but a housing project is under way and will have small homes available in the $17,500 price range. Most of the present homes are of wood-frame construction, a few of stucco or cement, and a few log houses, but none of brick. Most homes are heated with oil, and cooking is done on oil, electric, or bottled gas ranges.

Valdez

Valdez is the farthest north ice-free port in North America, and the shortest route to interior Alaska via the Richardson all-weather Highway, 363 miles from Fairbanks and 305 from Anchorage.

The famed Captain James Cook sailed into the northern arm of the Gulf of Alaska in May 1778 and named the area Prince William Sound. Then, in 1790, the Spaniard, Lieutenant Fidalgo, renamed it Puerto de Valdez.

In the first few months of the gold rush, prospectors used the

Chilkoot pass en route from Haines to the interior. This route was not satisfactory because it meant passing through Canada and paying a toll fee. The need for a shorter, more direct route resulted in the Richardson Trail from Valdez, and Valdez grew to a population of over ten thousand and for many years was the largest city in Alaska.

Freighting was a mainstay in the economy of Valdez until a fire destroyed the Federal Building in Valdez and the seat of the third judicial division was moved to Anchorage. With freighting largely taken over by the government-subsidized railroad, Valdez declined in importance and became a ghost town of little over three hundred people.

In the late 1940's, military and government officials, realizing the vulnerability of Alaska, developed the old Richardson Trail from a summer road into a modern paved highway designated as Route #1, extending from Valdez all the way to Fairbanks.

At the same time there was other road building in the north and the Alaska Highway was pushed through the wilderness, and once again Valdez boomed as a natural shipping port for the interior of Alaska.

Today Valdez has a population of about six hundred. It is known throughout the state as the "Switzerland of Alaska"; it is situated at the head of mountain-ringed Valdez Bay which is much like a deep fiord cutting in the rugged coast of Prince William Sound and forming one of Alaska's principal harbors. Surrounding it is an exciting combination of every type of scenery—jutting mountains, placid bays, glaciers, and forests in great abundance.

The summer fishing fleet and cannery are not as important industrially as Valdez's trucking and freight, with offices of thirteen large trucking concerns; it is the main terminal point for over ninety additional trucking outfits, serviced by three repair shops and one heavy-duty trucking equipment depot. The port of Valdez handles considerable incoming and outgoing ocean freight for the government, as well as for private steamship companies. The Bureau of Public Roads maintains offices in Valdez and employs a number of local residents.

TRANSPORTATION

Valdez is one and one-half hours from Anchorage via Cordova Airlines; by car one travels via the Alaska Highway, Glenn Highway to the Richardson Highway, or direct between Fairbanks or Anchorage and intermediate towns via the Alaska highway system. There is summer bus service between Valdez, Anchorage, and Fairbanks. Valdez has a local twenty-four-hour taxi service and charter boat service. Planes are for hire at the airport or at the seaplane base on Robe Lake, two miles from town.

HOTELS

Rates in the various hotels and motels in and around Valdez range from $3 to $7 for singles and from $5 to $12 for doubles. The hotels include the Alaskan Hotel; Port Valdez Motel, which has nine rooms with bath, central heating, and showers; Vista Motel; Valdez Hotel with forty rooms; Beals Hotel, and Johnson's Trailer Court. There are many lodges and roadhouses along the Richardson Highway approaching Valdez, including Aurora Lodge, Junction Inn, Copper Center Roadhouse, Silver Fox Lodge, Tiekel Roadhouse, and Tsaina Lodge, which is open twenty-four hours a day and serves fine food.

RESTAURANTS AND BARS

A wide choice of restaurants and bars in and near Valdez includes the Canteen, Copper Center Bar, Glacier Bar, Pinzon, Virginia's Café, and The Village Morgue Cocktail Lounge. The food is plain, American style. Occasionally the bars have live music and one, The Acres, offers surrey buggy rides to Valdez Glacier and sled rides in winter.

SCHOOLS AND CHURCHES

The public educational system has a kindergarten and twelve grades in three school buildings, including a new junior-senior high school. The Russian Orthodox, Roman Catholic, Episcopal, Assembly of God, Baptist, and Free Methodist faiths have churches in Valdez.

SHOPPING AND SERVICES

The business district of Valdez is full of contrast with the many old buildings of the gold-rush days standing alongside the most modern structures. Stores are modern and include grocery and drugstores, hardware and marine shops, dry goods and novelty stores, laundry and cleaning services, a bank, and a number of small business firms that are usually found in a community of similar size. The new community hospital has a resident physician and staff. There are modern dial telephones and mail service is weekly by ship and daily by air.

ORGANIZATIONS

There are many members in the American Legion, VFW, Masonic Lodge, Eastern Star, Women's Civic Club, PTA, Chamber of Commerce, Boy and Girl Scouts, adult and teen-age square dance groups, sewing clubs, and a number of local societies and clubs.

ACTIVITIES

Valdez is the home of the annual Truck Road-eo, the exciting roundup for Alaskan truck drivers. The annual Silver Salmon Derby, which is known locally as the Fish-for-Fun Derby, is held from about the first of June to the first of August, with weekly and daily prizes for the largest catch.

Hiking and motor trips are some of the local activities, including trips to the base of Valdez Glacier by foot trails or gravel road over the trails which were first used by the prospectors during the early gold-rush days, to the huge ice barrier which was known as the "ice demon" because of the great number of pioneers killed in attempting to climb the surface.

Richardson Highway goes to Thompson Pass, 26 miles from town and 2,700 feet high, to the breathtaking panoramic view of the mountain peaks, deep canyons, snow fields, and the Worthington Glacier, which may be seen from the highway or by driving to the glacier front.

Fifteen miles from Valdez is the tunnel cut by hand into the solid rock of Keystone Canyon, the only remains of the railroad era when nine companies fought to take advantage of the short route from the coast to gold-rush country. This is also the site of Hangman's Tree where it is said many bloody battles were fought.

Bridal Veil Falls is thirteen miles from Valdez, cascading into Lowe River from Keystone Canyon, less than one hundred feet from the highway, and opposite Horse-Tail Falls, which moistens the highway with its spray. Out Mineral Creek Road, southwest of town, are several campsites on the way to the abandoned mining areas.

Valdez has a movie theater, ball park, public library, gymnasium, and playground. There is an ice-skating rink and a ski tow located eight miles from town.

Campgrounds—Eagles Falls, 7 miles west of Valdez, Glacier Road, 5 miles west of Valdez, and Nine Mile at Mile 9 on the Richardson Highway are good locations for camping, fishing, mountain climbing, and hunting. They are sites maintained by the Bureau of Land Management and designated primarily as campgrounds and picnic areas without facilities for trailer houses. Stays are permitted in each campground for one week. A pile of fuel wood is normally available in each area and additional wood may be gathered using only dead or fallen timber; the cutting of standing trees is prohibited. All fires should be built in the existing fireplaces and thoroughly extinguished before leaving the campgrounds. Sanitary facilities are available at each site.

SIDE TRIPS

W. S. Upson, of the Sextant Marine Corporation in Valdez, conducts sight-seeing trips by cruise boat in the Prince William Sound area. One of the trips is to the Columbia tidewater glacier, a seven-hour journey with a thirty-minute stop at the glacier, costing $15 per person and including one meal. Another trip lasts four days, leaving Valdez every Monday, from Memorial Day through Labor Day, for fishing, crabbing, a clambake, sight-seeing tours of the islands, a trip through LaTouche, and a deserted mining town which can be reached only by boat at a cost of $50 per day per person. This tour may be taken as a package tour from Seattle, with a plane to Fairbanks, then to Anchorage, tours of both areas, the four-day boat trip in Prince William Sound, and return to Seattle, at a total cost of $491.75.

Sextant Marine also has a boat-chartering service and hunting and fishing guide service. The boats are of the newest steel construction with staterooms, showers, and toilets. These trips offer an opportunity to see much sealife and wildlife, and enjoy a leisurely informal cruise of the south central coastal area.

The Indian village of Tatilek with its small museum of artifacts and native lore is twenty miles south of Valdez by charter boat near the fishing village of Ellamar, a short but worth-while side trip.

Cordova

Cordova is known throughout Alaska as the "Friendly City" because of the hospitality and the relaxed way of life in the community. About two thousand people live in Cordova and the small village of Eyak, seven miles away by road. During the summer, seasonal workers increase the population at least another one thousand, depending on the fishing conditions.

Cordova, 50 miles southeast of Valdez and 142 miles southeast of Anchorage, is located in the Copper River Delta. It was founded in 1905 because of great interest in the Berring River coal deposits and the townsite's favorable location as a seaport; however, there was very little development of the coal fields.

Cordova was the distributing center for the now-abandoned Kennecott Mine, which was located some two hundred miles upstream. The two were connected by the Copper River Railroad which cost $23,500,000 to build. During the period from 1911 to 1938, $100,000,000 in copper ore traveled through Cordova via the railroad for transshipment to the rest of the world. Today the old roadbed for the railroad is being converted into a new highway to connect Cordova with the network of Alaskan highways.

Since the closing of the copper mine and the diminished interest in the coal fields, Cordova's industry has been largely fishing with some fourteen canneries responsible for 65 to 75 per cent of the Pacific Coast razor clam pack and the packing of Dungeness crab, amounting to over half of the Alaska pack, with salmon production in the Prince William Sound areas between $2,000,000 and $4,000,000 annually.

Trapping fur animals is a winter occupation for the residents who fish, mine, or prospect during the summer months. The estimated value of the annual trap is over $50,000, consisting of beaver, marten, land otter, mink, ermine, and other high-grade furs.

Logging and lumbering operations within the Chugach National Forest are a part of the industrial activity, and the lumber from Cordova's modern sawmill is used to supply local demands.

To the south of Cordova lie the Berring River coal fields and the Katalla and Yakataga oil fields. Many years ago oil of exceptionally fine quality was produced in the Katalla district and a refinery was built and operated until it was destroyed by fire. Currently three test wells have been drilled in the Yakataga area but none have been opened to commercial production primarily because of the lack of roads and the high cost of transporting equipment to the site. Other lands have been leased in the area for additional exploration and potential development.

Recently interest was revived in the Berring River coal fields and private capital has obtained sufficient leases to go into operation. Much of the deposit is considered to be of good quality coking coal. The field is estimated by the United States Bureau of Mines to contain 1,100,000,000 tons of bituminous coal and 2,100,000,000 tons of anthracite.

Transportation

Pacific Northern and Cordova Airlines offer daily service between Cordova and Anchorage. Cordova Airlines flies between Cordova and Seward, Valdez, Chitina, Gulkana, Middleton Island, Icy Bay, and Yakataga. The same air line has ski, wheel, float, and amphibious aircraft available for charter to all Alaskan points. There is bus service to and from the airport and three taxi services in the community offer twenty-four-hour service. The Alaska Steamship freighters from Seattle make frequent stops in Cordova.

HOTELS AND FOOD

The four hotels, with rates ranging from $3 to $9, are the Windsor, Northern, Cordova, and Alaskan. Cordova has its share of cocktail lounges and bars, nine in all, and the three restaurants serve plain meals but feature well-prepared seafood in season. There is always an influx of summer workers and visitors, and reservations at hotels should be made well in advance if a summer trip is planned.

SCHOOLS, CHURCHES, AND ORGANIZATIONS

The local school system consists of a new grade school and a high school with 18 teachers, one superintendent, and a total enrollment of 380 students.

The churches include Episcopal, Catholic, Russian Orthodox, Baptist, Assembly of God, Pentecostal, Lutheran, a Gospel Chapel and Little Chapel. The Lutheran Church also maintains a Children's Home in Cordova.

There are nineteen national and international fraternal and social organizations in the community, as well as the local ski club, women's clubs, and youth organizations.

SHOPPING AND SERVICES

Cordova is quite a modern little city with many fine stores, giftshops, sporting goods suppliers, jewelers, a barber and beauty shop, cleaners, flower shop, the Cordova Co-op Association, the First Bank of Cordova, North Star Theater, KLAM radio station and the local weekly newspaper, the *Cordova Times*. There is a public library and city-owned public utilities.

Health—The community has a twenty-two-bed hospital, two doctors, a dentist, a public health nurse, and a health center.

ACTIVITIES

Lake Eyak and the village of Eyak may be reached by road from Cordova for good fishing, swimming, boating, and hiking trails up Mount Eyak for the spectacular views of the mountains, forests, and waterways. Orca Inlet and Lake Eyak are the sites of Cordova's annual Silver Salmon Derby held on the

Labor Day week end. The sawmill on Orca Inlet at Three-Mile Bay, the canneries, and the cold-storage plants are interesting places to visit, and arrangements can be made to charter boats for crabbing, fishing, or clam digging.

From Cordova there are fifty-three miles of trails through hunting and recreation areas where five cabins and the trails are maintained by the United States Forest Service. The trails lead to Cabin Lake, Lake Elsner, Sheridan Glacier, and other lakes in the region for the fine trout fishing.

The near-by slopes of Mount Eccles are considered excellent for skiing. Facilities include a shelter, cabin, and portable ski tow. There is ice skating on Lake Eyak and a shelter cabin maintained by the Forest Service. Cordova residents are subscribers to the Alaska Music Trails concerts, bringing in vocal and instrumental artists during the winter concert season. The biweekly dances sponsored by the Cordova square dance clubs and the basketball games are community favorites.

SIDE TRIPS

The ghost town of Chitina, 131 miles northwest of Cordova, is one of Cordova Airlines' scheduled stops. It may also be reached by road from the Richardson Highway. There are only a few residents still living in this town that was once an important railroad, trapping, and prospecting center, but it has retained all the color of a deserted pioneer town. There are many Chitina or Copper River Indian artifacts and a few Indians in the vicinity making moccasins and doing wood carvings.

Cordova Airlines runs bush flights from Cordova as well as Anchorage to Kennecott and McCarthy, the abandoned Kennecott Mine's company towns which were deserted after the mines closed. These ghost towns are almost as they were in their bonanza days, and the remains of hotels, stores, homes, trails, and wagon roads are still there to be explored.

PROSPECTIVE SETTLERS

There are seldom jobs available for newcomers but when the highway is completed and the mineral resources developed there will be new business opportunities.

Homesteading lands are not available in or around Cordova because of its location within a national forest. There are pieces of ground available for homesites adjacent to the town; however, they are not suitable for commercial farming and only a small amount of farming is done in the area.

Housing—The shortage of houses for rent in Cordova has boosted two-bedroom house rentals from $35 per month to $75 to $125 in ten years. Apartments are currently renting from $75 to $125 per month. Many families in the rural areas and some within the city limits live in substandard housing.

Kodiak

The home of the Kodiak bear is world famous for hunting and fishing, and the town of Kodiak offers some of the best guides and outfitters in Alaska. It is the largest community in the Kodiak Island group and the oldest permanent settlement in Alaska, founded in 1792 by Alexander Baranof. The island on which the city stands is the largest of the group, rich in rugged mountainous territory and inhabited almost exclusively along its shore. Numerous long, fingerlike bays extend into its depth, creating magnificent scenery, and in the summertime its green vegetation against the azure of the sea has given it the local name of the "Emerald Isle." Many of the bays afford shelter for small fishing villages and cannery towns.

Kodiak is situated on the northwestern corner of the island at the base of 1,400-foot Pillar Mountain, overlooking the island-studded harbor of St. Paul. The population of the city is about 4,000 and the near-by naval station and Coast Guard detachments contribute another 3,700. Small villages around the islands number about 3,000 permanent residents, but during the fishing season this figure swells to about 5,000.

In 1784 the first settlement established on Kodiak Island by the Russians was at Three Saints Bay on the southeastern shore, established by Grigor Shelikof for the purpose of serving as a fur-trading center for the Shelikof-Golikof Fur Company. Three Saints Bay remained headquarters on Kodiak for eight years and then Alexander Baranof, chief of the company, moved to the present site of Kodiak.

Kodiak was company headquarters from 1792 to 1804 when the company was known as the Russian-American Company. In 1804 headquarters were moved to Sitka. Kodiak remained a fur-trading center and small fishing village until the construction of the naval station in 1939, when Kodiak began to grow and the population increased from 550 to the present 4,000.

Today its economy depends about half on the naval station and half on the fishing industry. The local fishing industry has been expanding in recent years to include the famous Kodiak king crab, a giant crustacean that reaches six feet in spread and weighs thirty pounds. The salmon industry has long been a major contributor to the economy, crab and clam industries are second in importance, with two crab canneries in the town and one on the other side of the island, and several clam canneries. There are known to be numerous shrimp and scallops in the area, and immediately off Kodiak Island are some of the most productive halibut banks in the world. Adjacent Afognak Island harbors a small lumbermill which supplies lumber locally. There are six cattle ranches scattered about the island group; the beef is sold locally and in Anchorage. Sheep are raised, the wool is good quality, and is shipped commercially. A small dairy supplies fresh milk to the pasteurizing and bottling plant in Kodiak.

TRANSPORTATION

Kodiak is serviced by Pacific Northern Airlines twice a day from Anchorage. The mailboat M.V. *Expansion* carries passengers between Kodiak and Seward on a once-a-month schedule. There are several taxi services in the community and U-Drive cars can be rented from the Holman Auto Mart. Planes can be chartered from Harvey Flying Service or Kodiak Airways, Inc., which handles air freight from their offices and hangars on Tagura Road. Charter boats are available also. Alaska Steamship and Martin Van Lines handle freight and shipping household furnishings.

HOTELS

The two hotels in Kodiak are the Kodiak Hotel on Main Street and the Montmartre Inn on Mission Road. Rates are from

$5 for a single to $10 for a double, and reservations are essential. There are a few rooms in private homes and rooming houses.

RESTAURANTS

Nine restaurants in the community include Max's Drive Inn serving fish'n'chips, prawns, steaks and fried chicken, breakfasts at any hour, sandwiches, malts, and milk shakes. The Polar Bear features homemade pies; the Montmartre Inn has excellent steak dinners and serves Chinese foods in a spacious dining room where there is dancing in the evening. The Beachcombers serves large ranch-style breakfasts.

CHURCHES

The oldest church, and the most historic, is the Russian Orthodox Church, originally founded in 1795. The Community Baptist Church is the oldest Protestant church in Kodiak. The Roman Catholic, Church of God, and Assembly of God are each housed in new buildings. The Kodiak Christian Center is a new addition, and the Christian Science group holds services in the city. Kodiak is headquarters for the Baptist Church evangelist and his family who sail the *Evangel* boat to native Aleut villages and season canneries around the islands. The boat has a movie and slide projector, an amplifying system, two-way radio telephone, and a portable organ. In summer, it visits the villages of Karluk, Alitak, Kaguyak, Old Harbor, Sitkalidak, Afognak, and Ouzinkie, plus twenty outlying canneries, where church services are mostly held by loudspeaker from the bow of the boat with the congregation standing on the shore. At other places the boat puts in and services are held in one of the local buildings. In Kodiak there is a Baptist Mission for dependent children two miles from the center of town.

SCHOOLS

One of the two school buildings in the city of Kodiak was completed in 1955 at a cost of $1,500,000 and is a combination grade and high school boasting a gymnasium-auditorium seating over one thousand people. The old school is located downtown and is used presently for some of the lower grades.

Shopping and Services

Kodiak has large supermarkets, general merchandise stores, including Kraft's and Knudsen's, a cleaning plant and laundry, garages, service stations and auto dealers, the Bank of Kodiak, beauty and barber shops, a Swedish massage, steam bath and reducing salon, a florist, giftshops, sporting goods, and photo supply shops. The local weekly newspaper is the *Kodiak Mirror*.

Health—The Griffin Memorial Hospital is a twenty-three-bed institution operated by the Grey Nuns of the Sacred Heart. It is well equipped with the latest diagnostic facilities and is operated on a nonprofit basis. The city is served by three doctors, one of whom is a surgeon, one dentist, and a health center.

Radio and Television—The Kodiak area is served by Armed Forces Radio and Television located at the naval station. In the winter months regular radio reception gets stations from Los Angeles and Salt Lake City with short-wave reception from many points in the world.

Organizations

The community of Kodiak has many active organizations. Among them are the Chamber of Commerce, Rotary, Elks, Masons, Business and Professional Women's Club, Emblem Club, Eastern Star, Rainbow Girls, VFW and auxiliary, American Legion and auxiliary, Toastmasters, Kodiak and Aleutian Islands Historic Society, Kodiak Guides Association, Teen-Age Club, Kodiak Conservation Club, Winter Sports Club, PTA, Kodiactors Drama Club, and the Kodiak Welcome Club.

Activities

Winter sports are popular at Kodiak and the skiing is good. In summer there are swimming and many outdoor sports. Sightseers enjoy visits to the canneries, the historic landmarks, trips out Old Mill Road and Mission Road where there are beaver dams, the Russian cemetery, magnificent scenery, places to picnic, and bathing beaches. The Orpheum Theater is the movie house; billiards and pool are played in the taverns, and some of the twelve cocktail bars have dancing and entertainment. Special permission is required to visit the large Naval Air Base installation, Old Fort Greeley, and to travel on portions of the numerous roads in the Buskin River, Old Woman Mountain, and Chiniak Bay areas. Applications are made to Base Headquarters.

On the beaches, during low tide, catching and digging shoreline sealife is a favorite pastime. Crabs similar to Dungeness can be picked up or dug out from beneath the sand. Purple mussels are easily obtainable. Cockles lie just under the sand at low tide, butter and littleneck clams are somewhat deeper, and the razor clams, largest of all, are buried farthest down. Shrimp may be caught in traps or nets in the tidal pools.

Kodiak and Aleutian Islands Historical Society has relics and artifacts of the pioneer days of Kodiak, the Russian settlements, forts, and native villages in their local museum. Conducted tours of the sites of these historical establishments and the remaining buildings, including the first Russian house built in Alaska, the old churches, and the ancient stonewall moorings, are a part of the society's program for visitors and residents.

PROSPECTIVE SETTLERS

Job opportunities are scarce in Kodiak and most of the basic service and shopping businesses are already established, so that opportunity for a new small business is limited. Industrially there is still much to be developed in the area but a major problem of development is transportation from the island to the markets.

Housing—Very limited housing is available for rent in and around Kodiak, and the demand is heavy because of the concentration of military personnel and families. Inquiries should be directed to the Chamber of Commerce or to Aleutian Homes, 1111 Carolyn Avenue, Kodiak.

King Cove

King Cove is one of many similar native villages that exist along the Alaska Peninsula and Aleutian Islands. There are no trees on the countryside but there are many wild flowers, spectacular mountains and volcanoes, including Pavlof which erupted in 1937 and 1950, covering the area with ash from its peak thirty miles away.

The economy of King Cove's 250 people is based on salmon and crab fishing and processing. The local cannery is open from the latter part of May until the first of September for salmon canning, and stays open all winter for the processing of crab if the weather permits good fishing. Among the village's fishermen are experienced guides for the hunting of the big-game varieties found in this area.

A general store carries basic foods and supplies needed by the residents, and the school has four teachers for its sixty-five to seventy-five pupils. The King Cove Chamber of Commerce handles the arrangements for visitors desiring sleeping accommodations, food, chartering local boats, and guide services. It should be contacted before visiting the village.

Reeve Aleutian Airways maintains air service with nonscheduled flights from Anchorage. Air-mail parcels and letters reach the village about two or three times a week, and there are planes for charter flights from Kodiak and Homer airports. The mailboat M.V. *Expansion* stops once a month on the trip from Seward, carrying the larger cargo and mail for the village.

Pribilof Islands

In July and August the Reeve Aleutian Airways offers a fascinating tour of the Pribilof Islands, nine hundred miles west of Anchorage. The all-expense cost is $160 for the three-day trip on a flight over the Valley of Ten Thousand Smokes, volcanoes, Japanese crab-fishing fleets, whales, thousands of wild animals, and Arctic birdlife.

The island destination offers the most interesting show of wildlife on earth, the romantic and mysterious life and propagation of the Alaska fur seal, which is reported to be one of the great wonders of nature.

Once a year the fur seals go to the Pribilofs to bear their young and to breed, because, from spring to fall, the islands are almost always overcast, a perfect condition for the seal, which does not enjoy direct sunlight. Although the islands are barely visible from the air and sea during these months, the constant, never-ending roar of the bull seals, their harems, and young can be heard a great distance away.

The vanguard of the great fur seal herd are the bulls, or "beachmasters," who reach the Pribilof rookeries early in May. These massive bulls are tremendously powerful animals, six to eight feet in length and actually five times as large as the females. They arrive weeks in advance and pre-empt the best positions on land for their forthcoming homes.

The unattached bulls form a solid fringe around the outside edge of the breeding rookeries, on the alert to take their many wives and establish their own families. The two-year-old females arrive and there is rugged and romantic competition by the bulls to win them. Once they are won, there is no divorce. If the female starts out to choose another husband, the bull rushes after her, grabs her by the back of the neck, and actually throws her over his head back into the harem.

Each breeding female bears but one pup a year and they have an uncanny instinct for recognizing their young. The mother, after being bred, frequently swims to the feeding grounds which may be as far as 150 miles distant. After swimming this great distance for squid, her favorite food, she will come back to the island and find her own pup from among the million others. She will never suckle any but her own and, if she is killed at sea, the pup also dies.

The native Aleuts and a small complement of government personnel at St. Paul and St. George, the two Pribilof Island communities, are employed to kill off the large numbers of male seals. Every day from the fifteenth of June until early August, just before daybreak, natives quietly approach the rocks where the young male seals are concentrated. They surround the animals, driving them back from the beaches inland to the tundra-covered fields a quarter of a mile or so away. From the large group of animals in the drive, smaller groups of about fifty animals are detached and surrounded by the natives who select the three-year-olds from the group, allowing the others to escape.

After killing and skinning, the pelts are transported by trucks to a modern plant on the islands where they are quickly cooled, washed free of dirt, blubbered, salted, and packed in barrels for shipment by the government to Seattle.

St. George Island

St. George Island has a population of approximately 185 persons. The hospital on St. George is a well-arranged, modern, building with two wards, one private room, and a total of nine beds. No surgery is performed except in extreme emergencies and food is prepared and brought in by patients' families. Passenger service is by air only and Reeve Aleutian Airlines schedules a mail run from Anchorage approximately once a week, arriving on Thursday. Mail is sometimes not received for weeks at a time, however, because of weather and other conditions. A Navy supply ship comes into the island the latter part of August or early September to pick up furs and deliver equipment and supplies. Accommodations are available through Reeve Airlines only.

Bethel

In the great tundra areas inland from the Bering Sea on the western coast of Alaska there are many isolated and tiny Eskimo villages serviced by the community of Bethel, four hundred miles west of Anchorage and about eighty miles from the Bering Sea, located on the Kuskokwim River, where there is a deep channel that permits freighters to come up the river with supplies and equipment. This access to deep-sea ships makes Bethel a center for trading stores, a jumping-off spot for bush planes carrying mail and supplies to the coastal villages, and to the Yukon and Kuskokwim river villages.

The town of Bethel has a constantly changing population of about one thousand persons, approximately two hundred whites and eight hundred Eskimos, Aleuts, and Indians. The white members of the community include teachers, storekeepers or traders, members of the Army, Air Force, and National Guard, temporary construction personnel, Bureau of Indian Affairs administrative personnel, Alaska Native Health Service hospital personnel, and employees of the Civil Aeronautics Authority who maintain the airport and other aviation services.

Bethel's two churches are the Moravian and the Roman Catholic, and the Baha'i Faith has several members in the community. The local combined grade and high school is attended by all children and is administered by the Alaska Department of Education; the high school is accredited by the Northwest Association of High Schools. The small public library is operated by the Women's Club and the two movie theaters are privately owned.

The PHS Alaska Native Hospital in Bethel is the largest field hospital in the Anchorage area and the Bethel Hospital, caring for most of the tubercular patients in the area, serves a territory the size of the State of Kansas, comprising fifty-five native villages and serving between eight and nine thousand natives. It is staffed by eighty-seven persons, which includes a professional staff consisting of three doctors, one dentist, and a nursing staff of thirty-two.

A radio transmitter and receiver set is installed in the hospital to contact all the villages in the area every evening. Cases are diagnosed and prescriptions made via this radio contact, and, if cases are in need of specialized care, they are brought to the hospital via bush plane. One of the doctors in the hospital advises officials, schoolteachers, or nurses in the various villages as to the type of drugs to use and how to administer them. If proper drugs are not available in the village, they are sent from the hospital by bush plane the following morning.

TRANSPORTATION AND ACCOMMODATIONS

Transportation between Bethel, the surrounding villages, and Anchorage is supplied by Alaska Airlines and Northern Consolidated Airlines by scheduled bush plane service. The planes are equipped with pontoons or wheels in the summer and skis in the winter. The river usually provides landing facilities for small planes except during freeze-up and breakup when all transportation is at a standstill.

Accommodations for overnight stops or longer visits should be arranged in advance with the air-line ticket agents. All housing and transient facilities are scarce.

Hooper Bay

Typical of one of the Bering Sea coastal villages served by Bethel is Hooper Bay, 150 miles from Bethel. It is a very old village; archaeological exploration and excavations have proven that Eskimos have lived there since at least A.D. 1600. The first recorded visits of outsiders was by Catholic missionaries about 1890.

The Bureau of Indian Affairs operates a grade school for the local residents and has plans for a new junior high school. The grade-school students publish irregularly a four-page newspaper called *Hooper Dooper Happenings*, which carries the news of the school and accurately covers the village news. Feature articles review the movies, recommend recipes that have been tried in the local homes, review the Eskimo dances, and tell local folk stories, all written and illustrated by the children in fascinating style.

The Eskimo women weave grass baskets and mats for sale locally and through the Alaska Native Arts and Crafts Cooperative in Juneau. The two ivory carvers in the village are dependent on ivory being shipped in because there is no local source.

Christmas, Easter, and the Fourth of July are all celebrated with Eskimo games, dances, and kayak races, and, occasionally when there are visitors, the people stage special dances. Little girls from about four to fourteen carve pictures in the snow and moist earth to illustrate stories with their "story knives," an unusual art form not seen in other villages. It is difficult to observe the work of these youngsters as they are very shy and do not perform their art for strangers.

Hooper Bay has a Catholic and Swedish Lutheran church, a general store, and coffee shop. The community does not have a resident doctor or nurse but the short-wave clinic operated by the hospital in Bethel takes care of the medical needs of the villagers.

TRANSPORTATION AND ACCOMMODATIONS

Sleeping accommodations for visitors are not available; however, in an emergency it is possible to sleep at the schoolhouse or in one slightly furnished cabin that can be used by transients who bring their own sleeping bags and equipment. Drinking water is very difficult to obtain and should be boiled as a precautionary measure. The Northern Consolidated Airlines has scheduled bush flights to Hooper Bay twice a week to bring in supplies, mail, and passengers. The one-way fare is $35. Once a year the cargo boat, *North Star*, makes a freight-delivery stop that creates a holiday spirit in this coastal village.

CHAPTER VIII. INTERIOR AND ARCTIC ALASKA

Fairbanks — McKinley National Park — University of Alaska — Tanana Valley — Nenana — Tanana — Big Delta — Tok Junction — Fort Yukon — St. Lawrence Island — Unalakleet — Nome — Kotzebue — Barrow

To the north of the crescent formed by the Alaska Range lies a broad expanse of plateaus and lowlands, dotted by mountain groups and drained by several large rivers including the Yukon and its tributaries. The subsoil over most of this area is frozen the entire year but some of the thawed topsoil is relatively fertile. Tundra and wooded areas are the homelands of fur animals, game birds, and large numbers of big game, such as moose, caribou, mountain sheep, and black bear.

The Seward Peninsula, a major gold-mining area, was the scene of the fabulous gold rush of the early 1900's. At its tip the Bering Strait separates Alaska from Siberia and, in the middle of the strait, less than three miles apart, is Little Diomede Island of the United States and the Soviet Union's Big Diomede Island.

Farther north, above the Arctic Circle, the rugged Brooks Mountain Range cuts across the endless miles of tundra country, where most of the villages and settlements are inhabited by the Eskimo people, at the "top of the world."

Fairbanks

Five time zones west of New York City, less than two hundred miles south of the Arctic Circle in the Golden Heart of Alaska, is the city of Fairbanks.

This is a city of extremes where the round-the-clock daylight in summer is contrasted with round-the-clock darkness in midwinter, where the record low temperature is 66 degrees below zero and the record high is 99, and where log cabins of the early settlers stand alongside multistoried apartment buildings of concrete and steel.

The year of 1902 marks the earliest recorded history of Fairbanks, centering on Felix Pedro who made a gold strike on what is now called Pedro Creek near the present city, launching a gold rush to the area and the establishment of the community. But it was not the kind of gold rush experienced in other areas of the territory; there were no vast quantities of gold lying around just waiting to be picked up off the ground. It was buried under some one hundred feet of gravel and muck to the disappointment of the stampeders and, as a result, Fairbanks did not mushroom overnight and become a boom town like Nome and Hope. Instead, heavy machinery had to be brought for the deep placer mining. This required that shafts be sunk into the bedrock, tunnels made underground, and pay dirt hoisted by buckets. Hydraulic methods, derricks, and steam shovels were used until the advent of monster dredges, which were moved in and worked to speed the economical recovery of the ore. Gold mining was an expensive business beyond the reach of most individual prospectors, and today the greatest share of gold mining is carried on by large mining companies with dredges that bring in from ten to twelve million dollars a year.

Fairbanks, the largest gold-mining district in the United States, is a center for other mining operations and exploration with unlimited potential including coal, antimony, tungsten, and many others, but the extent of each is unknown. Oil and gas projects are in the process of development and the prospects of expanding all of the Fairbanks' area's natural resources production will contribute greatly to the economy of the city.

More than fifty construction contractors maintain offices in the city, making it the center of interior and Arctic construction, and one of the major sources of employment for the city's forty thousand residents.

Because Fairbanks is also a center of transportation and dis-

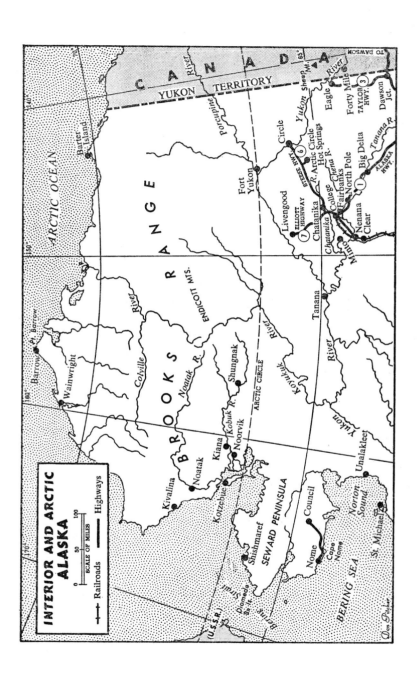

tribution for the railroad, planes, buses, trucks, freight, and transfer companies for an area consisting of 227,000 square miles, a
strategic military center with two huge airbases, Eielson and
Ladd, as well as a communication headquarters for the "White
Alice" network and the Alaska Communications System, and
for agricultural produce, it rightfully earns its name as the
"Golden Heart of Alaska."

TRANSPORTATION

Fairbanks has four airports, International, Phillips, and the
two military fields at Ladd and Eielson Air Force bases. Wien
Alaska Airlines provides the greater share of scheduled transportation facilities between Fairbanks and forty-six communities
north, all the way to the Arctic Ocean. In addition to scheduled
flights, Wien has charter service and operates summer tours of
the Arctic. Pan-American and Alaska Airlines give excellent
service to the city from every point in the nation, Canada, and
connecting overseas flights. The Alaska Railroad extends to and
from Anchorage, Seward, McKinley National Park, and all points
between. Fairbanks is easily reached by car and bus from the
Alaska Highway or from the communities along the Alaska highway system. The Alaska Motor Coaches has year-round service
three times a week from Fairbanks to the Canadian border and
makes summer connections for traveling to points in Canada or
other states. This bus line also has connections to Anchorage and
buses for charter. Alaska Overland, Inc., operates charter bus
services throughout the state.

All types of public transportation are available in Fairbanks,
including charter plane, boat and bus services, taxis, automobile
rentals, and dog teams. There are many moving and storage
companies, as well as freight and express services.

HOTELS

Though there are eighteen hotels, five motels, eight trailer
camps, and a few small rooming houses, accommodations in
Fairbanks are usually difficult to obtain, especially during the
summer months, and advance reservations should be made. Rates

range from $6 to $12 for singles, $7 to $17 for doubles, and $25 up for small suites. Two of the ranking places to stay are the Nordale Hotel which has 112 rooms and 48 baths, located at Center on Second Avenue downtown; the Traveler's Inn at Eighth and Noble streets, one of the handsomest establishments in Alaska, has seventy rooms with baths as well as suites, a fine dining room, cocktail lounge, coffee shop, banquet rooms, and twelve housekeeping units. The old Yukon steamer *Nenana* has been remodeled to serve as an auxiliary hotel and in summer it is tied up at the Fairbanks docks.

Four of the best-equipped trailer parks are the Marvel Mobile Homes at Twenty-ninth and Cushman streets, which has forty-foot wide, lighted streets, year-round sewers, water, and a completely equipped playground, rentals $32 monthly; the Timberland Trailer Park, with laundry, garbage disposal, and pets allowed; the Birch Tree Trailer Court, and the Golden Heart Trailer Village.

The Fairbanks Chamber of Commerce maintains a Hospitality Lob Cabin information center, keeping up-to-date listings of available accommodations in homes when hotels are filled.

RESTAURANTS

The Continental and Northward coffee shops specializing in steaks and seafood, the Redwood with its open-pit charcoal-broiled foods, the Hide-away with Mexican specialties, the Count's Dinner House and the Switzerland's Italian dinners, and Vi's Smörgåsbord with a different "foreign bord" each night are restaurants offering international varieties of foods. The Traveler's Inn serves excellent meals in handsome modern surroundings, and, in addition to the eighteen restaurants, Fairbanks has one drive-in.

CHURCHES

The many churches represent the Assembly of God, Baha'i Faith, Catholic, Nazarene, Latter-day Saint, Baptist, Methodist, Lutheran, Presbyterian, Pentecostal, Episcopal, Salvation Army, Seventh-day Adventist, Unitarian, and many others.

SCHOOLS

The Fairbanks schools rank with the best in the state. Lathrop High School and the five elementary schools each have a nurse and lunchroom facilities. A day nursery and secretarial school are privately owned.

SHOPPING AND SERVICES

Fairbanks has excellent giftshops, department stores, specialty shops, drugstores, jewelers, florists, a health-food products supplier, pet shops, photo equipment shops, and many others. In addition to all regular services, such as banks, cleaners, laundries, beauty and barber shops, automobile dealers and garages, there are also caterers, loan companies, public stenographers, a twenty-four-hour telephone-answering service, snow removal and landscaping companies, massage and steam-bath parlors, and an investment broker. The local travel agency is Arctic Alaska Tours and Arctic Travel Service in the Empress Building.

Health—Fairbanks has a model hundred-bed hospital, a Doctor's Medical and Surgical Clinic, and the Fairbanks Medical and Surgical Clinic. There are twelve physicians and surgeons in the city, many nurses, technicians, six dentists, four optometrists, one chiropractor, and a physiotherapy myopractic. When anyone is unable to reach a doctor at his home or office, it is necessary only to dial "operator" to obtain medical assistance.

Publications—Two newspapers are published in the city, the *Fairbanks Daily News-Miner* and *Jessen's Weekly,* plus the monthly *Guide to Fairbanks* and a television magazine, *TV Spotlight.*

Radio and Television—The two radio stations are KFRB and KFAR. KFAR-TV is one of the television stations, the other is KTVF, the C.B.S. affiliate in Fairbanks. These stations carry all popular radio and television shows with good reception in the area.

ORGANIZATIONS

The city has many social, civic, and business organizations typical of the other communities in Alaska, including the Chamber of Commerce, Daughters of the American Revolution, American Legion, Elks, Lions, Kiwanis, Rotary, Pioneers of Alaska, and many others.

ACTIVITIES

Summertime in Fairbanks offers baseball games at Griffith Park or on the Little League Baseball Diamond, car races at the Rendezvous Speedway, and boat races on the Chena River. Golf tournaments are weekly events at the nine-hole country club course, which is open to the public almost twenty-four hours a day. Rifle shoots and softball games, swimming in the gravel pits and in the city pool, picnics in town at Kiwanis Park on the south banks of the Chena River or out in the countryside, hiking, prospecting, and visiting the nurseries and greenhouses are part of the summer activities.

These are the months when the local garden clubs have flower shows and garden tours for visitors, and the many 4-H clubs put on demonstrations, fairs, and a cherry pie contest.

Winter activities include hockey, basketball, bowling, skiing, curling, folk dancing, attending concerts, and similar events. Skiing at Cleary Summit and Ester Dome is excellent. There are three rope tows at Cleary and the finest ski lodge in the state, in a ski area of 280 acres. Both ski areas are located about twenty-one miles from the city and transportation is easily arranged. The snow is always powder dry during the winter months.

Annual Events—On June 21 the annual Midnight Sun Baseball Game is a feature attraction, followed by the Golden Days Celebration in July. The high light during August is the Annual Tanana Valley Fair. The festive annual Winter Carnival and North American Sled-Dog Championship races are held in March and are the event of the season.

Night Life—There is more night life here than in other Alaskan cities. Two night clubs offer eight floor shows nightly; others have live music, small jazz combos, or pianists. There are many bars and cocktail lounges. The two movie houses are the Empress and Lacey Street theaters. Bowling, roller skating, dancing, swimming and even picnics in summer are all a part of the night-time activities and, like everywhere else in Alaska, everything is informal.

Campgrounds—Chatanika River, Mile 39 on the Steese Highway; Bedrock Creek, Mile 127 on the Steese Highway; Ketchem Creek, Mile 149 on the Steese Highway about 13 miles south of Circle, and Tolovana River, at Mile 59 on the Elliott Highway en route to Livengood, are all sites maintained by the Bureau of Land Management and designated primarily as campgrounds and picnic areas without facilities for trailer houses. One-week stays are permitted in each campground. A pile of fuel wood is normally available in each area and additional wood may be gathered using only dead or fallen timber. The cutting of standing trees is prohibited. All fires should be built in the existing fireplaces and thoroughly extinguished before leaving the campgrounds. Sanitary facilities are available at each site.

SIDE TRIPS

Motor trips are popular because there is so much of interest in the area. Traveling out Steese Highway is Pedro Creek where the first gold was discovered and a monument has been erected in honor of discoverer Felix Pedro. At Cleary Summit, twenty miles from the city, there are excellent views of the Tanana Valley, the Alaska Range, and Mount McKinley. Several gold dredges are at work in the area and, if you branch off this road to the Elliott Highway, it is about eighty-one miles to the community of Livengood, an interesting old mining camp. Continuing on Steese Highway from Fairbanks, through the mining town of Chatanika, motorists pass over the highest point on the Alaska highway system at Eagle Summit, then on to Arctic Circle Hot Springs or to the small village of Circle on the banks of the Yukon River at the end of the Steese Highway, about 163 miles from Fairbanks.

North Pole is fourteen miles southeast of Fairbanks on the Richardson Highway. This community of five hundred is also known as "the home of Santa Claus" because it makes a year-round business of Christmas and the tiny post office receives nearly half a million Christmas letters a year, canceling the stamps with its special "North Pole" inscription.

College Road goes northwest from downtown Fairbanks to the University of Alaska, passing the University Experiment Farm and Creamer's Dairy, to Farmer's Loop Road and the Golf and Country Club, the Tanana Fairgrounds, the North American Sled-Dog Race Course, and fish wheels, all within five miles of the city. Farther on are the gold dredges and mines.

The riverboat *Discovery*, a stern-wheeler, provides excursions on the Tanana River, stopping at native summer camps to watch salmon fishing on primitive fish wheels and the curing processes, and the demonstrations of tanning moose and caribou hides for clothing and shoes. There is a native guide in attendance to answer questions about the various locations visited. Daily sailings are from the river landing at a cost of $10 for the five-hour trip, including refreshments.

Wien Alaska Airlines' Arctic Coast Tour includes an overnight stop at Kotzebue, skin-boat ride, Eskimo dances, meals, and all ground and air transportation, with a stop at Nome to visit the King Island Eskimo ivory carvers and skin sewers and to sight-see in and around Nome's famous gold diggings. The two-day tour costs $135. The three-day tour, which includes an overnight stop in Nome, is $155.50.

Wien's Yukon Valley Tours offers a one-day conducted tour of Fort Yukon, the largest Indian village on the Yukon and a historic treat for tourists. After leaving Fort Yukon the trip goes to Arctic Circle Hot Springs for a tour, swimming, and gold panning, then back to Fairbanks on the same day. The cost of this tour is $44.50. There is a $62, two-day tour of the same area with an overnight stop at Arctic Circle Hot Springs, meals, accommodations, and all transportation.

The "Top o' the World Tour" by Wien is a trip to Barrow on the Arctic Ocean for a rare adventure, dog-team rides, skin-boat rides, Eskimo dances and games, and native craftspeople at work. A two-day tour is $135, a three-day tour with an extra day in Barrow is $155.50. Both include hotel, meals, guides, and all transportation, as well as parkas and other Arctic clothing.

RESORT

At Arctic Circle Hot Springs Hotel and Resort, the new out-door swimming pool is protected by plastic roof and sidewalls. The modern hotel and cabin accommodations for 160 people with family-style meals make it a popular vacation and health resort, located about 137 miles from Fairbanks. The water from the hot springs contains silica, iron, aluminum, calcium, potassium, bi-carbonate, chloride, and sulphate, as well as other chemicals. The temperature of the waters is about 139 degrees at the source and from 103 to 106 in the bathhouses, providing heat to the buildings, the gardens, and hothouses which produce abundant crops. This is an all-year-round resort and the rates are $6.50 for a single, $12 for a double per day, including use of the pools and bathhouse. Meals are $2.25 for breakfast, $2.00 for lunch, and $3.50 for dinner, all served family-style. The resort has a post office, landing field, grocery, giftshop, and service station. There is daily plane and limousine service direct from Fairbanks.

PROSPECTIVE SETTLERS

The average cost of living in Fairbanks runs approximately 45 per cent higher than Seattle. Food costs are 51 per cent higher and housing is 83 per cent higher, but contrary to popular belief the high wages cannot be relied upon to meet them.

The largest single industry in Fairbanks is construction, par-ticularly military construction, which has had a tremendous impact on the local economy, and news of these projects attracts hundreds of persons from the other states during the summer months. There are, however, only so many such jobs to go around, and with the continuing expansion of the resident labor force there is normally a sufficient supply of workers already in Fairbanks to take care of all employer demands except for temporary periods of spot shortages in some skilled crafts.

Mining is decreasing in its importance as a supporting industry of Fairbanks, but it is important to the economy and maintains a stabilizing influence even though it is seasonal. Mining activity is largely connected with placer gold operations. There are open-ings at times during the summer months to take care of replacement needs caused by labor turnover, but the local labor force can usually take care of most demands. There are a few coal mines along the Rail Belt between Anchorage and Fairbanks, but employment is relatively small.

If a newcomer goes to Fairbanks without a specific job commitment, he must have adequate funds to sustain him for a period of thirty to sixty days while seeking employment for which he is qualified. It is estimated that at least $500 per person plus return fare should be allowed for each month.

Employment in Fairbanks is highly seasonal, and there is a regular transient work force which goes to Fairbanks each year during the May to September work season, then returns home. These workers are already established and known to employers and they take many of the jobs that cannot be filled by the resident labor force and thus decrease the opportunities for newcomers.

The main occupations still needed are professional engineers, electronic technicians, and various technical or administrative government jobs. Most government jobs are now handled and filled through civil service procedures.

Job opportunities for qualified women office workers are fairly good. Employers prefer permanent residents but they do hire nonresidents who plan to remain eighteen months or more. Qualified stenographers, secretaries, bookkeepers, and clerk typists are customarily in demand. Worker surpluses usually exist in the classifications of sales clerk, receptionist, telephone operator, waitress, and nurses aide, and starting salaries are low in most cases.

Business opportunities are as varied in Fairbanks as they are in any city of comparable size with basic shops and services already established and needs primarily in improved facilities or specialized services. Ample consideration must be given to the fluctuating population and the effect climate has on business operations in the area. The Fairbanks Chamber of Commerce and Alaska Resource Development Board, P. O. Box 2391 in Juneau, are helpful sources for current information about business conditions and potential needs in and around Fairbanks.

Housing—The modern Polaris, one of the fifteen apartment

houses in the city, has 144 efficiency and one-bedroom, furnished or unfurnished, apartments with automatic laundry, linen, and maid service. Fairview Manor Apartments has 272 one- and two-bedroom and efficiency apartments, children's play areas, and garages. Additional housing is available at the Dixon Apartments, Queen's Court, Smith Apartments, Tamarac Inn, and Wickersham Street Hotel and Apartments. The Northward Building Apartments have a complete shopping center at street level, with a bank, café, pharmacy, taxi, supermarket, laundry, cleaners, cocktail lounge, air-line ticket office, and many other shops and services. The Northward has 210 efficiency and one-bedroom units, electric kitchens, and maid service. Prices for furnished efficiency apartments range from $100 per month and up.

Housing for transient workers is critical during the summer work season. Permanent housing dwellings and apartments usually have vacancies but they are expensive. Transient quarters, such as hotels and motels, are in short supply with rentals from $6 to $14 daily. Quarters in rooming houses range from $15 per week up.

A number of housing developments are in construction to meet the demand. Over a dozen real-estate agencies handle rentals, leases, and property for sale.

Utilities are furnished by the Municipal Utilities System with electricity costs ranging between 4 and 9 cents per kilowatt hour, and water service minimum charges from $5 to $10 per month. The city has a metered steam heat service for customers located adjacent to the steam heat mains for general heating purposes, and the base rates range from $2.47 to $3.51 for every 1,000 pounds of steam used per month with a minimum charge of $10 monthly. Telephones cost from $7.50 for a one-party line to $5.65 for a four-party line.

Mount McKinley National Park

June 10 to September 10 is the official season for Mount McKinley National Park, the more than 3,000 square miles of wilderness in south central Alaska, 233 miles north of Anchorage by train and 424 by highway, and 123 miles south of Fairbanks by train and about 350 by highway. Of all scenic features in the park, Mount McKinley, with its year-round sheath of ice and snow, is the most majestic. Denali, "The High One," was the name given by the Indians to this great mountain, the largest in North America, thrusting the higher of its two snow-covered peaks 20,320 feet into the clouds.

For tens of thousands of years glaciers have sculptured the mountains of the Alaska Range. Jagged spires, knife-sharp ridges, and broad U-shaped valleys are all results of glaciation.

They are still plentiful in Mount McKinley National Park, not remnants of the Ice Age, but valley glaciers resulting from today's climate.

The fronts of most of these glaciers are deeply buried by rocks that have been carried by ice and dropped as the glacier melts. Fronts of the larger glaciers are sometimes completely covered by vegetation, and many animals find their homes there, as they did on Muldrow Glacier, until the winter of 1956 when large waves of ice descended on the inactive front and thrust towering spires of ice to the base of Muldrow. Impressive views of the glacier and this recent spectacular activity can be seen at the Eielson Visitor Center at Mile 65 on the park highway.

Mount McKinley, with its abruptly rising icy slopes, is a bold challenge to mountain climbers. It was first climbed by a party of four sourdoughs in 1913. Every year mountain climbing expeditions from all over the world attempt to reach the top, taking a month or more for the round trip, which many experienced climbers find impossible to achieve. Because of the hazards, climbers must obtain the park superintendent's permission to attempt an ascent. Skill in the techniques of ice climbing must be demonstrated, because treacherous, crevasse-scarred glaciers have to be crossed, and avalanches of snow, rock, and ice are constant dangers.

Mount McKinley National Park is a true wilderness. It is the home of many native animals whose habits have been little affected by man. Animals, like plants, must be well adjusted to the northern climate. But some, such as most birds and the bats, spend only the warm summers in the park and several avoid the cold by hibernating during the long winter. Others grow thicker fur or feather coats, and layers of cold-resistant fat, and some spend much of the winter in burrows and nests deep beneath the insulating blanket of snow.

Visitors can observe most of the animals of the park, for beyond the forested section there are open and unobstructed views, and the rolling tundra of the intermountain areas gives excellent opportunities to see and study animal life.

Several large mammals are capable of inflicting serious injury. Observers should not attempt a close approach, nor should they stalk animals for close-up photos. Grizzly bears and moose are among the animals to watch and photograph from a safe distance. No one should try to attract animals with food. The regulations prohibit feeding and molestation of wildlife.

Bird students and watchers will observe an abundance and variety which includes 120 kinds of nesting birds in the national park. Ducks and other water birds frequent the many lakes and ponds; a plaintive cry identifies the loon on Wonder Lake; along the park road are the nests of gulls, terns, and plovers; and the thrush, redpoll, white-crowned sparrow, tree sparrow, longspur, snow bunting, and many kinds of warblers can be seen as well as heard during a summer visit. The golden eagle and gyrfalcon and several other hawks and owls are common sights to interested visitors.

Most of the rivers of the park are fed by glaciers and contain glacial silts that render them unsuitable for fish. However, in the clear mountain streams the Arctic grayling is caught with artificial flies. Mackinaw trout, twenty-four inches or more in length, are in the cold waters of Wonder Lake.

The daily creel limit is two Mackinaw and ten grayling. A fishing license is not required within park boundaries. Fishing in certain waters may be suspended by special regulations but a complete list of areas open and closed to fishing is available from the park superintendent's offices.

Hunting in the park is prohibited. All firearms must be sealed.

TRANSPORTATION

The Alaska Railroad leaves for the park from Fairbanks and Anchorage. Passenger-train service is available from both cities six days a week during the summer. To get there by automobile the Richardson Highway connects with the Denali Highway leading direct to the park entrance. A car can be shipped to the park by railroad from either Fairbanks or Anchorage. A three-thousand-foot landing strip for private planes only is located at McKinley Park Station near the hotel, and a second landing strip is at Kantishna near the western end of the park road near Camp Denali.

Park Road—Approximately one hundred miles of improved gravel road can be traveled comfortably through the tundra and mountain wilderness of Mount McKinley National Park. The road follows the picturesque intermountain valley north of the Alaska Range at elevations from 1,600 feet at McKinley Park Station to nearly 4,000 feet at several of the low passes between the park's north-flowing rivers. Many points provide excellent views of rolling tundra and valley glaciers, as well as of Mount McKinley and other major peaks of the range. Leaving the park near Wonder Lake, the road follows Moose Creek through historic Kantishna, now nearly deserted but once a thriving gold town of more than two thousand people. On the east, the park road meets the Denali Highway, which parallels the Alaska Range and joins the Alaska road system at Paxson, 156 miles from the park entrance.

ACCOMMODATIONS

McKinley Park Hotel is a modern hotel with eighty-four rooms, a dining room, recreation rooms with dancing, badminton, ping-pong, and other activities. Tennis courts adjacent to the hotel are for guests only. A giftshop, cigar counter, and cocktail lounge are in the hotel. Rates are: a single at $9 without bath; $11 with bath; a double at $13 to $17. There is no charge for children under five years of age if they occupy a bed with an adult, and there is a 10 per cent discount on weekly rentals. Breakfast may be ordered à la carte. The special breakfast is $2.25, luncheon is $2 and up, dinner is $3 and up. The hotel operates two tours along the Park Highway, an eight-hour tour including lunch is $15 and the twelve-hour tour is $20. Automobiles may be chartered with driver for $12.50 per hour. The hotel is open from June 15 to September 10 and advance reservations are a necessity.

Camp Denali is located two miles north of Wonder Lake on a high ridge with a sweeping view of Mount McKinley. Only thirty-two guests can be accommodated at this superior resort which can be reached by car, or in the camp's station wagon which meets guests at the railway station at a cost of $20 round trip for those who are not on the "Sourdough" plan. Chartered planes land at near-by Kantishna airstrip and, if the pilot guns his engine while flying over the camp, a pick-up service is sent out to the airstrip for passengers.

Reservations must be made well in advance for any of the varied accommodations. For two, three, or four persons the small, rustic, chalet-type cabins are fitted with built-in bunks and equipped with bedding, linens, cooking, and eating utensils, and clear spring water that has been piped three thousand feet down the hillside from No Name Creek to each cabin. These housekeeping accommodations are priced at $7 a day or $45 a week for singles, and $10 a day or $60 a week for doubles. Supplies are plentiful at the camp's new trading post.

The main lodge is built of logs, which give a sturdy and rustic atmosphere to the dining room where family-style, home-cooked meals are served, and to the lounge with its big, open fireplace and huge picture windows framing the view of Mount McKinley. American-plan accommodations are $18 a day, and the youthful and experienced hosts at Denali offer a Sourdough Vacation Plan which includes lodging, all meals, transportation, guide services, use of all recreational equipment, including fishing gear, foldboats, and canoes, shupacks, goldpans, knapsacks, and camping gear, at rates of $79 for two days, $101.50 for three days, and $198 for a week. There are also bedrock tents, which rent for $1 a night per person; those interested in renting them must supply all their own equipment.

Campgrounds—Near Savage River Mile 11, and at Wonder Lake at Mile 84 there are modern campgrounds with tables, fireplaces, water, and restrooms. At Teklanika, Mile 27, Toklat, Mile 53, and at convenient intervals along the park road, there are small campsites. Nights are chilly and campers should have tents and warm sleeping gear. Since firewood is scarce, camp-stoves are recommended. Permission must be obtained from park headquarters for authorization to camp at other than designated campgrounds or campsites.

Only dead, fallen timber may be used for fuel for those without a campstove. All refuse must be burned or buried. Permission to build fires outside of designated areas must be obtained from the superintendent. Fires must not be built in duff or in a location where a conflagration may result. After use, fires must be completely extinguished. Lighted cigars, cigarettes, or other burning material must be "dead out" before discarding them in the park.

ADMINISTRATION

Mount McKinley National Park is administered by the National Park Service of the United States Department of the Interior. A superintendent, whose address is McKinley Park, Alaska, is in immediate charge. Exhibit rooms at park headquarters are located two miles beyond McKinley Park Railroad Station on the park road. Every summer evening the park attendants have a color-slide and movie program about the park. Exhibit rooms are open daily and conducted nature trail hikes may be arranged. There are also dog-sled lectures and demonstrations at the kennels.

Boating—Permission to operate privately owned boats, canoes, rafts, or other floating craft must be obtained from the superintendent. The use of motors on boats is prohibited on Wonder Lake and other waters.

Prospecting—A special permit must be obtained from the superintendent for prospecting for minerals on park lands.

Dogs and cats—They are allowed on park lands only on leash, crated, or otherwise under physical restraint at all times. The park superintendent may designate areas where they are not permitted.

University of Alaska

Four miles west of Fairbanks is the unincorporated community of College. There is no industry or business except for two small grocery stores, two motels, a service station, and a restaurant. But on a 2,250-acre tract at College is the University of Alaska, one of the sixty-nine land-grant colleges established by the United States Congress.

With a student body of 650 and increasing numbers of non-Alaskan students, the university is growing academically and building a handsome campus, which includes among the many fine buildings modern dormitories for men and women overlooking the snow-covered Alaska Range, the Brooks Memorial Mines Building, the Student Union, and the Geophysical Institute. This latter building, the first earthquake-proof structure in Alaska, cost approximately $1,000,000. The purpose of the institute is to advance knowledge in the broad field of physics of the earth and to emphasize geophysics as related to the Arctic. Available at the institute are some of the finest facilities in the world for studying the Arctic, the stratosphere, and the space regions beyond.

The museum at the university exhibits only part of the large collection of more than 100,000 specimens of Eskimo and Indian artifacts, arts and crafts, native animals, and historic objects on its present limited floor space in the Eielson Memorial Building. The noted photographic exhibition, "Family of Man," is on permanent exhibit in the museum, which is open from nine to five daily. The library contains 42,241 volumes and receives 675 periodicals, including all daily and weekly newspapers of the state. Microfilm and microcard readers are available. The library is by law a depository of government publications and a map repository. The collection is particularly strong in books pertaining to Alaska.

The university is accredited as an institution of higher learning by the Northwest Association of Secondary and Higher Schools, and belongs to the Association of American Colleges and the National Commission of Accrediting.

Regular four-year courses are offered in agriculture, arts and letters, biological science, business administration, chemistry, civil engineering, education, electrical engineering, general science, geophysics, home economics, mining engineering, geological engineering, metallurgical engineering, geology, physics, and wildlife management, and all of them lead to various bachelor's degrees. The university offers courses in drama, art, journalism, music, and radio.

Civil, mining, and metallurgical engineering and geology students have an option of four-year courses leading to bachelor's degrees or professional degrees. Premedical, predental, and pre-nursing work is also offered. Graduate degrees are offered by various departments.

In the Department of Civil Engineering and the School of Mines, mining engineering and geological curricula are fully accredited by the Engineers Council for Professional Development. Hundreds of Alaskans each year take short courses in mining.

The work in mining extension is designed to give basic training in various phases of geology and mining as a service to those who are unable to take up resident study at the university, but who can study at the university's branches of community colleges in Anchorage, Ketchikan, and Juneau.

The university does co-operative extension work in agriculture and home economics with offices throughout the state, encourages home-making and 4-H clubs, and offers a homemaker's short course each year. It is also associated with the Frick Laboratories of the American Museum of Natural History in the recovery of large quantities of fossil skeletal remains of prehistoric animals that come to the surface as a result of dredging operations and mining on near-by creeks. The university also operates the Point Barrow Arctic Research Laboratory. It offers a six weeks' summer session on campus and a special five-day course dealing exclusively with Alaskan subjects that is attended by many newcomers to the state.

The university is free to residents of the state as well as students from Oregon, Washington, British Columbia, and the Yukon Territory, Canada. The nonresident tuition fee is $60, and the total fixed fees for matriculation, incidentals, Student Union, yearbook, insurance, registration, and library deposit are from $82.50 to $35, depending on the number of credits taken. Single rooms are $100, doubles $80, and board is about $320 for the semester. The total for nonresident students in a double room carrying seven or more credits is about $542.50 per semester. There are a number of scholarships, awards, loans, and aid programs for students, but most of the forty scholarships are limited to Alaskan residents.

A very high percentage of the students work while attending the university. There are many campus jobs available but returning students receive preference in filling these positions. Other students work in Fairbanks, but there are not always enough jobs in Fairbanks and the university recommends that no student enroll without sufficient funds to defray the expenses of one entire academic year.

There are accommodations for couples with not more than one child at the Stuart where there are furnished living room-kitchen, bath, and bedroom apartments. The rent is $100 a month; garages may be rented separately. The Trailer Court is also available for married students, the $15-a-month rent includes water, sewage disposal, and use of the utility house. Other off-campus housing is available at College and Fairbanks.

The Student Union building, renamed Constitution Hall because it was the scene of Alaska's Constitution Convention in 1955, has student recreational facilities, a cafeteria, and a snack bar. A meal ticket for the cafeteria costs approximately $80 a month.

Campus activities include hiking, photography, and winter skiing on local jumps or cross-country, as well as ice skating on the lighted outdoor rink. There are football, basketball, and baseball. There are co-educational picnics, dances, and the university has seventeen campus organizations including the Ski Club, University Band, A Cappella Choir and Vocollegians, the Wildlife Club, Playreading Group, and Sigma Xi. There is a drama workshop, radio workshop, and various music societies.

The university distributes a free-of-charge twenty-seven-minute motion picture, "Frontiers of Learning," telling the story of the college and its operation. The film is available upon request to Audio Visual Center, Inc., 1205 North Forty-fifth Street, Seattle 3, Washington.

Tanana Valley

The city of Fairbanks is a major trade center for the Tanana Valley, which became an agricultural settlement when gold mining and railroad construction hit a big decline.

Of the 65,000 residents and military personnel living in the valley, 150 are farmer-homesteaders who have jobs in Fairbanks or at military bases to meet the high costs of land clearing and well drilling, but more potential cropland is being added each year as knowledge of permafrost conditions is studied and tested with the present result that many bottomland acres, formerly considered useless because of permafrost, are now being cleared and drained.

Some 4,200 acres of farm land have been cleared in the Tanana Valley. Most homesteaders have only a few acres in crops, growing potatoes and truck crops for the bulk of their farm income. Several dairy farms and one large commercial dairy contribute to the economy of the valley, where livestock enterprises are limited because of poor domestic water supplies.

Considering market opportunities and soil resources, the Tanana Valley seems to have a larger agricultural future than Matanuska Valley. Improved transportation offers the opportunity to grow grain, hay, and straw for shipment to Matanuska Valley and the Kenai Peninsula. This inter-Alaska movement has not yet been developed, but it presents a real possibility for strengthening the agricultural economy of Alaska and the profits of farmer-homesteaders in Tanana Valley.

Nenana

Nenana is the famous home of the Ice Classic and the center of attention of all Alaska during the spring when the time draws near for the ice breakup. Because it is located at the point where the Nenana and Tanana rivers come together, it is an important cargo transfer point for river barges and the Alaska Railroad, making it a distribution center for many remote river villages and mining districts of the interior. It is easily reached by the Alaska Railroad and by Wien Airline's scheduled bush flights from Fairbanks; a new roadway connects Nenana to the Alaska highway system. Nenana has a movie theater with showings two evenings a week, a civic center for local meetings and social events, bars, cafés, a general store, and one hotel, the Tortella Inn.

Tanana

Tanana, which was once the site of old Fort Gibbons Army Post, is two hundred miles northwest of Fairbanks at the mouth of the Tanana River, the largest tributary of the Yukon.

This quiet little Indian village is rich in the lore of early Alaska and claims more old-timers among its 175 people than any other village on the Yukon. The oldest frame building on the Yukon River is the home of the manager of the Northern Commercial Company, Tanana's general store which stands near the government hospital for natives, and the school maintained by the Bureau of Indian Affairs with classes through the eighth grade.

In addition to the Athabascan Indians, there are a few employees of the Civil Aeronautics Administration, the Federal Electric Company, and the doctors and nurses stationed at the hospital. The villagers' and visitors' recreation is fishing, hunting, boating, hiking, and panning small gold nuggets in near-by streams. Movies are shown weekly at the CAA station and in the village.

The active Episcopal Mission and the irregular visits from a Catholic priest make their contributions to the life of the village where the wild flowers grow profusely in summer, and in the fall fields of berries grow and are gathered for canning and preserving.

Big Delta

Located on the Tanana River at the junction where the Alaska and Richardson highways meet, Big Delta is an important supply point for the area, and the site of the United States Army's Fort Greeley, where there is an atomic reactor and Arctic training center. The personnel of these outfits help support the town's trading post, the lodge, and the modern Bays Hotel of twenty rooms with bath, a coffee shop and bar, with single rates at $10 and doubles from $10 to $12. There are good motels, cafés, and automobile service and supply, a souvenir shop, a soft-drink factory, and well-attended schools and churches.

Tok Junction

Tok Junction is the place where the Glenn Highway to Anchorage enters the Alaska Highway. The United States customs and immigration offices are located at the junction, which is the inspection point for all traffic entering Alaska. The customs and immigration offices are open from eight in the morning until ten at night. Numerous facilities are available for the traveler, including a service station and garage, grocery store, church, an airstrip, telephone and telegraph service, and two hotels. Tok Lodge has sixteen rooms with or without bath, dining room, cocktail lounge, general store, and service station. The Parker House has rooms with or without bath, cabins and dormitory accommodations, room service, and dining room. Rates are from $6 to $8 for a single, $8 to $12 for a double.

Campgrounds—These sites are maintained by the Bureau of Land Management and are designated primarily as campgrounds and picnic areas without facilities for trailer houses. One-week stays are permitted in each campground at Tok River, 5 miles east of Tok Junction at Mile 1309 on the Alaska Highway; Moon Lake, at Mile 1334 on the Alaska Highway; Lakeview, Mile 1257 on the Alaska Highway; Deadman Lake at Mile 1249 on the Alaska Highway and 1½ miles southwest by side road; and Gardiner Creek at Mile 1247 on the Alaska Highway about 26 miles from the Canadian border. A pile of fuel wood is normally available in each area and additional wood may be gathered using only dead or fallen timber. The cutting of standing trees is prohibited. All fires should be built in the existing fireplaces and thoroughly extinguished before leaving the campgrounds. Sanitary facilities are available at each site.

Fort Yukon

Fort Yukon, one mile north of the Arctic Circle, was the chief trading post of the Hudson's Bay Company; it was established in 1847 and considered to be the oldest English-speaking community in Alaska. For a short visit it is an interesting and colorful place with landmarks and much of the old frontier flavor. It is fascinating to see the intricate beadwork done by the Athabascan Indian women on native tanned moose hides, and the native men catching salmon with the primitive fish wheels. The preparation of the fish for curing and storage, the demonstrations of sled-dog care, outfitting, and travel, and large vegetable gardens that produce abundantly are also of interest. Fort Yukon has the most extreme climate in Alaska, with winter temperatures recorded at 78 degrees below zero and recorded summer temperatures at 100. Game hunting and fishing are not considered good because the area is hunted out and the river is silty. As a result of inaccessibility, the town has not grown, but there is a trading post and two roadhouses providing lodgings and meals. The water supply is a problem and drinking water must be boiled before it can be used; showers and baths cost $1. The local transportation is provided by a new bus operated by Wien Airlines. There is also an ancient Ford car which is available in summer, but in winter dog teams are used almost exclusively. Fort Yukon can be reached by Wien Alaska Airlines from Fairbanks and the round-trip fare is $46, or by a guided one-day tour operated by Wien. The Yutana Barge Lines operate freight service from Nenana.

St. Lawrence Island

The last shot of the Civil War was fired near St. Lawrence Island from the Confederate ship, *Shenandoah*. This large island in the Bering Sea and dotted with mountains is nearly one hundred miles long, twenty miles wide, and forty miles from the shores of Russia. It is a volcanic island covered with moss and lichens, creeping willows, and birches. There are no trees, but many lakes, rivers, creeks, lagoons, and tundra ponds relieve the landscape. Over half of the year it is surrounded by the Arctic ice pack. The two communities on the island, Savoonga and Gambell, have about 550 people, mostly English-speaking Eskimos, and almost 1,000 dogs. The distance between the two villages is about forty miles and transportation consists of native skin boats fitted with outboard motors or dog team and sled, costing $30 per passenger for a round trip and 10 cents a pound for baggage or freight.

The island may be reached by plane from Nome airport via bush plane at a cost of $86.25 each way. At Savoonga and Gambell visitors can arrange to rent sleeping space in native houses, at the Presbyterian mission, or through the teachers at the Bureau of Indian Affairs schools located in both communities. There is a native store in each village where no meals are served but food items may be purchased. The government freighter, *North Star*, brings in supplies once or twice each summer, but all other freight and mail are brought by air.

The medical facilities consist of a public health nurse who alternates her time between the two villages; there are no doctors but cases of serious illness are reported by radio and the patient is flown out to the nearest hospital.

Many of the natives are fine craftsmen producing ivory carvings which are offered for sale in the local stores. One Eskimo woman, Florence Chaunsey, sketches and paints scenes of Eskimo life on paper and skins, and a native photographer, Clarence M. Irrigoo, Sr., at Gambell has received national attention for his color pictures of the island.

The one to two hundred reindeer on the island are all that remains of the original herd of ten thousand that was placed there by the government. There are white and blue foxes, polar bears, whales, seals, and shore and land birds that nest on the island in vast numbers. Hunting and fishing are good and the native guides are excellent hunters and guides.

The island is an archaeologists' paradise because of the great number of artifacts and other remains of settlements that lie close to the surface of the land. The St. Lawrence Eskimos and their island have been the focal point for many important explorations and expeditions by museums, universities, and explorers' societies.

The Fourth of July is the annual event celebrated by all the residents, with Eskimo games, skin tossing, and dances. On rare occasions during the year native ceremonials proclaim the whaling, walrus hunts, and moon worship.

Houses in the villages are mostly of frame construction; however, many of the Eskimos maintain shelters in summer camps where they gather food plants, hunt, trap, and fish. Telephone and telegraph communications with the island are transmitted via the "White Alice" communications system, as well as by radio.

Unalakleet

Unalakleet is a small Eskimo village, one of the scheduled stops for Alaska Airlines en route between Anchorage and Nome. The village has a small hotel and restaurant and additional guest accommodations at the home of Frank Ryan, the postmaster. There is very little for a visitor to see or do except to observe the life of a quiet Eskimo village where berrypicking, Arctic hunting and fishing, church socials, and hiking are the foremost recreations of the friendly, English-speaking people, whose children attend the grade school run by the United States Bureau of Indian Affairs and the high school of the Covenant Mission.

Nome

At the turn of the century Nome was the scene of one of the world's most famous gold rushes, when twenty thousand men and women landed on its sloping beach and established a frontier city with false-front buildings, narrow unpaved streets, and wooden sidewalks. Most of it was destroyed by fire in 1934 and in its place new buildings were constructed, streets widened, and sidewalks straightened, but even today the streets are unpaved and the wooden sidewalks remain. Many wood-frame homes are mounted on giant runners, like sleds, so that they can be moved when heat from the interior of the house thaws the permafrost, causing the houses to lean and cracks to form in the walls, unless the house is towed to a new location where the ground is still frozen and solid. Some buildings in Nome have foundations sunk many feet through the perpetually frozen subsoil to bedrock so that it is never necessary for them to be moved, but it is a very costly operation and recently some residents have imported house trailers and Arctic-type prefabricated living quarters.

Water is piped into homes during the summer months through exposed pipes that run along the streets on the surface of the earth. In winter the water supply is delivered by truck from the warm springs at the edge of town which resist the winter freeze. Many homes and business establishments have tanks built into the building for winter water storage but a slight leak or a faucet accidentally left open can create a hazardous water shortage.

Nome is the trading and distribution center for the Seward Peninsula, serving the mining districts and native villages for miles around. It is strategically situated along the radar defense DEW line, as well as the new "White Alice" communications system, which were responsible for much of the income and employment of local labor in recent years. The gold that made Nome famous still exists in great quantities, but because of rising costs in mining operations and the inflexible price of $35 an ounce, gold mining has been curtailed; dredges now operating in the area produce nearly $100,000 worth of gold every week. The mineral potential of the area includes not only gold but huge deposits of tin, iron, copper, lead, nickel, and many other ores.

There is no road connecting Nome with the Alaska highway system but much consideration has been given to a road link between Nome and Fairbanks, which is seven hundred miles east; this would mean cutting across the tundra, mountains, and forests and it is estimated that the project would require five years to build at a cost of many millions of dollars. Such a link would have an important effect on the economy of the city, which depends largely on tourist traffic and defense construction.

The population of two thousand includes many Eskimo families living in the city the year around, as well as King Island and Diomede Eskimos who come only for summer to fish and camp at the east end of town. The camp is strung out along the water front where the transient islanders form an unusual sight as they sit on the beach in the shelter of their walrus-skin boats making their famed ivory carvings. The production of native arts and crafts is considered one of the major industries of Nome. The Eskimo women have a co-operative skin-sewing organization called the Nome Skin Sewers; they own and operate a salesroom and produce fur garments, parkas, gloves, mittens, mukluks, boots, and dolls for sale around the world, and have made the clothing for many of the historic North and South Pole expeditions.

TRANSPORTATION

Nome may be reached direct by Alaska Airlines daily from Anchorage or by Wien Alaska Airlines daily from Fairbanks. The local transportation consists of a twenty-four-hour taxi service and a tour bus operated by Wien in connection with their Arctic tours to Nome. Cargo boats, which can reach Nome about five months of the year from June to October, make about four stops each summer to deliver freight and supplies to the city.

HOTELS AND FOOD

Three hotels, the modern Polaris, the new North Star, and the Wallace Hotel, have rates from $8 for a single to $14 for a double, and during the winter months special discount rates are offered.

The best restaurants in Nome are the Bering Sea Club, Polaris Dining Room and the North Star, all serving well-prepared American food. Reindeer steaks and seafoods are featured on the menus and the North Star has special "after the movie" suppers on Saturday night with Oriental, Scandinavian, and European specialties. There are other small cafés and coffee shops for quick snacks and a number of bars, several with entertainment and dancing on week ends.

SHOPPING AND SERVICES

A modern hospital servicing the large area, schools, churches, a public library, a bank, trading posts, department store, cleaning and laundry service, auto repair, telephone communications, many curio shops, and other service businesses make it a busy community. The only newspaper in all of northwestern Alaska is the triweekly *Nome Nugget*, the oldest newspaper in Alaska, established in 1899, which also publishes pamphlets containing stories and lore of the area. Nome has "paid" television broadcast by the local television station, KNOM-TV.

ACTIVITIES

In April of each year the Nome Dog-Team Sweepstakes are run with teams coming to Nome from all over the Arctic area. There is a giant-sized Fourth of July celebration with parades, Eskimo games, and many festivities and, in November, the Roof Garden Celebration is held when the largest gold nugget of the year is awarded to the lucky ticket holder.

Hiking, picnicking, hunting, and fishing are very popular. The local movie theater has good programs three or four nights a week. There are many church and other socials where the public is usually invited.

The gold dredges are very close to the downtown area and are still in operation, and during the summer visitors are shown how to pan gold which they may convert into cash at the local bank.

Short auto trips may be taken to Cape Nome, about fifteen miles east of the city on a road that continues to Council, the former center of a rich placer-mining district, passing through the old mining camp of Solomon along the way. This road is not kept in good repair and is sometimes impassable beyond Cape Nome, but even a short trip is worth while because it follows along the coast line and presents the summertime sight of the expanse of green tundra that surrounds Nome where over three hundred varieties of wild flowers and wild berries grow.

The seven-mile Wild Goose Railway to Anvil Creek is operated for visitors during the summer for sight-seeing trips over the same tracks used by the gold-rush pioneers.

PROSPECTIVE SETTLERS

Housing is a serious problem in Nome. There is rarely anything available. Living costs are high, food is 57 per cent higher than Seattle, housing is 68 per cent higher, and clothing is 14 per cent higher, and there is much local unemployment. The hiring offices in Fairbanks handle Nome's employment needs for industrial personnel.

Kotzebue

One of the major attractions on most package tours is the colorful and lively Eskimo village of Kotzebue, the Arctic playland for visitors during the summer months.

Governed by a native council which forbids the sale of liquor, this second largest village of Eskimos looks as if the streets and buildings were placed there by accident rather than plan.

Many natives from the Little Diomede Island come for a three-month summer visit to Kotzebue, increasing the population to approximately one thousand and participating in the many summer activities for visitors.

Transportation

Wien Alaska Airlines operates package tours out of Fairbanks, as well as a regular scheduled service, from Fairbanks and Nome to Kotzebue. The round-trip fare between Nome and Kotzebue is $50. Wien has bus service during the summer for tour guests. In winter during freeze-up, the planes operate on skis, landing on Kotzebue Sound.

Hotels and food

There are three places to stay. The Wien Arctic Hotel on the shore of Kotzebue Sound is operated by the air line. Rotman Hotel and Hanson's Trading Post also have modest accommodations. Hotel rates are from $4 to $7 per day per person. The Kotzebue Grill serves meals and at the hotels meals are served family-style. Wien Arctic Hotel has a number of specialties including sourdough hot cakes, Arctic sheefish, pickled beluga muktuk from the white whale, reindeer stew, and wild blueberries or cranberries when they are in season.

Clothing

Everyone must have a windproof jacket with a parka-type hood for head covering or a cap with ear flaps, wool slacks, warm socks, and gloves. Wien Airlines supplies these extra clothing articles to travelers on its regular tours.

ACTIVITIES

Of particular interest to visitors are the skin-boat rides, Eskimo games, kayak demonstrations, dog-sled rides, skin-blanket tossing, and Eskimo dancers who perform every summer evening, accompanied by taborin-type drums of walrus skin and singing of their strange music.

In March and April Kotzebue is headquarters for polar-bear and wolf hunters. During the first week in March there is a Winter Carnival with dog-team races. Between mid-May and mid-June the ice breakup pushes out of the rivers and into the sea in a dramatic spectacle, and, when the ice has gone out far enough from the coast line, there is the Beluga Whale Derby. Visitors may participate in this whale catch but they must give all captured whales to the Eskimos who use the entire whale for food, clothing, and decorative and utilitarian products such as baleen baskets and toys. The gristle from the whale is carved into ball shapes for the children's "bouncing balls" and even the shavings from the baleen are used for innersole linings in their shoes.

Also in May and June, arrangements can be made with Wien Airlines for trips to Kiana and the Kobuk River fishing camp for excellent shee fishing.

On June 3, the Midnight Sun remains above the horizon and does not set for thirty-six days. Following three weeks of this prolonged daylight, on June 21 there is a Midsummer's celebration with many activities and feasting. Before the midsummer's sun goes below the horizon, the Fourth of July festival is celebrated with the election of the Arctic Circle Beauty Queen who presides over foot races and Eskimo games, yo-yo contests, blanket tossing, muktuk eating, baby contests, boat races, Eskimo dancing, and the prizes awarded for the Whale Derby.

SIDE TRIPS

Three Eskimo villages are easily reached from Kotzebue and are especially interesting to visit because of the unusual handicraft projects in operation which are owned and operated cooperatively by the Eskimo residents.

Shungnak village is the home of a jade jewelry industry. It lies about 60 miles north of the Arctic Circle and about 160 miles east of Kotzebue, up the Kobuk River.

The timbered foothills and mountains to the north contain what is reported to be one of the largest nephrite jade deposits known to man. The jade is mainly picked up in the form of loose boulders in the creeks and rivers that have their sources in the Jade and Cosmos hills.

For many years the existence of jade has been known in this area, which is approximately ten miles wide by forty long; however, prospectors and natives of the region did not begin staking claims and gathering jade until quite recently.

Although there is a great deal of it in this area, only a small percentage is of true gem quality, but this cannot be determined by the outside of the jade boulders. Considerable labor is required to transport the raw material to the village, where it must be cut before it is known if it can be used for making high-quality jewelry. Boulders weighing over one thousand pounds are not unusual in the area.

As far as is known, the craftsmen at Shungnak are the first Alaskan natives ever to produce finished work in jade suitable for jewelry and other decorative purposes, but the use of jade by the natives for utilitarian purposes goes back to prehistoric times. Artifacts of jade at least several hundred years old have been found in a number of places in Alaska and are believed to have originated in this area. Because of the hardness of the jade, it was never worked elaborately but was used principally for tools such as knife blades, creasing tools for working leather, sharpeners, and ax blades. To work jade without modern tools requires incredible patience. One method used by the natives involved fastening a rough piece of jade to a willow branch and anchoring it in a stream of water in such a way that the current kept it moving against a hard sandstone boulder until the surface was smooth.

The Eskimo people of the village now use the latest modern equipment and have a power plant and all necessary tools to convert the jade boulders into beautiful jewelry in their log workshop. In addition to owning and operating the Shungnak Jade

Project in the village, they also maintain a summer retail shop at Kotzebue, which is open from about the middle of June to the first of September.

Noorvik village, also located on the Kobuk River closer to Kotzebue, has a crafts program which is patterned along the same lines as the one at Shungnak, but with emphasis on gold, silver, and copper jewelry with Eskimo designs. Jade work is done only on a very limited scale by the craftsmen.

Kivalina is the largest of the three villages. It is located on the Arctic Ocean roughly ninety miles north of Kotzebue.

Hand-made jewelry is indigenous, but the materials are unusual, even for Alaska. Here caribou hoof and reindeer hoof are combined with small amounts of gold and made into handsome, sophisticated jewelry that somewhat resembles tortoise shell with gold inlay.

In addition to handicrafts, the residents of Kivalina are heavily dependent on hunting and fishing for a livelihood. Some trapping is done for wolverine, Arctic fox, wolf, and muskrat furs. Seal and caribou are the most plentiful source of meat and a reindeer herd is part of the local economy.

The co-operatively owned projects at Shungnak, Noorvik, and Kivalina are assisted by the Indian Arts and Crafts Board, the Bureau of Indian Affairs, and the Alaska Rural Development Board.

Transportation—During summer Wien Alaska Airlines has scheduled bush flights from Kotzebue to Shungnak twice weekly at $60 round trip, three times a week to Noorvik at $34, and three times a week to Kivalina at $25.

Accommodations—It is not advisable to plan overnight trips to these villages because accommodations and eating facilities are not available except at the invitation of the schoolteachers stationed there. If it is necessary to stay overnight, Wien Airlines will attempt to make arrangements if notified well in advance of the trip.

Barrow

The time to visit Barrow, the largest Eskimo village in the world, is between June and September because the weather and the native activities for visitors are at their height in this interesting community of 1,500 people, located on the ice-packed Arctic Ocean at the most northerly tip of Alaska.

It was first visited by English whalers in 1826 and settled by American whalers around 1870, when it was a whaling center and primitive village. But today it is a community of frame houses with only a few reminders of the past, consisting of the buildings built of whalebone, strips of baleen, and blocks of sod, or the natural ice caverns which are still used for storing foods. And there is still the old and certain way of getting water, an involved and fascinating method which consists of blocks of ice approximately two feet square sawed from a near-by lake, loaded on a sled, and hauled to storage shacks which have underground tunnels that are reached through a hole in the shack floor. Ice is also packed all around the interior of the shack and covered with a tarpaulin to keep it as clean as possible.

When water is needed for drinking purposes, ice is chipped from the blocks, placed in five-gallon containers with spigots and melted. Water for bathing and washing clothes is obtained by processing ice blocks in a wanigan, a small shack built on a sled with a stove and large tank which can be moved to the lake and loaded with ice. A fire is started in the stove and the melting ice fills the tank.

Barrow has a theater, general stores, cafés, an Alaska Native School and United States Public Health Service hospital. Near by the United States Navy operates an Arctic Research Laboratory. The Presbyterian minister-missionary of the 561-member church at Barrow relies on a plane, the Arctic Messenger III, to bridge the miles between home base and scattered Eskimo camps and villages.

Visitors to Barrow are treated to kayak demonstrations, Eskimo dances and games, skin-boat and dog-team rides, and Eskimo craftspeople at work, the women sewing skin and making parkas, gloves, mukluks, and other clothing, while the men carve ivory and make baskets of baleen.

The big annual celebration at Barrow is an Eskimo feast and dance called "nulukatuk," which takes place after a successful whaling season around July fourth.

TRANSPORTATION AND ACCOMMODATIONS

Wien Alaska Airlines has scheduled flights from Fairbanks at $110 round trip, as well as two- and three-day guided tours. Wien operates the Top o' the World Hotel, which has plain but comfortable accommodations and a dining room where food is served family-style with unusual specialties of reindeer steaks, Arctic fish, and chewy chunks of muktuk.

CHAPTER IX. PROSPECTIVE SETTLERS

To those seeking a permanent home, Alaska presents a great challenge. In the abundance of the state's natural resources, the lands, the forests, the minerals, the fish and game, and water power there are unsurpassed opportunities. But they do not assure success for new settlers. A pioneering spirit, bolstered by all the knowledge and resources at the settler's command, is essential to the beginnings of success under the forty-ninth star.

Homesteading

Public domain lands are available for agricultural home-steaders in many parts of Alaska. The better farm lands are located in the Tanana River Valley near Fairbanks, in the Anchorage-Cook Inlet area which includes the Matanuska Valley, and on the Kenai Peninsula. A maximum of 160 acres may be secured by complying with the requirements of homestead laws.

Great care must be taken by the prospective settler in the selection of suitable land. Not only cultivation but also residence on the land is a requirement, and it is important to be located in an area reasonably accessible to schools, churches, medical care, and stores or trading posts. The homestead must be near a sanitary water supply on cultivable land, adequate in quality and size for profitable farming, and a satisfactory market for the produce.

There is no single indicator of good land, although the presence of a heavy stand of white spruce and white birch is sometimes a clue to good agricultural soil, but sometimes those trees are found on relatively thin soil that will not sustain crop production. Soil surveys and reports are available as a guide to the selection of land at the Soil Conservation Service, Alaska Agricultural Experiment Station, Box F, Palmer, Alaska, or the Land Management Offices, Box 1740, Anchorage, or Box 110, Fairbanks, Alaska.

It is extremely important for the prospective homesteader to have financial assets to take care of living costs during the development period, to cover expenditures for clearing and preparing the land, constructing the necessary roads and buildings, and getting the essential equipment. These costs are much higher in Alaska than in other states.

There is very little good agricultural land available for homesteading within short distances of roads and electricity. The best procedure for prospective homesteaders to follow is to go to Alaska with a round-trip ticket, look over the country, find a suitable area, mark the boundaries, and file an application with the nearest Land Management office. Since applicants are not required to establish residence for at least six months there is time to return home and prepare for the move to the new homestead.

The number of homesteads that have been developed into going farms is very small, because, to a great extent, of the lack of adequate financing and the cost of transporting farm products to available markets.

Only one homestead entry may be made in the State of Alaska, and only land which is adaptable to agricultural use, and which contains no minerals other than coal, oil, gas, or other leasable minerals, is subject to homestead settlement.

Additional information about homesteading or settling in the Matanuska Valley, Tanana Valley, and Kenai Peninsula is given in the sections of this book that describe each area.

QUALIFICATIONS FOR HOMESTEADING

An applicant must be twenty-one years of age or over or the head of a family. He must be a citizen of the United States or have formally declared his intentions to become a citizen, and must not own more than 160 acres of land in the United States. Anyone who has previously made a homestead entry in Alaska for 160 acres is not qualified. A married woman is not qualified if she is residing with her husband and he is the head and main support of the family. All applications must be made in person at the Land Management offices in Anchorage or Fairbanks.

HOW TO ESTABLISH AND FILE A HOMESTEAD CLAIM

Settlement may be made on either surveyed or unsurveyed public land. The settler must first check in person with the Land Management offices to determine what lands are available. After choosing a location, the four corners of the land must be marked on the ground by monuments, such as large wooden posts, iron pipes, or other markers of a permanent type. To secure the land against counterclaims, the settler on unsurveyed land must make a substantial improvement, such as part clearing, building a driveway, or putting up buildings. He must also file a notice of his settlement in the nearest land office within ninety days after the initial settlement.

If settlement is made on surveyed land, the homesteader should file a homestead application in the land office within ninety days of settlement and pay a fee of $5 if the land area is less than eighty-one acres, $10 if it is larger.

Forms for giving notice of settlement and for making homestead applications are obtainable from the land offices in Anchorage or Fairbanks.

SIZE AND SHAPE OF HOMESTEAD CLAIMS

Homestead claims in Alaska are restricted to 160 acres. A claim on unsurveyed land must be made in rectangular and compact form, not more than one mile long, with side lines running only in north and south or east and west directions. Where conditions of the terrain make such boundaries impossible, other directions may be used.

A homestead on surveyed land must include adjoining subdivisions as determined by survey charts, and may not extend more than a half mile along the shore of any navigable water unless a special waiver is obtained and there is proof that conditions warrant an extension.

RESIDENCE REQUIREMENTS

From the time the homestead claim is filed, the settler has six months in which to establish residence; however, upon special application, an extension may be granted up to one year. Then, for a period of three years, residence must be maintained in good faith as a home, to the exclusion of any other home.

During each year, beginning from the original date of residence, the settler may leave the homestead a maximum of five months. The five months may be divided into two periods of time if the settler desires; however, these absences must be recorded with the land office, including the dates of leaving and returning.

In cases where there is unavoidable hardship as a result of crop failure or sickness resulting in failure to support the family by cultivating the land, application may be made for a one-year leave of absence which begins on the date of approval granted by the land office.

Additional relief is available to homesteaders in localities where severe climate makes residence for seven months a year a hardship. Any reduction in the months of residence extends the length of time necessary to fulfill homestead requirements and, for each month deducted, one year is added. For example, the settler who is granted the privilege of homesteading only five months a year is required to homestead for five years instead of the usual three.

CULTIVATION REQUIREMENTS

During the first year there are no requirements, but during the second a homesteader must cultivate not less than one-sixteenth of the land. During the third year a total of two-sixteenths must be cultivated. Proof of cultivation must be filed in the third year. One exception of this requirement is when there is evidence that the settler's claim is situated on land that cannot be cultivated, a condition the settler was not able to foresee when he filed his claim. The only other exception occurs when the homesteader, after establishing residence, meets with misfortune which makes him unable to cultivate the required area.

SURVEYS

When the homesteader has complied with the terms of the homestead laws and submitted evidence to the land office, a free survey will then be made by the government.

FINAL PROOF

In order to make acceptable three-year proof, the homesteader must show three years' residence on the land, cultivation of one-eighth of the land, and a habitable house on the land. Upon acceptance of the evidence by the land office, the homestead becomes the property of the settler and no payment is required except for fees and commissions. Proof must be made within five years from the date the settler filed his original claim with the land office.

FEES AND COMMISSIONS

A fee of $10 must be paid for recording a notice of homestead settlement. A fee of $5 is charged when final proof is filed. The homesteader must also pay the cost of advertising the final proof notice and a testimony fee at the rate of twenty-two and one-half cents for each one hundred words.

A fee of seven and one-half cents per acre is paid, half when the original application is filed and the remaining half when final proof is filed.

CREDITS FOR MILITARY SERVICE

Veterans of World War II and the Korean conflict, with at least nineteen months of service and an honorable discharge, are allowed a two-year deduction from the three-year requirements, but they must cultivate one-eighth of the acreage before submitting final proof.

There are a number of regulations covering credits for military service that apply to veterans of the Indian wars beginning in 1817 up to the present. The complete regulations may be obtained from the land offices.

COMMUTED PROOF

"Commutation" is a term applied to an alternate form of proof, which permits the homesteader to avoid the third year's residence and cultivation by paying for the land and fulfilling fourteen months' residence during the first two years. The requirements consist of proof of residence, the cultivation of not less than one-sixteenth of the area, and a habitable house on the land. If commutation proof is submitted after the second year, one-eighth cultivation must be shown. When commutation proof is submitted, the homesteader must make payment for the land at the rate of $1.25 per acre in addition to the fees and commissions.

HOMESTEADING IN NATIONAL FORESTS

Homesteads and homesites are available in national forests. Information about available lands may be obtained by writing to the Chief, Forest Service, Washington 25, D.C., or the Regional Forester, Juneau, Alaska. However, available homesteads are located in remote areas and are not near any existing communities.

GRAZING LEASES AND PERMITS

Leases and permits are issued to qualified livestock operators for a period not exceeding twenty years. Grazing fees are charged in proportion to the economic value of the area leased. Free permits are issued for grazing when small numbers of livestock are kept for domestic purposes only. Application is made through the Land Management offices in Anchorage or Fairbanks.

HOMESITES

A person desiring a tract of land for rural residence only may apply for a homesite. Essentially, this is a homestead limited to five acres with no cultivation requirement and a reduced residence requirement.

To qualify, a person must file a notice of location in the appropriate land office. Then, within the following five years, he must live on the land in a habitable house for at least five months during each of three years. After complying with these requirements, the settler may purchase the land at a cost of $2.50 per acre and not less than $10.

Credit equal to the length of military service is given to veterans of World War II and the Korean conflict, but it may not exceed more than two years of the requirement.

PUBLICATIONS

In addition to the government publications distributed by the Land Management offices, the Ninilchik Parent-Teacher Association, Ninilchik, Alaska, has a helpful booklet called *The Homesteaders Handbook,* which contains information about everyday living—how to construct utility buildings, hints for homesteaders' wives, and recipes using local ingredients such as wild game, fish, vegetables, berries, and so on. The booklet, written by homesteaders on the Kenai Peninsula, sells for $1.50.

Job Opportunities

The labor force of the new state has grown rapidly and this increase in the resident working force has changed the picture from a labor shortage to a surplus. The local attitude on the part of employers and business people is nearly always "take care of Alaskan residents first."

When there is urgent need for certain occupations in Alaska, information about it is usually sent out at once and distributed, so that it is always available at state employment offices throughout the nation. Union members can usually get information from locals or by corresponding with the union headquarters located in the various cities in Alaska. When the need is great, employers often advertise in the city newspapers all over the United States asking for applications from experienced workers.

Many persons, when considering a job-seeking trip to Alaska, have visions of a vast land of opportunity where highly paid jobs are plentiful. This concept stems largely from the publicity Alaska has received since World War II concerning the multi-million-dollar federal expenditures in connection with defense construction projects. It also stems from word-of-mouth success stories from individuals who were successfully employed in Alaska and returned to their homes with glowing reports. But the proportion of "success" stories must be balanced with the facts about the Alaskan employment picture.

The chief Alaskan industries before World War II, upon which the territorial economy was based, were the fishing industry, based primarily on salmon, the mining industry which was primarily gold, and the trapping of animals for fur.

The impact of World War II created many changes in Alaska. Its strategic location provided the need for immediate construction of military bases and defense installations. These projects required additional workers, so that during the war years thousands of temporary workers were brought in from other states. Wages soared, particularly in the construction industry. Other supporting industries also increased employment. Only the gold-mining industry received a setback since its product was not in demand. The growing population, which reached 128,643 in 1950, and the outside interest in Alaska, resulted in the expansion of federal agencies and increased government employment. There was a labor shortage in Alaska then, but it no longer exists.

With the granting of statehood, Alaska is now the largest of the fifty states; outsiders are intrigued with the challenge offered by a new state in a "last frontier" but statehood is not expected to create hundreds of new job opportunities. It is expected to stimulate the business climate, but in all probability it will take considerable time before there is a significant increase in new and additional work opportunities requiring workers over and above the available resident work force.

The cost of living, job opportunities, housing, and living conditions are described in detail under each of the major cities in the southeastern, western and interior-Arctic chapters of this book. The following brief summary of significant industries on which the Alaskan economy is based gives an indication of general conditions:

CONSTRUCTION

The amount of federal expenditures, particularly for defense construction, has been the largest single factor in sustaining the Alaskan economy during recent years. This is the industry which attracts the greatest interest for job-seekers because of its higher wages and possibilities of premium overtime pay. A substantial portion of construction work is caused by military defense expenditures, primarily in the Anchorage and Fairbanks areas, as well as in the remote areas north and west of these cities. The industry is seasonal with peak employment in the summer months around August. During the winter, construction employment plunges rapidly and unemployment is widespread. Resident construction workers frequently rely on two or more kinds of work to carry them through the year; some become fishermen, some own private business establishments, others attend the university, and there are many who have to scratch out a living in the winter.

The growth of the resident population in both Fairbanks and Anchorage has resulted in sufficient workers available to meet most normal requirements. But there are occasional peak periods when temporary shortages in some trade classifications occur. These instances are the exception. Local employment offices of the Alaska State Employment Service report a surplus of laborers, carpenters, truck drivers, heavy-duty operators and mechanics, plumbers and electricians, almost year-round. During the spring and early summer, additional hundreds of job-seekers migrate to Alaska hoping to land a lucrative construction job. This merely adds to the surplus of workers and creates a situation whereby, while employment is increasing, unemployment also increases because enough additional job openings are not available to absorb the continuing influx.

The construction industry is completely unionized, and employment is governed by collective bargaining agreements and hiring practices. In addition, preference is ordinarily given to the resident worker. Therefore, the construction job-seeker who goes to Alaska without any job offer or prospects may have a long wait before he finds the job for his qualifications and interests.

A great many large construction projects are awarded to general contractors, such as Western Electric and Morrison and Knudsen, who have headquarters in other states and who bring to

Alaska a certain number of their own key personnel and other company employees for their Alaskan projects.

Since federal expenditures occur on a year-to-year basis, any cutback of such expenditures administered by federal agencies has an immediate effect on employment and employment possibilities.

FISHING

The fisheries and fish-processing industries are seasonal and the employment trend in recent years has been downward because of a diminishing supply of salmon and increased use of machines in processing. Federal fishing regulations imposed for conservation purposes have further curtailed fishing operations and made the work season shorter. Increasing productivity and mechanization in canning plants have decreased the need for as many workers in fish canneries.

It is difficult for newcomers to enter the fishing industry because of an oversupply of fishermen and boats in the state. Investment in a boat and gear takes capital, and the consistent catching of fish takes know-how and a good fish run, but the decreasing fish pack hurts the individual fisherman's catch and income, and limits the opportunities of newcomers.

LUMBERING, LOGGING, AND PULP

These industries have expanded in the postwar years and offer a good potential for the future. However, except for the peak periods during the summer months when the turnover of labor consists of experienced men because of competition from other industries, there is usually sufficient local manpower to meet most demands except in the few highly skilled classifications.

The bulk of logging activity centers in southeastern Alaska, particularly around Ketchikan and Sitka, with some activity in the Chugach Forest areas of the Kenai Peninsula in south central Alaska. The lumbermill's labor requirements are normally confined to replacement needs, and hiring is at a minimum.

FEDERAL EMPLOYMENT

A considerable portion of Alaska employment is related to work in federal agencies and is now in classified civil service. Applicants for such jobs are normally selected through civil service registers. Opportunities are available for top-qualified stenographers, professional engineers, radio and electronic technicians, nurses, and medical technicians. Applicants qualified in these occupations should first check with their state employment office to find out if such openings are listed as current Alaska shortages. Inquiries to the nearest Civil Service Commission office should also be made for specific needs of government employment.

Inquiries regarding employment, wages, transportation, and other pertinent details may be addressed to the following agencies, and should be sent via air mail to those in Alaska:

Offices of the Alaska Employment Service are located at Box 2250, Anchorage, Alaska; Box 1010, Fairbanks, Alaska; 25 Marine Way, Juneau, Alaska; Box 159, Ketchikan, Alaska; Box 282, Petersburg, Alaska; and Box 100, Homer, Alaska. The Alaska Employment Service furnishes only information concerning employment for wage and salary workers.

For specific information write the following:

Department of the Interior
  Area Director, Bureau of Indian Affairs, Juneau, Alaska
  Regional Director, Bureau of Sport Fisheries and Wildlife, Juneau, Alaska
  Regional Director, Bureau of Commercial Fisheries, Juneau, Alaska
  Alaska District Manager, Bureau of Reclamation, Juneau, Alaska
  Area Administrator, Bureau of Land Management, Juneau, Alaska
  Regional Director, Bureau of Mines, Juneau, Alaska
  General Manager, The Alaska Railroad, Anchorage, Alaska
  Personnel Officer, U.S. Geological Survey, Washington 25, D.C.
  Regional Director, Region Four, National Park Service, 180 New Montgomery Street, San Francisco, California
  Director, Alaska Public Works, Juneau, Alaska
Department of the Army
  Civilian Personnel Division, Corps of Engineers, Gravelly Point, Washington 25, D.C.
  Overseas Affairs Division, OCP, DCSPER, Department of the Army, 2nd and Pennsylvania Ave., N.W., Washington 25, D.C.

Department of the Navy

Navy Overseas Employment Office, Headquarters Thirteenth Naval District, Seattle, Washington

Department of the Air Force

Overseas Employment Branch, Directorate of Civilian Personnel, Headquarters, U.S.A.F., Washington 25, D.C.

Medical and Public Health

Medical Officer in Charge, Alaska Native Health Service, Department of Health, Education and Welfare, Anchorage, Alaska

Alaska Department of Health, Juneau, Alaska

Board of Medical Examiners, Juneau, Alaska

Aviation

Regional Manager, Civil Aeronautics Administration, Box 440, Anchorage, Alaska

Alaska Department of Aviation, Anchorage, Alaska

Forestry

The Regional Forester, U.S. Forest Service, Juneau, Alaska

Mining

Alaska Department of Mines, Juneau, Alaska

Road Construction and Maintenance

Regional Engineer, Region 10, Bureau of Public Roads, Juneau, Alaska

Weather Bureau

Department of Commerce, Washington 25, D.C.

Other branches of Civil Service

Alaska Branch, Eleventh Civil Service District, Seattle, Washington

Accountancy

Board of Accountancy, Juneau, Alaska

Chiropractic

Board of Chiropractic Examiners, Box 1192, Juneau, Alaska

Contractors and Construction

Associated General Contractors, Central Building, Anchorage, Alaska

Cosmetology

Board of Hairdressing and Beauty Culture, Juneau, Alaska

Dentistry

Board of Dental Examiners, Juneau, Alaska

Engineering or Architecture

Board of Engineers' and Architects' Examiners, Box 1511, Juneau, Alaska

Law

Board of Law Examiners, Juneau, Alaska

Optometry

Board of Optometry, Box 468, Ketchikan, Alaska

Pharmacy

Board of Pharmacy, Box 800, Anchorage, Alaska

Teaching
   University of Alaska, College, Alaska
   Alaska Commissioner of Education, Juneau, Alaska
   Area Director, Bureau of Indian Affairs, Juneau, Alaska

Business Opportunities

Alaska has a need for creative and farsighted businessmen and women who have the capital to invest and the determination to succeed in spite of the problems that exist in Alaska.

Throughout the state there are evidences of the need, such as those reported by the small community of Bethel which needs a dry-cleaning establishment, a bakery, and a telephone system, or Kenai which needs a theater and good restaurants.

An example cited by the Civil Aeronautics Administration is the need for people to handle food and gasoline service at twenty-six airports in the state. The CAA is in the position to lease land for commercial use at these airports and they may issue concessions for shops and services which are potential business opportunities they would like to see developed.

A major problem for the businessman who would like to take advantage of the opportunities offered by the CAA is the difficult choice of things which would sell at a profit at the variety of air transportation points along Alaska's eight thousand miles of airways. Some stations consist only of the field and a few government houses and buildings. Others have near-by native villages and few traveling visitors. Others are sizable villages with established commercial enterprises and populations that increase and decrease seasonally. It is a problem to determine which of the airports have a transient and local population large enough to support a new business. It is known that gasoline is one commodity in demand at all the air stations. Many airlines in Alaska now provide their own fueling facilities, but only because no one else is selling the fuel at the stations.

At some stations, the hungry traveler, waiting for his plane, is reduced to cheese and crackers from the village store, if there is a store. At most stations there is no such thing as a room where passengers can wait. This situation provides an opportunity for some kind of a chain operation selling fuel and food at airports along the major lanes of travel. Food that is packaged or that can be kept in storage until it is cooked for a customer might well solve the existing problem at most stations. However, as with any potential business in Alaska, it takes careful planning based on knowledge of Alaskan communities.

Many business enterprises do not yet exist in the new state, and many of those that do are inadequate. It must be taken into account whether or not the community can support any new enterprise and how it will be affected by the changes in population, business conditions, and transportation facilities. So many communities are affected by large transient populations near military installations and seasonal industries that any new business must be adaptable to these conditions.

Transportation costs vary greatly during the year, especially in the northern part of the state where weather conditions influence the shipping and handling of freight. However, in areas where new roads are being built or transportation routes are being improved, costs become more predictable and there is less chance of risk.

With a knowledge of some of the problems of operating a business in Alaska the interested businessman should know more of the facts. The cost of personnel in a retail shop, in Anchorage for example, averages $2.45 an hour. Local capital is scarce. Bank-interest rates on loans average 8 per cent throughout the state. Lease and rental rates for business property are in proportion to the higher cost of living.

Businesses in Alaska are subject to the same federal income and corporate taxes as their counterparts in all other states. The Alaska state personal income tax is figured at the rate of 14 per cent of the individual's calculated federal income tax. There are local, city, but no state, sales or real-estate taxes.

On the other hand the Alaskan consumer is conditioned to the higher costs that the businessman must pass along as a result of higher overhead and operating expenses, and there is a market for quality products and services.

A business tailored to the needs of the community will get enthusiastic support from Alaskans. On the other hand "get-rich-quick" operations frequently fail. The residents want stable businesses that will be helpful not only to themselves but also to the local and state economy.

Because of the emphasis Alaskans are placing on attracting tourists to the state, and the great shortage of rooms, resorts, restaurants, hotels, and other tourist facilities, this is one area where business opportunities should be investigated.

Particularly in such a vast but sparsely populated state as Alaska, anyone contemplating a business investment must investigate the potential in person. It is important to visit a few well-chosen communities to talk with the members of the chamber of commerce and become acquainted with local conditions. Whatever results from the investigation, one thing is certain—the friendly people of Alaska will do everything they can to insure success for the newcomer.

APPENDIX

All air lines, boats, steamship lines, bus companies, and railway lines operate tours in addition to regular scheduled service. Information may be obtained regarding special tours or general schedules, rates, and services by contacting any of the following transportation services:

AIR TRANSPORTATION

Alaska Airlines, 2320 Sixth Avenue, Seattle 1, Washington
Alaska Coastal Airlines, Juneau, Alaska
Canadian Pacific Airlines, Ltd., Vancouver Airport, Vancouver, B.C., Canada
Cordova Airlines, Box 1149, Anchorage, Alaska
Ellis Airlines, Box 1059, Ketchikan, Alaska
Northern Consolidated Airlines, International Airport, Anchorage, Alaska
Northwest Orient Airlines, 5563 White-Henry-Stuart Building, Seattle 1, Washington
Pacific Northern Airlines, 1626 Exchange Building, Seattle 4, Washington
Pan-American World Airways, 1320 Fourth Avenue, Seattle 1, Washington
Reeve Aleutian Airlines, Box 559, Anchorage, Alaska
Scandinavian Airlines, 138-02 Queens Blvd., Jamaica, Long Island, New York
Trans-Canada Airlines, 730 Fifth Avenue, New York 19, New York
United Airlines, 5959 South Cicero Avenue, Chicago 38, Illinois
Wein Alaska Airlines, Box 649, Fairbanks, Alaska
Western Airlines, 6060 Avion Drive, Los Angeles 45, California

BOATS AND STEAMSHIP LINES

Alaska Cruises, Inc., 420 Joseph Vance Building, Seattle 1, Washington
Alaska Riverways, Inc., Riverboat M.V. Discovery, Box 636, College, Alaska
Alaska Steamship Company, Pier 42, Seattle 4, Washington
Canadian National Steamships, 214 Vance Building, Seattle 1, Washington
Canadian Pacific Steamships, Passenger Traffic Department, Vancouver, B.C., Canada
M.V. Chilkat Car and Passenger Ferry, Auke Bay, Alaska
Ritchie Transportation Company, Wrangell, Alaska
Sextant Marine Corporation, Box 2233, Anchorage, Alaska

BUS TRANSPORTATION

Alaska HYway Tours, Inc., Fairbanks, Alaska
Alaska Motor Coaches, Box 1048, Fairbanks, Alaska
Alaska Overland, Inc., 305 Noble, Fairbanks, Alaska
Canadian Coachways, Ltd., 10805 120th Street, Edmonton, Alberta, Canada
Greyhound Highway Tours, Inc., 71 West Lake Street, Chicago 1, Illinois
National Trailways Bus System, Room 803, Continental Bldg., 1012 14th Street, N.W., Washington 5, D.C.
Northern Carriers, Inc., Box 1619, Anchorage, Alaska
Northern Stages Ltd., Box 613, Prince George, B.C., Canada
Western Canadian Greyhound Lines, 222 First Avenue West, Calgary, Alberta, Canada
White Pass and Yukon Route, Box 1846, Seattle 11, Washington

RAILWAY LINES

Alaska Railroad, Box 7-2111, Anchorage, Alaska
Canadian National Railways, 630 Fifth Avenue, New York 20, New York
Canadian Pacific Railways, 581 Fifth Avenue, New York 17, New York
Great Northern Railway, 2 Wall Street, New York, New York
Northern Pacific Railway, 120 Broadway, New York, New York
Southern Pacific Railway, 65 Market Street, San Francisco, California
Union Pacific Railway, Pettock Building, Portland, Oregon
White Horse and Yukon Route, Box 1846, Seattle 11, Washington

INDEX

(Main references within each entry are indicated in italics.)

A

Accommodations, 16-18: at Admiralty Island, 195; airplane, see Transportation, air; on Alaska Highway, 70, 73-75; on Alaska Railroad, 211-12; at Anchorage, 210, 212-13; at Angoon, 192; at Arctic Circle Hot Springs, 271, 272; Arctic tours, 271; at Barrow, 297; at Bethel, 260; at Big Delta, 284; on bus routes, 67, 68-69; cabin, 196, 251, 261, 272; Camp Denali, 277, 278; campgrounds, 74-75, 167, 191, 195, 200, 219, 237, 242, 247, 270, 278-79, 285, see also Camping; camps, hunting and fishing, 155-56, 222-23; at Cordova, 250; dormitory, 285; at Fairbanks, 266-67; at Fort Yukon, 286; at Gambell, 287; at Haines, 198-99; at Homer, 235-36; at Hoonah, 192; at Hooper Bay, 18, 261-62; hotels and motels, see each city, town, village, highway; house boat, 267; housekeeping (transient), 213, 235-36, 267, 278; at Juneau, 187-88; at Katmai National Monument, 222-23; at Kenai, 234; on Kenai Peninsula highways, 232, 242; at Ketchikan, 163; at King Cove, 18, 257; at Kivalina, 295; at Kodiak, 253-54; at Kotzebue, 292; lodges, 17, 117, 242, 245, 284; lodges, ski, 103, 189, 269; at Moose Pass, 242; in Mount McKinley National Park, 277-79; at Nenana, 284; at Nome, 290; at Noorvik, 295; at Palmer, 227; for pets, 26, 62, 215; at Port Chilkoot, 198-99; reservations for, 17-18, 55-56, 74; resorts, 102-04, 169, 175, 196, 270, 271, 272, 277-78;

on Richardson Highway, 245; roadhouses, 230, 245, 286; rooming houses, 254, 266-67, 274; at St. George Island, 259; at St. Lawrence Island, 287; at Savoonga, 287; at Seward, 239; shelter cabins, 166, 195, 251; ship, 59-60, 62-63, 187, 248; at Shungnak, 18, 295; at Sitka, 181; at Skagway, 201; tipping at, 47; at Tok Junction, 285; trailer camps, 212, 219, 247, 266-67, 270, 285; at Unalakleet, 288; at University of Alaska, 282; at Valdez, 245; villages and outposts, 17-18; at Wasilla, 230; at Whitehorse, Y.T., 203; White Pass and Yukon Route, 64; at Wrangell, 172; at Yakutat, 204

Adak Island, 87

Admiralty Island, 31, 119, 144, 192, 194-96

Afognak Island, 119, 127, 142, 148-49, 253

Afognak River, 148

Agriculture (see also Homesteading): Alaska Dairy Products Corporation, 226; at Angoon, 193; cattle farming, 224, 253; chicken farming, 224, 238; Cooperative Association, Matanuska Valley Farmers, 226-27; at Cordova, 252; cost of farming, 231-32; cropland for, 223, 224-25, 233, 298-99; dairy farming, 186, 224, 226, 231, 253, 283; experimental stations, 131, 223, 227, 229, 232, 298-99; at Fairbanks, 266; fairs and expositions, 113-14, 116, 117, 190, 199, 229, 236, 269; Farmers Home Administration, 232; farming equipment, 225-26; financing for, 132; at Fort Yukon, 286; fur farms, 131, 178; grazing lands, 233; grazing leases

315

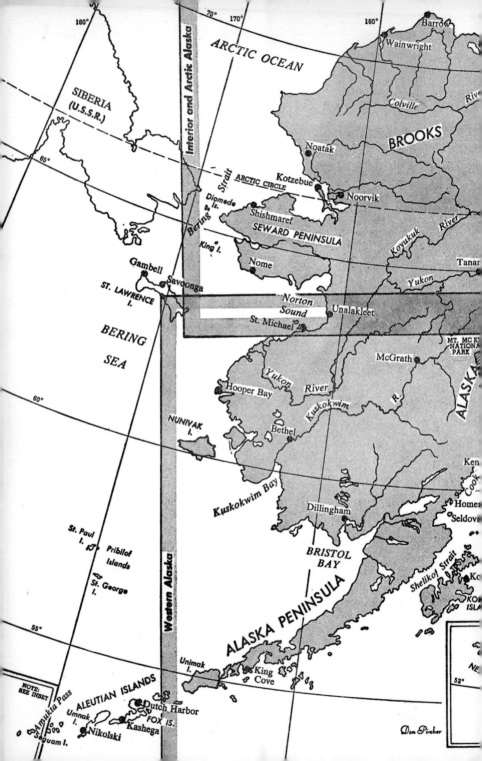